Contents

This aims to be the new, definitive guide to the magical world of an Orlando holiday, especially for first-time visitors to the area. It is written with a real tourist's eye for detail and includes all the information you *really* need to know, not just what the brochures want you to know. It will give you a good idea of what to expect and how to plan for it, how to budget for things like hotels, meals and days out at the theme parks as well as being a useful ready reckoner while you are there.

Have a nice day now …!

1. Introduction

(or welcome to the holiday of a lifetime) including getting to grips with Orlando, facts and figures, outline of the main attractions.

2. Planning and Practicalities

(or how to do it all and live to tell the tale) including when to go, the main tourist areas, the big holiday companies, holiday strategy, how to beat the crowds, clothing and health, travellers with disabilities and American-speak.

3. Driving and Car Hire

(or the secret of getting around on interstate 4) including arriving at Orlando Airport, the main roads and tourist roads, car-hire guide and how to drive on the wrong side of the road!

4. Accommodation

(or making sense of American hotels, motels and condos) including understanding American-style accommodation, Walt Disney World resorts and the best of the rest.

5. The Big Six Theme Parks

(or spending the day with mickey mouse and co) including full guides to the Magic Kingdom, Epcot 96, Disney MGM Studios, Universal Studios, Sea World and Busch Gardens.

6. The Other Attractions

(or one giant step for tourist kind) including the other theme parks and activities, the water parks, off the beaten track, sports and Orlando by night.

13. Copyright Notices

Introduction
or welcome to the holiday of a lifetime

It's the biggest, brashest theme park on the planet – and we're not talking just about Walt Disney World.

For Orlando itself is now the nearest thing there is to an Amusement City, an almost non-stop land of adventure rides, thrills, fun and fantasy. It is so bewilderingly vast that any holiday to Florida's Funland now needs to be organised with the precision of a military operation.

In the course of a week or two, your senses will be bombarded by an absolutely dazzling array of attractions, from the corny to the highly sophisticated, all vying for your attention and exacting a high physical toll. There is something to suit all tastes and ages, and it is guaranteed to bring out the kid in everyone. You'll walk a lot, queue a lot and probably eat a lot. You'll have a good time, but you'll end up exhausted as well!

Six theme parks

In simple terms, there are six big theme parks which are now generally reckoned to be essential holiday fare, and at least one of those will require two days to make you feel it has been well and truly done. Add on a day at one of the water fun parks, a trip to see some of the wildlife or other more 'natural' attractions, or the lure of the nearby Kennedy Space Centre, and you're talking about 10 days of pure adventure mania. Then add in the night-time attractions of Church Street Station, Pleasure Island and the various and numerous dinner shows, and you start to get an idea of the awesome scale of the entertainment on offer. Even given two weeks, something has to give — just make sure it isn't your patience/pocket/sanity!

So, how do we Brits, many of us making our first visit to the good ol' US of A, make the most of what is still without doubt the most magical of holidays?

There is no set answer of course, but there are a number of pretty solid guidelines to steer you in the right direction and help you avoid some of the more obvious pitfalls. Central to most of them is planning. At the back of this guide there is a useful 'calendar' to fill in and use as a ready reference guide. Don't be inflexible, but be aware of the time requirements of each of the main parks, and (importantly) allow yourself a few quiet days either by the pool or at one of the smaller attractions to recover your strength!

Also, be aware of the vast scale and complexity of this theme park wonderland, and try to take in as much of the clever detail and great breadth of imagination on offer, especially in Walt Disney World.

Orlando

Orlando itself is a relatively small but bright young city which has been taken over to the immediate

FLORIDA

How far to ...

Bradenton	130 miles	Key West	375 miles
Clearwater	110 miles	Miami	220 miles
Cocoa Beach	40 miles	Sarasota	140 miles
Daytona	60 miles	St Petersburg	105 miles
Fort Myers	190 miles	Tampa	75 miles
Jacksonville	155 miles	Venice	160 miles

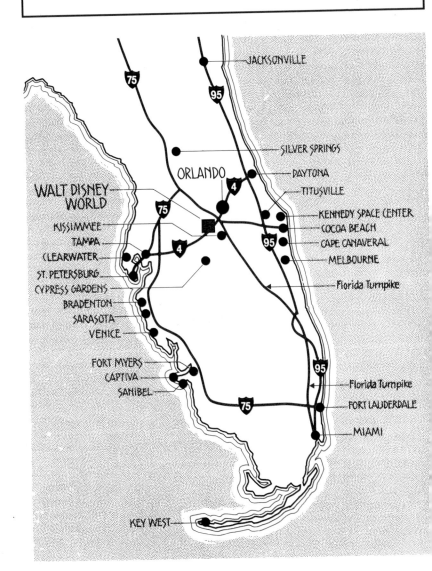

south-west by the Walt Disney World Vacation Kingdom, to give it its full title, which opened with the Magic Kingdom in 1971 and has encouraged a massive tourist

Lake Eola, downtown Orlando

expansion ever since. New attractions are being added all the time and the city of Orlando is in danger of being swamped by this vast out-pouring of rampant commercialism and aggressive tourist marketing. However, there is still a genuine concern for the environment and the dangers of over-commercialism and the development should not get out of hand, at least in the near future (although it is easy to imagine it already has in some parts of Kissimmee, notably along Highway 192). But more of that later.

The current area of Orlando is roughly equal to that of Greater London or Manchester. The local population numbers barely 1.3 million, of which some 144,000 are actively employed in the tourist business, but in 1995 more than 30 million people were forecast to decide on Orlando as the place for their holiday, spending in excess of $6 billion in central Florida! Britain accounts for a third of all foreign visitors to Orlando, and in 1995 that was likely to be more than 900,000. Those figures represent a near 100 per cent increase in just the last eight years, with the international airport seeing its traffic boom from eight million passengers in 1983 to a massive 22 million just eleven years

later. In addition, the full city area boasts around 85,000 hotel rooms and 3,500 places to eat.

Walt Disney World

Walt Disney World consists of three distinct, separate theme parks, in addition to 20 speciality hotel resorts, a camping ground, a nature reserve, three water fun parks, a shopping village and an evening entertainment complex. It covers some 43 square miles (27,520 acres): Alton Towers and Thorpe Park would comfortably fit into one of its car parks. Indeed, Alton Towers, Britain's biggest theme park, is 60 times smaller than Walt Disney World. Disney's most-frequented park, the Magic Kingdom, has a single-day record attendance in the region of 92,000 — Thorpe Park in Surrey (size 500 acres) peaks at around 20,000. The Disney organisation still does things with the most style, but the others have caught on fast and they are all creating new amenities almost as fast as they can think of them. Intriguingly, less than half of Disney's massive site is currently developed, leaving plenty of room for expansion of accommodation and attractions.

Here's a quick run-down of what's on offer. **The Magic Kingdom**: this is the essential Disney, including the fantasy of all its wonderful animated films, the adventure of the Wild West and African Jungles, and the excitement of some classy thrill rides like Space Mountain, a huge indoor roller-coaster, and the new Alien Encounter. **Epcot 95:** This is Disney's look at the world of tomorrow (formerly known just as the Epcot Center) through the gates of Future World, plus a potted journey around our planet in World Showcase. It's more educational than adventurous, but still possesses some memorable rides and some great places to eat. The **Disney**

MGM Studios: here you can ride the movies in style, meeting up with Star Wars, the Muppets and Indiana Jones, and learn how films are *really* made. **Typhoon Lagoon**: bring your swimming costume and spend a lazy afternoon splashing down water slides and learning to surf in the world's biggest man-made lagoon. **River Country**: more water fun 'n' games, with some great slides and the accent on nature. **Blizzard Beach**: just opened, this will be the big brother of all the water parks, with a massive spread of rides 'n' slides all in a snowy environment. **Discovery Island**: a man-made 12-acre zoological garden attraction of peaceful walks and local wildlife habitats. **Pleasure Island**: here every night is New Year's Eve and one big party, with an impressive choice of live music, comedy, discos, shops and restaurants. For Disney's hotels, see Chapter Four.

Most people buy one of two four-day passes or a five-day pass, two of which allow you to move between the various parks on the same day, while all three grant unlimited access to Disney's transport system of monorails, buses and ferries (always get your hand stamped if you leave one park but intend to return later on). Make no mistake here, you can't expect to walk between the various parks, and trying to do more than one in a day in any depth is a recipe for disaster. The four-day Value Pass provides a day at each of the three main parks, plus an extra day at one of them, while the four-day Park Hopper means you can also visit any combination of the three on one day. The five-day World Hopper Pass adds unlimited admission to Typhoon Lagoon, Blizzard Beach, River Country, Discovery Island and Pleasure Island for a full week after the pass is first used at one of the main three parks.

A first word of warning here: you really don't want to try to do Walt Disney World in one, big chunk. Apart from ending up with serious theme park indigestion, you'll probably also hit one of the parks on a busy day (generally Monday, Tuesday and Wednesday). Instead, space out your Disney days over the full duration of your holiday. The Magic Kingdom and Epcot 96 can be particularly exhausting, and you'll need a quiet day afterwards.

The others

If Disney is what you think Orlando is all about, then you'll be in for a very pleasant surprise when you

Universal Studios

encounter the likes of Universal Studios, Sea World, Busch Gardens, Cypress Gardens, the Kennedy Space Center and Silver Springs. Universal Studios is barely five years old, while the others have all expanded in recent years. They may be built along smaller lines (although Universal have some grand plans), but they deal successfully in the same areas of excitement and sophistication. **Universal Studios**: this features the state-of-the-art simulator ride Back to the Future, Jaws, King Kong, Earthquake, the Blues Brothers and Ghostbusters. **Sea World**: don't be put off thinking it's just another dolphin show, this is *the* place for the creatures of the deep, with killer whales being the main attraction, a

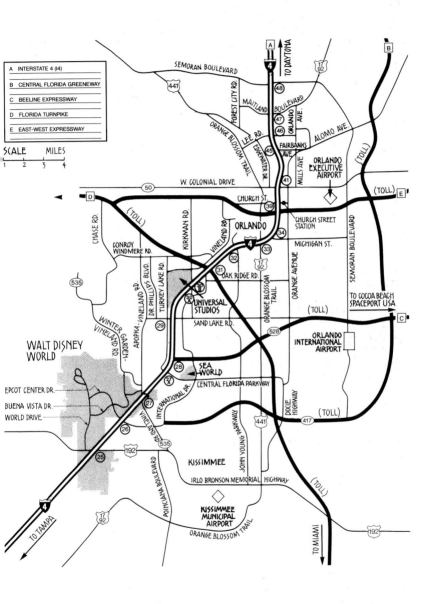

Sea World

bright, refreshing atmosphere and a pleasingly serious ecological approach. **Busch Gardens**: the sister park to Sea World, here it's creatures of the land, with the highlight being the new Myombe Reserve and a close-up look at the endangered Central African highland gorillas. A real treat, plus a number of brain-numbing roller-

Cypress Gardens

coasters and other rides. **Cypress Gardens**: a chance to slow down and take in the more scenic attraction of beautiful gardens, water-skiing shows and circus acts. **Kennedy Space Center**: otherwise known as Spaceport USA, is a must for anyone even vaguely interested in One Giant Leap for Mankind. Many free attractions, plus coach tours and giant-screen film shows. **Silver Springs**: a close look at Florida nature via jeep and boat safaris through real swampland, with the addition of several alligator displays. **Splendid China**: a magnificent new attraction, a 5,000-mile journey through the country of China with elaborate miniaturised

reproductions of features like the Great Wall, the Terracotta Warriors, plus films, live shows and great shopping and food. **Fantasy o Flight**: a brand new aviation

Kennedy Space Center

museum experience, featuring the world's largest collection of vintage aircraft plus fighter-plane simulators.

So that's what's on offer, the next question is when to go? Florida's weather does vary a fair bit, from

BRIT TIP: The humidity levels – up to 90 per cent – and fierce daily rainstorms in summer take a lot of visitors by surprise, so take a lightweight, rainproof jacket with you if possible.

bright but cool winter days in November, December and January, with the odd drizzly spell, to furiously hot and humid summers punctuated by tropical downpours.

The most pleasant option is to go in between the two extremes, ie, in spring and autumn. You will also avoid the worst of the crowds. However, as the majority of families are governed by school holidays, July to September remain the most popular months for Brit visitors, and so there will also be some pertinent advice on how to get one jump ahead of the high-season crush.

And now to business. Hopefully,

KEY TO ORLANDO – MAIN ATTRACTIONS

A = MAGIC KINGDOM
B = EPCOT 96
C = DISNEY MGM STUDIOS
D = UNIVERSAL STUDIOS
E = SEA WORLD
F = BUSCH GARDENS
G = KENNEDY SPACE CENTER
H = U.S. ASTRONAUT HALL OF FAME
I = SPLENDID CHINA
J = CYPRESS GARDENS
K = SILVER SPRINGS
L = GATORLAND
M = TYPHOON LAGOON

N = BLIZZARD BEACH
O = RIVER COUNTRY
P = WATER MANIA
Q = WET 'N WILD
R = DISCOVERY ISLAND
S = MYSTERY FUN HOUSE
T = RIPLEY'S BELIEVE IT OR NOT
U = TERROR ON CHURCH STREET
V = CHURCH STREET STATION
W = PLEASURE ISLAND
X = CYPRESS ISLAND
Y   FANTASY OF FLIGHT

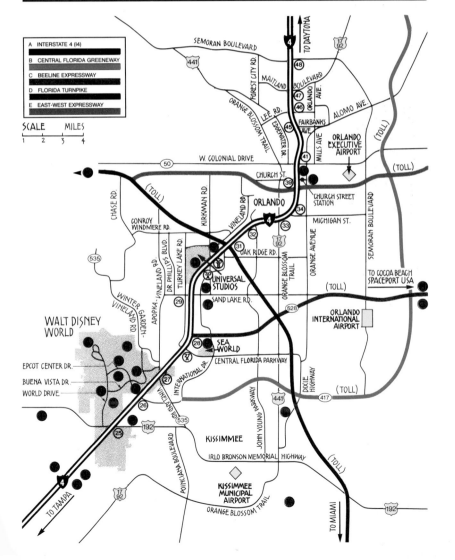

we've whetted your appetite for the excitement in store. It's big, brash and fun, but above all it's American, and that means everything is exceedingly well organised, with a tendency towards the raucous rather than the reserved. It's clean, well-maintained and very anxious to please: Floridians generally are an affable bunch, but they take affability to new heights in the main theme parks, where staff are almost painfully keen to make sure you Have A Nice Day. Also close to every American's heart is the custom of TIPPING. With the exception of petrol pump attendants and fast-food restaurant servers, just about everyone who offers you any sort of service in hotels, bars, restaurants, buses, taxis, airports and other public amenities will expect a tip. In bars, restaurants and taxis, 10–15 per cent of the bill is the usual going rate while porters will expect $1 per bag. Brits are notoriously forgetful of this little habit but, as all service industry workers are automatically taxed on the assumption of receiving 15 per cent in tips, you will be doing a major service to the local economy if you remember those few extra dollars each time, and you'll be helping to rebuild our tourist image as well! While on the subject of money, it is useful to know that nearly all shops, hotels and restaurants will accept dollar travellers' cheques in payment as they would with cash, so it is not necessary (as well as not being advisable) to carry large amounts of cash around. Take note also that all Orlando prices, both where indicated in this book and on every price-tag you see over there, DO NOT include the 6 percent Florida Sales Tax.

Holiday visitors to America also do **not** need a Visa providing they hold a valid British passport showing they are a British Citizen (and which does not expire before the end of

BRIT TIP: Sterling travellers' cheques will cause only confusion. Americans are notoriously bad at dealing with 'foreign' money.

your holiday). Instead, all you do is fill in a green Visa waiver form (from your travel agent or airline) and hand it in with your passport to the US immigration official who checks you through first thing after landing. However, British Subjects **do** need a Visa, as do Irish and Australian passport holders, and you should apply at least a month in advance to the US Embassy. In England and Wales, write to the Visa Office, US Embassy, 5 Upper Grosvenor Street, London W1A 2JB (tel 0891 200 290); in Scotland, it's the US Consulate General, 3 Regent Terrace, Edinburgh EG7 5BH; and in Northern Ireland write to US Consulate General, 3 Queens House, Belfast BT1 6EQ.

Plan your visit

The next few chapters will help you plan your Disney days and lazy ways and include a tourist's guide to American-speak so you know what they mean when they ask if you have any change in your fanny-pack and so you don't ask for a packet of fags!; the perils and pleasures of driving on the wrong side of the road; understanding American motels and other accommodation; the secrets of the main theme parks; the best of the rest; where, when and how to eat; being safe in this tourist wonderland (this is not as big an issue as the British media would have you believe, but it is important to be safety-conscious); and how to become a world-class shopper.

Planning and Practicalities

or how to do it all and live to tell the tale

There are several simple rules involved once you have decided Orlando is the place for you.

Rule No. 1: Sit down and plan what you want to do very carefully.

No. 2: Plan what you want to do after sitting down very carefully.

No. 3: After sitting down, very carefully plan what you want to do.

No. 4: Very carefully sit down and plan, etc.

You get the idea. This is NOT the type of holiday you can take in a freewheeling, carefree 'make it up as you go along' manner. Frustration and exhaustion lie in wait for all those who do not have at least a basic plan of how to fill in their seven to fourteen days in the fun capital of the world.

So this is what you do. First of all work out WHEN you want to go, then decide WHERE in the vast resort is the best place for you. Then consider WHAT sort of holiday you are looking for, WHO you want to entrust your holiday with and finally HOW much you want to try to do.

When to go

If you are looking to avoid the worst of the crowds, the best periods to choose are October to early February (but not the week of the Thanksgiving holiday in November or the Christmas to New Year period), mid-February (after George Washington's birthday holiday) to the week before Easter, and April (after Easter) to the end of May. Orlando gets down to some serious tourist business from Memorial Day (the last Monday in May, the official start of the summer season) to Labor Day (the first Monday in September and the last holiday of summer), peaking on the 4th of July, a huge national holiday. The Easter holidays are similarly uncomfortable (although the weather is better), but easily the busiest is the Christmas period, starting the week before December 25 and lasting until January 2. It is not unknown for some of the theme parks to close their gates to new arrivals as their massive car parks become full by late morning.

BRIT TIP: Thanksgiving is always the fourth Thursday in November, while George Washington's birthday, or President's Day, is the third Monday in February. The weeks including those dates are to be avoided!

The months offering the best combination of comfortable weather and smaller crowds are May and October, but never let the weather put you off. Few of the main theme

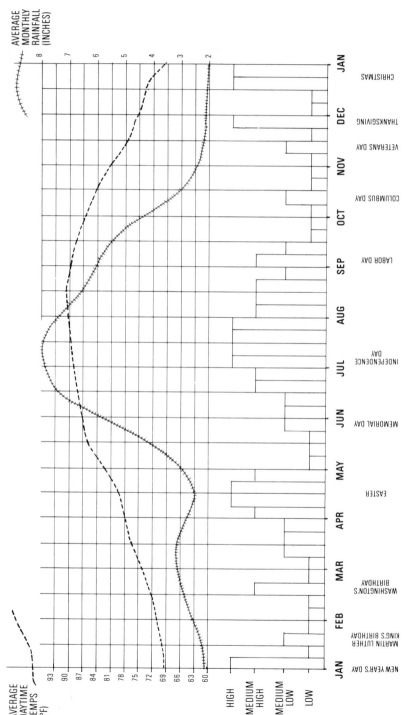

DIAGRAM 1

2

park attractions are affected by rain, and you will be one jump ahead if you have remembered to bring a waterproof jacket as the crowds noticeably thin out when it gets wet. Don't worry if you haven't brought rain-gear — all the parks do a major trade in cheap, plastic ponchos to keep you dry while you carry on queuing! In the colder months take a heavy sweater or coat for early-morning queues, then, when it warms up later in the day, leave it in the handy lockers that are provided in all of the parks. And, when it's too hot, take advantage of the air-conditioned facilities (of which there are many) during the warmest parts of the day.

Where to stay

The choice of where to stay is equally important, especially if you have a family who will demand the extra amenities of swimming pools and games rooms. Having the use of a swimming pool is also a major plus for relaxing at the end of a busy day. Inevitably, there is a huge choice of hotels, motels, apartments and private houses, and there are pros and cons to each of the main tourist areas, as well as a slight difference in price. As a guideline, there are four main areas that make up the greater Orlando tourist conglomeration.

Walt Disney World: some of the most sophisticated, convenient and downright fun places to stay are to be found in Disney's 'resort' hotels sprinkled around its main attractions. The same sort of imagination that has gone into the creation of the theme parks has been at work on the likes of the Wilderness Lodge and Contemporary Resort. They all feature free, regular transport to all of the attractions and guests also get extra perks like special baby and child-care services, early admission to theme parks on selected days, free

Florida's east coast beaches are just an hour's drive from Orlando; west coast beaches are two hours away

parking and being able to book in advance for restaurants and shows in the parks, while Disney characters pop up for breakfast at some of them. The drawbacks here are that, with the exception of the new All Star Resorts, the Disney resorts are among the most expensive in Orlando, especially to eat in, and you still have a fair drive to get to the other attractions like Universal Studios and the Kennedy Space Centre. For a one-week holiday it takes some beating, though.

Lake Buena Vista: this is a loosely-defined area around some very pretty lakes to the eastern fringes of Walt Disney World and along Interstate 4 that again features some of the more up-market hotels. It also has the convenience of being very handy for all the Disney parks, with most hotels offering free transport, and some excellent leisure and shopping facilities. Once again it tends to be a bit pricey, but its proximity to the main highway, Interstate 4, makes it pretty convenient for the whole of Orlando.

International Drive: this ribbon development lies midway between Walt Disney World and downtown Orlando and is therefore an excellent central location. Running parallel to Interstate 4, you are not much more than 15–20 minutes away from the main theme parks, while it is also a well-developed tourist area in its own right, with some great shopping, restaurants and minor attractions like Wet 'n' Wild, Ripley's Believe It Or Not, mini-golf and go-karting. The down side is it can get rather congested with tourist traffic in peak periods and you have to make a slightly earlier start in the morning for Walt Disney World. But it does represent good value for money and it also possesses a rarity in Orlando in that you can go for a long stroll along real, well laid-out pavement!

Kissimmee: budget holiday-makers can be found in their greatest numbers along the tourist sprawl of Highway 192, an almost unbroken 12-mile strip of hotels, motels, restaurants and shops. It offers some of the best economy accommodation in the whole area and is *very* handy for Disney's attractions, although it gives you the longest journey to Universal Studios and downtown Orlando. A car is just about essential here, though, as you are not intended to walk anywhere, and the area generally lacks that little bit of sophistication to be found elsewhere.

Split holidays

The type of holiday you fancy also comes into the equation at this point, although it is fair to say you can't really go far wrong no matter what you're looking for. The Atlantic coast and some great beaches are only an hour's drive away to the east, the magnificent Florida Everglades are little more than two hours to the south, and there are more wonderful beaches and pleasant coast roads to the west. There are great shopping opportunities almost everywhere you turn, while Orlando is also home to some of the best golf courses in the world, and there are plenty of opportunities to either play or watch tennis, baseball and basketball as well. There really is something for everyone, and it just serves to

emphasise once again the need to plan what you want to do. An increasingly popular choice these days is to split the holiday by having a week or two in Orlando as well as a week on the Florida coast or somewhere more exotic like the Caribbean. The main tour companies have caught on to this trend very quickly and now offer a huge variety of different packages.

If you can afford the time (and the expense), the best combination is to have two weeks in Orlando itself and then a week relaxing and recuperating on one of Florida's many fabulous white-sand beaches. A half-and-half split is a popular choice, but can tend to make your week in Orlando especially hectic fitting everything in, unless you pick your additional week on the Atlantic coast at somewhere like Cocoa Beach. This resort, near to Cape Canaveral and the Kennedy Space Center, is only an hour from Orlando and offers the choice of being able to return to Walt Disney World for the day. A few companies offer a 10-day Orlando and four-day coast split, and this is worth seeking out if you are limited to two weeks. Fly-drives obviously offer the greatest flexibility of doing Orlando and seeing something else of Florida, but again there is a lot to cram in in just two weeks and you may find it is better to book a one-centre package that includes a car as well as your accommodation so you can still travel around a bit and avoid too much packing and unpacking in different hotels and motels.

Travel companies

The briefest of glances into the nearest travel agent will reveal there is some serious competition for your hard-earned money before you have even left these shores. In the last couple of years the travel companies have worked very hard to keep the cost of an Orlando holiday down, making it excellent value for money, whether you fly-drive, book your own flights or take a straightforward package. A return adult air fare can be had for as little as £210, and, with local car hire and a reasonable quality motel, it is certainly possible to work out a little cheaper than a typical package holiday. However, you are more likely to get a better quality of accommodation, attention to detail and security from one of the many standard packages.

At the last count there were some 60 companies offering package holidays or fly-drives to Orlando, with 13 of them in the Big League catering for at least 10,000 passengers a year. They all offer a sound, well-established product, with free rental cars now almost standard and many 'kids eat free' deals. The majority of the 13 are all well-known names in the travel business, but here is a quick run-down of who they are and what they have to offer in this market.

Virgin holidays: The biggest operator to MCO (that's Orlando in travel-agent speak), Virgin also have the biggest and most exhausting brochure. They offer the largest variety of combinations, including other American cities like Boston, New York and Nashville, nine different Caribbean islands and some tempting cruises, as well as the Florida coasts. A strong selling point is Virgin's non-stop scheduled service to Orlando with award-winning in-flight entertainment. They have a veritable army of representatives in Orlando and a good, all-round choice of accommodation in the different areas and are popular for fly-drives, flying into Orlando and out from Miami. They average out slightly on the expensive side, but there are some special deals to be had every year, including 'kids eat free' and single parent offers, and you are

assured of top-quality service. Orlando is also an increasingly popular choice as a wedding venue, and Virgin have their own wedding co-ordinators, even featuring balloon weddings! For golf, tennis and scuba-diving enthusiasts there are also activity packages.

Thomson: Another of the largest, mass-market operators, Thomson have an excellent reputation in Orlando and offer one of the widest choices of departure airports in the UK, including Cardiff and Newcastle. Nearly all of their flights, with Britannia Airways, are non-stop (only Cardiff and Bristol touch down before Orlando, at Bangor in Maine and Glasgow respectively), but they are very competitively priced and also feature great in-flight entertainment and the Jets Cadets Club for kids. Thomson place their main emphasis on families and couples, with special children's fares and extra value bonuses like 'kids eat free' which are especially useful for large families, while they are another company to organise special wedding packages. An exciting new development for '96 is a weekly flight to Palm Beach, north of Miami, which opens up new beach resorts like Hollywood and Naples, adding to an impressively up-graded range of two-centre holidays and self-drive tours from Orlando.

Airtours: They complete the Big Three group who each take in the region of 100,000 British tourists to Orlando every year. They now have their own airline and so offer the majority of flights non-stop, with a comprehensive in-flight entertainment programme and fun-pack for kids. They slot into the mid-price range and also offer some imaginative two- and three-centre combinations, including the Cayman Islands and New Orleans. They offer a seven-day ticket package, including Disney, Universal, Sea World and Busch Gardens, which offers the convenience of pre-booking but NOT a cheaper rate than buying the tickets individually. Airtours also make a feature of their fly-drive packages, with a range of 'Drive and Stay' holidays which offer a wide choice to the Florida sun-seeker, especially return visitors, with a good value hotel pass as well.

Unijet: One of the fastest-growing companies to Orlando, Unijet benefit from a direct air service courtesy of Leisure Air which features the Airshow system, a handy 'Where are we now?' screen that is sure to keep the kids amused on the nine-hour, non-stop flight. Unijet also pride themselves on their value-for-money family packages (including 'kids eat free' hotel deals) and offer an increasing number of holiday homes as well as hotels, which are great value for larger families or groups. They also feature six of Disney's big resort hotels, from budget to top of the range, an expanded range of two-centre holidays (including some popular Caribbean cruises), and, new for '96, some special deals with British Airways to Miami and Tampa.

British Airways Holidays: Another company to benefit from their direct, scheduled air service, with the option of an (expensive) upgrade to the more comfortable Club service, BA also offer a great variety of combinations, including some first class cruises, and have a very experienced staff in Orlando. They are offering a good range of Disney properties in 1995 and also provide a 'Without cash' holiday deal that enables you to pay a one-off price that includes tickets for Disney, Universal, Sea World and Busch Gardens, as well as a buffet breakfast daily at your hotel, but this again is not a cheap option.

Jetsave: Also a direct-flight operator, courtesy of Britannia Air, Leisure Air and British Airways, Jetsave reckon to get half their

business from second and third-time Orlando holiday-makers and so provide a large selection of up-market holiday homes as well as budget-priced hotels. For more confident travellers and larger family groups, these work out better value for money and Jetsave's proud boast as the first major operator in this field gives them the edge in experience. They also offer a terrific

Downtown Orlando

range of Florida combinations, plus the Bahamas and Caribbean cruising.

Cosmos: Another familiar name in the travel world, although they tend to concentrate more on the European market. Their Orlando operation is nonetheless very well organised with one of the most readable brochures, catering as it does mainly for the family market and offering a good variety of middle-range accommodation, and featuring one of the most entertaining welcome meetings in the resort. Flights, operated mainly on chartered airlines, are not always non-stop, but they do offer a large variety of departure points, including Newcastle, Cardiff and Birmingham, and they are one of the most competitively-priced operators. 'Dream Weddings' was a new feature for 1995 and is likely to be extended for '96.

First Choice: Formerly Falcon Holidays, they aim firmly at the family market and offer some of the best value deals, with price reductions, low-start prices and 'kids eat free' options. Again, you can pre-book tickets to most of the attractions, which means you can budget for a large part of your spending in advance, but it does not work out cheaper than buying them yourself over there. Usual range of Orlando-plus-beach combinations.

Sunworld: Another firm which concentrates on family appeal, Sunworld also offers very competitive rates for kids and some of the best middle-range prices in the market. Free kids passes to some attractions, more villa accommodation and a 'Florida Gold' hotel selection are all recent additions to their programme. They use Monarch Airlines, hence no non-stop flights on the way out (Monarch have a refuelling stop at Bangor in Maine, a bizarre contrast if you travel during the winter months as there may be as much as two feet of snow around the airport!). They offer Dollar hire cars with free rental, plus a new range of two-centre options, including the Florida Keys, Jamaica and a Bahamas cruise.

Jetlife: Another company who specialise in a tailor-made service, Jetlife are especially popular with second-time visitors as they offer an increasing number of what they call 'easy living' homes — private villas and apartments that represent great value for larger family groups, and three- and four-bedroom houses with a private or communal swimming pool — plus the full range of Disney accommodation. Jetlife also use all scheduled airlines, with a large number of non-stop flights, offer an excellent variety of two-centre holidays, including Barbados, St Lucia, Hawaii and various American cities, and their packages are all very competitively priced.

Kuoni: As in all their holidays, Kuoni offer the up-market version of Orlando, with some of the best

hotels, what they call their Florida Classics, and a strong tie-up with Walt Disney World. The bonus of booking Disney accommodation with Kuoni comes in the form of a

Busch Gardens, Tampa

seven-day unlimited pass to all Disney attractions which lasts for *any* number of visits for the duration of your stay. New for this year are the exclusive and picturesque Gulf Coast resorts of Sanibel and Captiva plus a range of executive holiday homes in keeping with Kuoni's high-class profile. The average price reflects the more exclusive nature of the packages, but there are some big child reductions and Kuoni use only scheduled air services, which means non-stop flights (except for United Airlines, who go via Washington).

US Airtours: Not so much a package holiday operator as a travel agent offering a tailor-made service utilising the latest discounted scheduled airline fares. You are more likely to find their full travel service on Teletext rather than in a travel agent, but new for '96 is their handling of Delta Air Lines Dream Vacations brochure, which WILL be in most agents' shops. This features a strong Disney tie-up, optional ground transport, fly-drives and two-centre packages. Their overall appeal is greater flexibility of choice, although that comes at a slightly increased price.

Transolar: A rather fussy and confusing main brochure (although they now produce a smaller version on Walt Disney World that is easier to read) hides some surprisingly good deals with this long-established company which has been taking Brits to Orlando for more than 25 years. Transolar also have their own hotel at Cocoa Beach which makes a good combination with the main business of getting stuck into the theme parks. Like Kuoni, Transolar add an unlimited Disney pass to customers staying at Walt Disney World resort hotels and offer a scheduled airline service from Gatwick and Manchester (although Manchester flights, operated by Delta, go via Atlanta, and Northwest flights from Gatwick go via Boston).

There are, of course, plenty of other options apart from the main tour companies, and scanning the holiday pages of the national press or Teletext will often reveal many special deals on full packages or flights alone. As with any holiday abroad, the essential thing is to make sure the company is ABTA or ATOL-bonded, which assures you of proper assistance should anything happen to your holiday or the tour company.

The best idea is to establish some sort of plan of what you want to do and then get a selection of brochures and compare the various prices and attractions of each one.

What to see when

Once you arrive, the temptation is to head immediately for the nearest theme park, then the next, and so on. Hold on! If there is such a thing as theme park indigestion, that's the best recipe for it, so once again try to establish a basic plan of campaign. Some days at Walt Disney World, Universal Studios, etc, are busier than others, while it is simply not possible to take in more than one a day, and is sometimes inadvisable to attempt two of the main parks on successive days. So here's what you do.

With the aid of the Holiday Planner at the back of this book, make a note of all the attractions you want to try to see and then pencil them in over the full duration of your holiday (the book's example of a typical two-week stay will give you the idea).

The most sensible strategy is to plan around the six 'must see' parks of The Magic Kingdom, Epcot 96, Disney MGM Studios, Universal Studios, Sea World and Busch Gardens. If you have only a week to try to pack everything in, consider dropping Busch Gardens from your itinerary (it's furthest away from Orlando and doesn't have quite the same magical appeal of the others) and concentrate on the Disney parks and Universal Studios, with Sea World as an 'extra' if it fits into your plan. Science fiction addicts like myself and others fascinated by the realities of space travel will be hard-pressed not to include the Kennedy Space Center in their 'must see' list, but it will probably bore small children and the adventure-ride seekers.

As a basic rule, the Magic Kingdom is the biggest hit with children, and families often find it requires two days to feel they have seen and done everything on offer. The same can be said of Epcot 96, but there are fewer rides to keep small children happy, and more of the emphasis is on education as well as entertainment, although it all has Disney's slick, easily-digestible coating. Only the most fleet of foot, coupled with the benefit of a relatively crowd-free period, will be able to negotiate Epcot successfully in a day. Disney MGM Studios is a 9–5 park (where you can comfortably fit in all the attractions in the daylight hours), while Sea World needs rather longer and Universal Studios can be a two-day park when Orlando is at its busiest. Busch Gardens is another full day affair, especially as it is 75–90 minutes drive away to Tampa in the south west, but an early start to the Kennedy Space Center (an hour's drive to the east coast) will mean you can be back in your hotel swimming pool by tea-time, confident you have fully enjoyed One Small Step For Man. All the main attractions, plus the smaller ones, are detailed in Chapters Five and Six, so try to get an idea of the essential time requirements of them all before you pick up your pencil!

Smaller attractions

Of the other, smaller-scale attractions, the nature park of Silver springs is a full day out as it also involves a near two-hour drive to get there, but everything else can be fitted around your Big Six Itinerary. The water fun parks of Typhoon Lagoon, River Country, Blizzard Beach, Wet 'n Wild and Water Mania are all a good way to spend a relaxing afternoon, while Cypress Gardens is another quieter place to while away four to five hours. There are also a number of smaller-scale attractions in Orlando which will probably keep the children amused for several hours. Gatorland is a unique look at some of Florida's oldest inhabitants, with three different shows to display the various reptilian creatures. The Mystery Fun House is a good bet for two to three hours, as is Ripley's Believe It Or Not, an American version of the Guinness World of Records. Terror on Church Street (not for the faint-hearted — see Chapter Six!) guarantees a 20 to 30 minute journey through various indoor horrors, while Disney's Discovery Island is quite the opposite, two or three hours of gentle Florida nature, with a walk-through aviary and animal shows. Each main tourist area is also well served with imaginative mini-golf and go-kart tracks that will happily absorb any

excess energy for an hour or two from those who haven't, by now, been exhausted!

Evenings

Then, of course, there is the evening entertainment, with a similarly wide choice of extravagant fun-seeking. By far the best two, and a must for at least one evening each, are Disney's Pleasure Island and Church Street Station in downtown Orlando. Both will keep you fully entertained from 5pm until the early hours if you so wish — and you don't want to have an early start planned for the next morning! An increasingly popular and rapidly-proliferating source of evening fun are the various dinner shows Orlando has to offer, a two- to three-hour cabaret based on themes like the Wild West (predictably), Medieval England (not so predictably) and Sleuths (wildly unpredictable, a real, live version of Cluedo) that all include a hearty meal.

What to do when

Getting down to the fine detail: there are a couple of very handy general guidelines for avoiding the worst of the tourist hordes, even in high season. It may well be stating the obvious, but the vast majority of fun-seekers in town are American, and they tend to arrive at the week-ends, get settled in their hotels, and then head for the main theme parks, ie, Walt Disney World, first. That means that Mondays and Tuesdays are generally bad times to join the queues for the Magic Kingdom and Epcot 96. In addition, Thursdays and Saturdays are almost as con-gested at the Magic Kingdom, while Fridays and Saturdays are above average for crowds at Epcot. Disney MGM Studios is slightly different in that their busiest days tend to be

Wednesdays and Sundays, while Disney's most popular water parks, Blizzard Beach and Typhoon Lagoon, tend to hit high tide at the weekend and Wednesday to Friday during the summer. Like MGM Studios, the best days to visit Universal Studios are Friday and Saturday, with Mondays also a little quieter. By the same logic, if Walt Disney World is positively humming in the early part of the week, that makes it a good time to visit Sea World, Busch Gardens, Cypress Gardens, Silver Springs or the Kennedy Space Center. Wet 'n Wild and Water Mania are best avoided at the weekends when the locals come out to play.

Making sure you get the most out of your days at the main theme parks is another art form in itself, and again there are a number of very practical policies to pursue. The official opening times of the Big Six are all well-publicised in and around Orlando and don't vary much between 8.30 and 9am. However, apart from the obvious advantage of arriving early to try to get at the head of the queues (and you will encounter some VERY formidable queues — or lines, as the Americans call them — at regular intervals), all the parks will often open earlier than scheduled if the crowds build up quickly before the official hour. So, you can get a step ahead of the masses by arriving at least 30 minutes before the expected opening time, or an hour early during the main holiday periods. Apart from anything else, you will be better placed to park in the vast wide open spaces of the public car parks and catch the tram service to the main gates (which can be anything up to half a mile away!).

Once you've put yourself in pole position for that eagerly-anticipated opening, don't waste time on the shops, scenery and other frippery which will lure the unprepared first-timer through the gates. Instead head straight for some of the main rides and get a few big-time thrills under your belt before the main hordes arrive. You will quickly work out where the most popular attractions are as the majority of the other early birds will be similarly prepared and will flock in the appropriate direction. Go with the flow for the first hour or so and you'll enjoy the general tourist buzz as well as some of the best rides in relative comfort. Chapter Five provides a full run-down of exactly what's what, so you can plan your individual park strategies.

As another general rule, you can also benefit from doing the opposite of what the masses do after the initial rush has subsided into a steady stream. But a word of warning first: the Disney parks, notably the Magic Kingdom, stay open late in the evening during the main holiday periods, occasionally until midnight, and that can make for a very long day, especially for young children.

Pace yourself

Therefore it is important to pace yourself, especially if you have been one of the first through the gates. There are plenty of opportunities to take time-outs and have a well-earned drink or bite to eat, and you can take advantage of the American propensity to take meal-times very seriously by avoiding lunchtime and dinnertime (around 6pm) for your own breaks. So, after you've had a couple of hours of real adventure-mania, it pays to take an early lunch (ie, before midday), plunge back into the hectic thrill of it all for another three hours or so, have another snack-sized meal in mid-afternoon and then return to the main rides, especially if your appetite has been only whetted by the early morning fun, as the parks tend to quieten down a little in late afternoon. If your hotel is not far from the park, it is worthwhile even taking a couple of hours out to return for a dip in the pool, providing you have your hand stamped for re-entry when you leave (your car park ticket will also be valid all day so you won't have to pay for re-admission there either), and then enjoying the evening entertainment back at the park, which is often the most spectacular part of the day.

Finally, if all this talk of how to tackle the main attractions isn't enough to wear you out, a word about shopping in Orlando — it's world class. Chapter Nine deals fully with the huge variety of temptations guaranteed to lure even the most miserly shopper, but suffice it to say here that your battle plan should also include at least an afternoon to visit one of the spectacular shopping malls in Orlando, as well as a chance to sample some of the discount outlets and speciality centres like Old Town in Kissimmee, the Church Street Exchange in downtown Orlando, and the Mercado Centre on International Drive.

Clothing and comfort

The most important part of your whole holiday wardrobe is your footwear. Hopefully the message will now have sunk home that you are going to spend a lot of time on your feet, even during the off-peak periods. The smallest of the parks covers 'only' 100 acres, but that is irrelevant to the amount of time you will spend queuing. Your feet will definitely not thank you, therefore, if you decide this is the trip to break in those new sandals or trainers. Comfortable, well-worn shoes or trainers are ESSENTIAL. Otherwise, you need dress only as the climate dictates. T-shirts and shorts are quite acceptable in all of

the parks (but not bare torsos, even for men!) and most restaurants and other eating establishments will happily accept informal dress.

If, after a long day, you feel the need for a change of clothes or a sweater for the evening, use the handy lockers which all the theme parks provide to leave personal belongings. For parents with small children and babies, Walt Disney

BRIT TIP: Watch out for the unofficial sun-tan merchants who have taken to visiting hotel pool areas trying to tell you that the Ambre Solaire or whatever you have brought with you is not good enough for the Florida sun. All the familiar name products sold at home are quite adequate for a spot of Orlando sun-bathing, providing the *protection factor* is high enough.

World in particular is well equipped to ease your stay. Push-chairs (or strollers in American-speak) are available for a small charge at all parks, while baby services — for nursing mothers and nappy-changing — are to be found at strategic points.

It is often necessary to point out the absolutely vital need to carry and use high-factor sun creams at all times, even during the winter months when the sun may not feel that strong but can still burn all the same. Nothing, but nothing is guaranteed to make you feel uncomfortable for several weeks like severe sunburn. Orlando has a sub-tropical climate and requires higher factor sun creams than our summers or even a holiday in the Mediterranean. Use sun blocks on sensitive areas like your nose and ears, and splash on the after-sun cream liberally once you are back in your hotel room. Local skin-care products are widely-available in Orlando and usually inexpensive (especially at Wal-Mart or K-Mart stores), while many tour operators now have a skin care specialist available for advice at their welcome meetings.

Be aware, however, that if you are in and out of the pool, or spending a day sliding down all the fun rides

> BRIT TIP: The summer is also the time when the local mosquito population starts to get busy. Make sure you take a spray-on insect repellent, especially for evening use.

and slides of one of the water fun parks, you will need a waterproof sun cream to avoid becoming lobsterised! Wear a hat if you are out theme park-ing in the hottest parts of the day, and try to avoid alcoholic drinks until the evening as there is nothing like alcohol for making you dehydrated (except, perhaps, strong coffee) and susceptible to heatstroke, a more advanced stage of sunburn. You will need to increase your fluid intake significantly during the summer months in Orlando, but stick to lemonade or water!

Should you require medical treatment, whether it be for sunburn or other first aid, dial 911 in the event of an emergency or consult your tour company's information about local hospitals and surgeries.

It cannot be over-stressed that you should have comprehensive travel and health insurance for any trip to America as there is NO National Health Service and ANY form of medical treatment will need to be

paid for — and is usually very expensive.

Emergency out-patients departments can be found at Florida Hospital Medical Center on 601 East Rollins Street and Sand Lake Hospital on 9400 Turkey Lake Road, while the East Coast Medical Network (407 657 0739) and House Med Inc (407 648 9234) both make hotel 'house calls' 24 hours a day. House Med also operates MediClinic, another walk-in facility on 2901 Parkway Boulevard, Kissimmee, which is open daily from 9am to 9pm. If you visit a doctor during your stay, make sure you let your tour rep know afterwards. For a chemist (the Americans call them drug stores), the two biggest chain stores are Eckerd Drugs and Walgreens. Eckerd Drugs on 8330 International Drive is an easy-to-find chemist that is open until midnight, while their branch at 908 Lee Road is open 24 hours a day, as is Walgreens at 6201 International Drive (opposite Wet 'N Wild).

Travellers with disabilities

Holiday-makers with disabilities will be pleased to note that the main parks pay very close attention to their needs, too. There are very few rides and attractions that cannot cater for them, while wheelchair availability and access is almost always good. Disney also publish a *Guidebook for Disabled Guests* which is available in all three of their main parks. Life-jackets are on hand at River Country and Typhoon Lagoon, while there are special tape recorders and cassettes for blind visitors, and guide dogs are in no way discouraged.

American-speak

Another thing to watch out for are those words or phrases that may have different meaning across the Atlantic, or which need a complete translation. When I sat down to compile this list, I surprised even myself at how many words need to be 'translated' back into English. Some of them are obvious, others more obscure.

American	English
Check or Tab	Bill
Restroom	Public toilet
Bathroom	Private toilet
Eggs 'over easy'	Eggs fried both sides but soft
Eggs 'over hard'	Eggs fried both sides but hard!
Eggs 'sunny side up'	Eggs fried on just ONE side (soft)
French fries	Chips
Chips	Crisps
Cookie	Biscuit
Grits	Porridge-like breakfast dish made out of ground, boiled corn
Hash browns	Grated, fried potato (delicious!)
Jelly	Jam
Liquor	Spirits
Seltzer	Soda water
Shot	Measure
Liquor store	Off licence
Broiled	Grilled
Sub	French bread roll
Shrimp	King prawn
Sherbet	Sorbet
To go	Take-away (as in food: 'I'd like a Big Mac and fries to go, please').
Candy	Sweets
Drug store	Chemist
Sidewalk	Pavement
Pavement	Roadway
Bill	Note (as in $5 note)
Crib	Cot
Rollaway	Fold-up bed

Diaper	Nappy
Stroller	Pushchair
Lines	Queues (Very important here! You'll often get told to 'Stand in line' rather than 'Queue up.')
Elevator	Lift
Underpass	Subway
Subway	Underground
Mailbox	Postbox
Faucet	Tap
Collect call	Reverse charge phone call
Gas	Petrol
Trunk	Car boot
Hood	Car bonnet
Fender	Car bumper
Antennae	Aerial
Windshield	Windscreen
Stickshift	Manual transmission
Trailer	Caravan
Freeway	Motorway
Divided Highway	Dual carriageway
Denver boot	Wheel clamp
Turn-out	Lay-by
No standing	No parking OR stopping
Parking lot	Car park
Yield	Give way
Purse	Handbag
Fanny pack	Bumbag
Pants	Trousers
Undershirt	Vest
Vest	Waistcoat
Pantyhose	Tights
Shorts	Underpants
Quarter	25 cents
Dime	10 cents
Nickel	5 cents
Penny	1 cent

American clothes sizes are less than we are used to, hence a woman's size 12 dress over there is really a size 14 to us, or an American jacket sized 42 is really a 44. Shoes are the opposite: if an Orlando shoe shop reckons that wicked new pair of trainers are a size 10, they should fit a British size 9 foot! Their measuring system is also still standard and NOT metric, so we have to get used to everything being in feet and inches, ounces and pounds, pints and quarts and mph (not kmh — watch those speeds!)

Finally, be aware that when Americans say the first floor, they actually mean the ground floor, the second floor is really the first, and so on.

(Last PS: NEVER ask for a packet of fags! Fag is, ahem, a crude, slang term for homosexual, hence you will get some VERY funny looks. 'A packet?' etc.)

Okay, now we've established all that, it's time to get you up and running on the roads of Florida's funland …

Driving and Car Hire
or the secret of getting around on interstate 4

For the vast majority, introduction to Orlando proper comes immediately after clearing the airport via the potentially bewildering complexity of the local road systems in a newly-acquired hire car. Driving is a lot more simple and, on the whole, enjoyable than driving in the UK. In particular, anyone used to the M25 will certainly find Orlando's motorways more sedate.

Before you get to your hire-car, however, a quick note about Orlando International Airport. There is a full breakdown of how the airport works in Chapter Ten, but you need to be aware of a couple of little quirks on your arrival.

Orlando is one of the most modern and enjoyable airports you will encounter, but it does have a double baggage collection system that is a bit bewildering at first. You disembark at one of three Satellite terminals and have to collect your luggage immediately, then put it on another baggage carousel that takes it to the main terminal while you ride the passenger shuttle. Once in the main terminal you will be on Level Three and need to descend to Level Two for baggage reclaim. Package holiday-makers with Dollar Rent-a-Car will be able to hand their luggage straight over here to the porters who will take it down to Level One to await your car pick-up.

The Big Five hire companies who all have check-in desks at the airport are Dollar, Hertz, National, Budget

International Drive at night

and Avis and all offer the most comprehensive hire services. However, there is also a telephone desk at Level One that connects you directly to one of another 11 hire companies who often work out

> BRIT TIP: Make sure you follow the correct instructions to collect your hire car. There are several different desks for each of the main hire companies and if you do not check in at the right one you will waste a lot of time.

better value if you haven't already booked your car. A quick call brings their bus to pick you up and take you to their nearby depot, which also gives you a look at the surrounding roads before you have to drive on them. Alamo are a particularly popular and noteworthy company, as are Americar and Value, while Ugly

Duckling have the best advertisement: 'Save a buck, rent a duck!'

Being mobile is very nearly essential in most American cities and Orlando is no exception. Very few of the attractions are within walking distance of anywhere and there are few pavements (sidewalks). You can get around to a certain extent by bus, and many hotels are linked to private mini-bus charter firms who charge reasonable rates to the main attractions, while some hotels operate a free shuttle service to Walt Disney World and some of the other attractions. Taxis tend to be pretty expensive for more than one-off journeys. For example, the journey from the airport to International Drive would cost you the best part of $30, while from International Drive to Universal Studios would be $10–$12. Three companies who operate a handy fleet of shuttle buses are Mears (tel 407 839 1570), World Transportation (407 826 9999) and Transtar (407 856 7777), with a typical journey from I Drive to Walt Disney World costing $9/10 a head. International Drive also now has its own extensive multi-coloured bus service, I-Ride, which runs the full length of the main tourist area, from Sea World in the south right up to the Belz Factory Outlets Malls at the top of the Drive. It is great value at 75 cents each journey (children 12 and under ride free!) and buses run daily every 10 minutes from 7am until midnight, with more than 50 stops. There are also 1, 3, 5 and 7–day passes for $2–$7, while senior citizens' journeys are only 25 cents each. I-Ride bus-stops are indicated by a circular sign with a large pink paw-print (for the Lynx bus system) and you must have the right money as drivers do not carry change. Your hotel front desk will have all the details, but otherwise Orlando's public transport is pretty sketchy and can involve long waits which are especially inadvisable in the hot

BRIT TIP: The boot size on American cars tends to be much smaller than the British equivalent.

summer months.

The car

Ultimately, having a car is the key to being in charge of your holiday, and on a weekly basis it tends to work out very reasonable price-wise, too. Expect to pay as little as $30–$40 a week, plus insurance and taxes, for the smallest model, $50–$60 a week for a family saloon. The three main types are known generally as **Economy** (usually a small, Fiesta-sized two-door hatchback), **Subcompact** (a two- or four-door Escort-sized car) and **Compact** (a four-door, small family saloon like an Orion). Going up in scale, a **Mid-size** car should comfortably seat five, or you can get much larger still!

Once again, the scale of the car hire operation is huge, and with upwards of 300 tourists arriving at a time it can be a pretty formidable business getting everyone off and running. In all, there are around 50,000 hire cars available in Orlando and it is one of the cheapest places in the world to hire a car! The currently widespread practice of British holiday companies offering Free Car Hire with their packages does NOT mean it won't cost you anything. It is only the rental cost which is free and you will still be expected to pay the insurance, taxes and other extras BEFORE you can drive the car away. Having a credit card is essential, and there are two main kinds of insurance, the most important being the Loss Damage Waiver, or LDW. This currently costs $12.99 a day and covers you for any damage to your hire car. You can manage without it, but the hire company will then insist on a huge deposit in the order of $1,000 on your credit card, and that could wipe out your credit limit in one go (and you are also liable for ANY damage to the car). You will also be offered top-up insurance at around $8 a day. This covers you against being sued for astronomical amounts by any court-happy American you may happen to bump in to. Drivers under 25 have to pay an extra $8–10 per day, while all drivers must be at least 21. Other additional costs (which all mount up over a two-week holiday, so be sure to take out only what you need) include local and Florida state taxes which can add another $3 a day to your final bill, Airport Access Fee at $2 per day and then there's your

> **BRIT TIP:** Be FIRM with the hire company check-in clerk as many are quite pushy and will try to get you to take extras, like car up-grades, you don't need. You should also be given the choice of whether to return the car with a full tank of petrol yourself or take their petrol fill-up. Take the former course — hire companies have the most expensive petrol in Florida!

petrol, although that's only around $1.30 a gallon for unleaded.

Drivers also please note: You may feel the effects of jet-lag for a day or two after arrival, but this can be reduced during the flight by avoiding alcohol and coffee and instead drinking plenty of water and other non-alcoholic drinks.

The thought of tackling American roads can be the main cause of pre-holiday anxiety, but most soon find it is a pleasure rather than a pain, mainly because nearly all hire cars these days are automatics and rarely more than a year old. And, because speed limits are lower than we're used to at home (and rigidly enforced), you won't often be rushed into taking the wrong turn. Keep your foot on the brake when you are stationary as automatics tend to creep forward, and always put the automatic gear lever in 'P' (for Park) after turning off the engine.

> **BRIT TIP:** You probably won't be able to take the keys out of the ignition unless you put the car in 'Park' first. This sometimes causes much consternation!

Controls

All cars are also fitted with air conditioning, which is absolutely essential during spring, summer and autumn. The button to turn it on will be marked A/C, Air, or will be indicated by a snowflake symbol. (Handy hint: to make it work, you also have to switch on the car's fan!). Note also that air conditioning takes power from the engine and with smaller cars you may notice a bit of a struggle going uphill. To get full power back, simply turn off the A/C until the road levels off again. Power steering is also a common feature on many hire cars, so if you're not used to it be very gentle around corners until you get the feel of it. Some larger cars also have Cruise Control which lets you set the desired speed and take your foot off the accelerator (or gas pedal in American speak). There will be two buttons on the steering wheel, one to switch the Cruise Control on, the other which you push to set the desired speed. To take the car off Cruise Control either press the first button again or simply touch the brake. Wait until you have a clear stretch of motorway before you try this, though! The handbrake may also be different to the standard British pull-up variety. Some cars have an extra foot pedal to the left of the brake, and you need to push this to engage the handbrake. There will then be a tab just above it which you pull to release it, or a second push on the pedal if there is no tab. The car probably won't start unless the gear lever is on 'P', which can be confusing at first. To put the car in 'D' for Drive, you also have to depress the main brake pedal. D1 and D2 are extra gears which need to be engaged only when encountering steep hills (of which there are none in central Florida!)

Getting around

Once you are familiar with your car's controls you will want to head straight for your hotel. Your hire car company should provide you with a basic map of Orlando plus directions for getting to the hotel. Insist that these are provided as all the hire companies make a big point of this in their advertising literature. To begin with, familiarise yourself with the main roads of the area and learn to navigate by the road *numbers* (it's much easier than names, and the directional signs will feature the numbers primarily) and the exit numbers of the main roads.

When you drive out of the airport (or the hire company's off-airport depot) don't look for signs to 'Orlando'. The main tourist areas are all south and west of the city proper, so follow the appropriate signs for your hotel. For the International Drive area you want the Beeline Expressway (Route 528) all the way west until it crosses

International Drive just north of Sea World. The main hotel area of I-Drive (as it is known locally) is to the north, so keep right at the exit. For western Kissimmee and Walt Disney World, go south out of the airport and pick up the new Central Florida Greeneway (Route 417) all the way west until it intersects with the main local motorway, Interstate 4, or I4. You can then follow it straight across into Walt Disney World or take I4 south for one junction until it hits the main Kissimmee Routeway, Highway 192 (or the Irlo Bronson Memorial Highway). For eastern Kissimmee, come off Route 417 at its junction with the Orange Blossom Trail (Highway 441), and going south brings you into Highway 192 at the other end of the main tourist drag.

BRIT TIP: The Beeline Expressway (528) and Central Florida Greeneway (417) are both toll roads, so it's ESSENTIAL to have a few dollars worth of change before you leave the airport.

Signposts and road names

Right, that gets you to your holiday base, but there are still a few other pitfalls, and it's best to be aware of them in advance. First and foremost, the Americans have invented a system of signposting and road-naming, the wisdom of which is known only to them. For instance, you cannot fail to find the main attractions, but retracing your steps back to the hotel afterwards can prove tricky because they often take

Orlando: International Drive

you out of the parks a different way. Also, exits off the Interstate and other main roads can be on EITHER side of the carriageway, not just on the right as you would expect. The Interstate 4 exit for Universal Studios is on the LEFT, for example. This potential worry is offset, though, by the fact you can overtake in ANY lane on multi-lane highways, not just the outside ones. Therefore, you can happily sit in the middle lane and let the rest of the world go by until you see your exit. To get their own back at this obviously unfair ploy by visiting tourists, American road signposters have another sneaky trick in that they don't give you much advance notice of turn-offs. You get the sign and then the exit in very quick succession. No nice, handy, 3-2-1 countdown as you get on our motorways. The local police also take a dim view of late and frequent lane-changing. But once again, the speeds at which you are travelling tend to minimise the dangers of missing your turn-off. Local drivers

also tend to be very courteous, so if you signal properly they will always let you pull out. It is handy if your front seat passenger acts as navigator though. Orlando has yet to come up with a comprehensive tourist map of its city streets and the maps supplied by the car rental companies tend to be rather simplified. It helps that none of the main attractions are off the beaten track, but the support of your navigator can be very useful, especially while you are still getting your bearings in the first few days.

Around town, and in the main tourist areas like International Drive and Kissimmee, you will come across another way of confusing the unwary with the way road names are displayed. At every junction you will see a road name hung underneath the traffic lights, which are always suspended ABOVE the road. This road name is NOT the road you are on, but the one you are CROSSING. Once again there is no advance notification of each junction and the road names can be difficult to read as you approach them, especially at night, so keep your speed down if you think you are close to your turn-off so you can get in the correct lane. Don't worry, though, if you do miss a turning, as nearly all the roads are arranged in a simple grid system so it is usually easy to work your way back. Occasionally you will meet a crossroads where no right of way is obvious. This is a four-way stop, and here the priority goes in order of arrival, so when it's your turn you just indicate and pull out slowly (Americans don't have roundabouts, so this is the closest you will get to one!).

Several major highways, notably the Beeline Expressway and Florida Turnpike, are also toll roads, so have some change handy in varying amounts from 25 cents to $1. They all do give change (in the GREEN lanes), but you will get through much quicker if you have the correct money (in the BLUE lanes).

As well as the obvious difference of driving on the 'wrong' side of the road in the first place (a particular hazard in car parks, some people find), there are also several differences in procedure of which it is handy to be aware. The most frequent British errors occur at traffic lights, where there are two variations to catch out the uninformed. At a red light it is still possible to turn RIGHT, providing there is no traffic coming from the left and no pedestrians and unless otherwise specified. Turning LEFT at the lights, you have the right of way with a green ARROW, but you have to give way to traffic from the other direction on a SOLID green light. The majority of accidents involving overseas visitors take place on left turns, so do take extra care here. There is also no amber light from red to green, but there IS an amber light from green to red!

Speed limits and restrictions

Speed limits are always well marked with black numbering on white sign and, again, the police are pretty hot on speeding and on-the-spot fines are steep: $57 for being stopped in the first place, plus $5 for every mile an hour you are over the limit. Limits vary from 55 to 65 mph on the Interstates (and can change frequently), where there is also a 40mph MINIMUM speed, to just 1 or 20mph in some built-up areas. Flashing orange lights suspended over the road indicate a school zone and you should proceed with caution, while school buses CANNOT be overtaken in either direction when they are unloading and have their hazard lights flashing. U-turns are forbidden in built-up areas and where a solid line runs down the middle of the road. It is also illegal to park within 10 feet of a fire hydrant or a lowered kerb, and NEVER park in front of a yellow-painted kerb — they are stopping points for emergency vehicles and you will be towed away! Never park on a kerb, either. Seat belts are also compulsory for all front seat passengers, while child seats MUST be used for children under four and can be hired from the car companies at around $3 a day. Children of four or five must either use a seat belt, whether sitting in the front or back, or have a child seat fitted. Florida has two additional quirks that should be noted. Firstly, you MUST put your lights on in the rain, and secondly you MUST park bonnet first. Reverse parking is illegal because number plates are often found only on the rear of cars and patrolling police cars like to be able to read them without the officers having to stop and walk round the car. If you park parallel to the kerb you must also be facing in the

irection of the traffic. Also, a word
n drinking and driving — don't do
t! Florida has very strict laws on
riving under the influence of
lcohol, with penalties of up to six
months in prison for first-time
offenders. The legal limit for the
lood-alcohol level is lower than in
Britain, so it is safer not to drink at
ll if you are driving. It is also illegal
o carry open containers of alcohol
n the car itself.

Accidents

n the unlikely event of having an
ccident, no matter how minor, the
police must be contacted before the
ars can be moved (except on the
busy I4). Car hire firms will insist on
full police report for the insurance
paperwork. In the case of a breakdown, there should be an emergency
number for the hire company among
their essential literature, or, if you
re on a major highway, raise the
bonnet of your car to indicate a
problem and wait for one of the
frequent police patrol cars to stop
or you. Remember also always to
carry your driving licence and your
hire agreement forms with you in
ase you are stopped by the police at
ny time. Should you be pulled over,
emain in your car and be polite to
he officer who comes over. Once
hey learn you are British you MAY
ust get away with a ticking-off for a
minor offence!

Key routes

As already mentioned, the main
route through Orlando is **Interstate
4** (or I4), a six-to-eight-lane
motorway linking the two Florida
costs. Interstates are always
indicated on blue shield-shaped
signs. For most of its length I4
travels almost directly east–west,
but, around Orlando it swings
annoyingly north–south. Annoying,

because directions are still given
either east or westwards, so be aware
that in this case east means north in
real terms and a sign saying west
means you are going south! All main
motorways are prefixed I, the even
numbers generally going east–west
and the odd numbers north–south.
Federal Highways are the next grade
down, and are again all numbered
with black numerals on white
shields, while state roads are known
as Routeways (black numbers on
white circular or oblong signs). All
the attractions of Walt Disney
World, plus those of Sea World and
Universal Studios, can be found and
are well signposted from I4. Cypress
Gardens is a 45-minute drive from
central Orlando (South) west on I4
and Highway 27, while Busch
Gardens is 75 minutes down I4 to
Tampa. The Kennedy Space Center
is a good hour's drive along the
Beeline Expressway which intersects
I4 at junction 28 and can also be
joined by driving east on Sandlake
Road, an alternative route into the
north of International Drive from
the airport.

International Drive is the
second key local roadway, linking
as it does a five-mile ribbon of
hotels, shops, restaurants and some
of the smaller attractions like Wet
'n' Wild, the Mercado Shopping
Centre, King Henry's Feast and
Belz Factory Outlet shopping
malls. From I4, take junctions 27A,
28, 29 or 30B. To the north,
International Drive runs into
Oakridge Road and then the South
Orange Blossom Trail, which leads
into downtown Orlando, (junctions
38–41 off I4). International Drive
is also bisected by Sandlake Road
and runs away into Epcot Drive to
the south, which is another handy
way to the attractions of Walt
Disney World. It is a major tourist
centre in its own right and makes
an excellent base from which to
operate, especially to the south of

3

Sandlake Road, near to the Mercado Shopping Centre, where you can actually enjoy a walk around on real pavement (and it's perfectly safe, too)! It's a 20-minute drive from Walt Disney World's attractions and 10–15 minutes from Universal Studios and Sea World. However, I-Drive can become congested at peak times, especially at the junction with Sandlake Road, so it can be better to use I4 for north–south journeys.

The other main tourist area is the town of Kissimmee to the south of Orlando and the south–east of Walt Disney World. Again, it's an attraction in its own right, being the home of Water Mania, the Old Town shopping complex, Gatorland, Jungleland and the Medieval Nights, Arabian Nights, Fort Liberty and Capone's dinner shows, plus more hotels and restaurants. It is all grouped in a rather untidy straggle along a 12-mile stretch of **Highway 192** (The Irlo Bronson Memorial Highway), which intersects I4 at junction 25B, and is not much more than 10 minutes from Walt Disney World, 15 from Sea World and 25 from Universal Studios. The downtown area of Kissimmee (off Main Street, Broadway and Emmett Street) is much prettier and accessible by foot!

Fuel

Finally, a quick word about re-fuelling your hire car at a typical American gas station (never 'petrol' remember). You will often have a choice of attendant or self-serve. You do not tip the attendant but you do pay a slightly higher price to cover the service. Most gas stations will also require you to pay in advance, ie, before filling the car, and will require the exact amount in cash or your credit card. Some pumps also allow you to pay by credit card directly, without having to go in to the cashier's office. The American gallon is also slightly smaller (by about a fifth) than the

> BRIT TIP: The Kissimmee/St Cloud tourist information office on east Highway 192 has the best free map of the area, clearly indicating all the main routes and attractions.

British version. Always use unleaded fuel, and, to make American petrol pumps work, you must first lift the lever underneath the pump nozzle.

Local maps

While a lot of the freely distributed tourist maps of the Orlando area tend to be pretty sketchy, there are couple which are better than others. For the best maps of Walt Disney World, International Drive and the main theme parks get MapEasy's Guide to Orlando ($5.50 at Benjamin Books in Orlando International Airport) while AA members can also get hold of the most detailed road maps of Central Florida courtesy of the American version of their organisation, the AAA. Check with the AA before leaving home or visit the AAA in Orlando on East Colonial Drive in the Colonial Promenade shopping plaza (tel 407 894 3333) with your AA membership card and get their maps for Southern Metropolitan Orlando and Kissimmee (at $3 each). The Universal Map is almost as comprehensive and is available from most petrol stations, priced $2.50.

Now, fully armed with the essential knowledge to be auto-mobile in Orlando, let's tell you a little more about what to expect from your holiday accommodation ...

Accommodation
or making sense of American hotels, motels and condos

To list all the various hotels, motels, holiday homes, guesthouses, condominiums, campsites and other forms of accommodation available in the Orlando area would fill up this book, so it is not the intention here to attempt a comprehensive guide. The metropolitan Orlando area can boast the highest concentration of hotels anywhere in the United States and more are being built all the time, with the number of rooms forecast to exceed 100,000 by 1997. The vast majority of British tourists (in excess of 95 per cent on the last figures supplied by the various holiday companies) will also have their accommodation arranged through the numerous package deals on offer, so the following detail is intended only as a taste of the bigger, better or budget types.

Hotels

The first thing to be aware of is that American hotels, particularly in the largest tourist areas like this, tend towards the motel type, even among some of the bigger and more expensive 'hotels'. This doesn't mean you will be short-changed as far as facilities and service are concerned, but you won't necessarily be located in one main building. The chances are your room will be in one of several blocks, arranged around the other facilities such as the swimming pool, restaurant, etc.

This is a significant distinction because of the safety aspects — it is possible for non-hotel guests to gain access to parts of a motel-style hotel, so it is important to be security conscious in little matters like ensuring the room is locked and checking the ID of anyone who knocks at the door (although it is not something to be worried about. See also Chapter Eight, Safety First). The size of rooms rarely alters, too, even between two-star and four-star accommodation. In general, it is the extra amenities of the hotel which give it extra star rating and not the size of the rooms themselves. A standard room usually features two double beds and will comfortably accommodate a family of four.

> BRIT TIP: Few hotels have got round to providing hair-dryers as standard in their rooms and if you bring your own you will need a US plug adaptor (with two flat pins). Their current is also different, 110–120 volts AC, as opposed to our 220, so your hair dryer/electric razor will work rather sluggishly.

As a general rule, hotels in Orlando are big, clean, efficient and great value for money. However, one area where they do lag behind their British counterparts is in the provision of tea- and coffee-making facilities. At present there are very few hotels that provide these as a matter of course, but they are slowly coming round to the demand. You will probably find that, in the absence of this facility, your tour rep will be able to sell you a handy tea-making kit for a nominal charge. What American hotels do all provide in abundance, however, are soft-drink and ice-machines, with ice buckets in all the rooms (although you may find that you are paying well over the odds for a can of Coke, or whatever, from the machine at the end of your corridor).

BRIT TIP: Buy your soft drinks at the nearest supermarket, who will also be able to sell you a neat polystyrene cooler for about $4 that you can fill with ice from your hotel ice machine to keep your drinks cold.

All types of accommodation will also be fully air-conditioned and, when it is really hot, you will have to learn to live with the steady drone of the A/C unit in your room at nights. NEVER turn the air-conditioning off when you go out, even when it is cool in the morning because, by the time you return the chances are your room will have turned into an oven.

Note also that the most expensive place to make a telephone call from is your hotel room! Nearly every hotel adds on a whacking 45–70 per cent surcharge on every call (you can also be charged for a call even if no-one answers if it rings five or more times). A better way to make your calls is to buy a local phonecard, which even the holiday companies

now sell, and use a normal payphone. There will be a 1–800 number to their central computer and you then punch in the special number on your card to bring up the dialling tone (give it plenty of time to connect — it can take up to 40 seconds before the dialling tone comes through in some instances). To call Britain from the USA, dial 011 44, then drop the first 0 from your area code.

Wilderness Lodge

Remember also that hotel prices (both in this book and in Orlando) are always per room and NOT per person. Where they are listed here it is always at standard room rates (without local taxes) during PEAK season. This means they will be cheaper out of the main holiday periods, but prices are still likely to vary from month to month and with special deals offered from time to time. Always ask for rates before you book and check if any special rates apply during your visit. There can also be an additional charge ($5–$15 per person) for more than two adults sharing the same room. It pays to book in advance in high season because Orlando's additional popularity as a convention centre

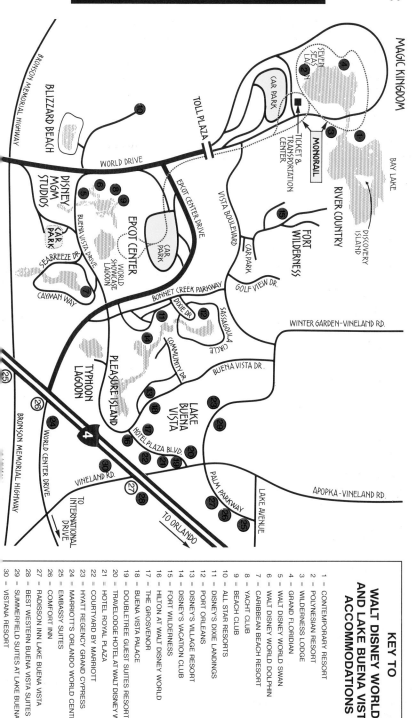

means it can get very busy at peak times, despite the 80,000-plus rooms the area boasts.

About the best course of action, if you've just arrived and are looking for accommodation, is to head for one of the two official Visitor Centres in the area, one on International Drive in the

> **BRIT TIP:** It is standard practice for American hotels to take a credit card imprint when you check in to cover any incidentals ('phone calls, etc) during your stay. Make sure, therefore, you have plenty to spare on your credit card limit!

Mercado Mediterranean Village and the other at the eastern end of Highway 192 in Kissimmee, where they keep an up-dated list of all the hotels and their rates, with dozens of brochures on display advertising the latest special deals to be had.

Walt Disney World

In keeping with the rest of this guide, a review of Orlando's hotels starts with Walt Disney World. With the convenience of being almost on the doorstep of the resort's main attractions, and linked by an excellent free transport system of monorail, shuttle buses and boats, Disney's hotels, holiday homes and campsites are also all magnificently appointed and maintained. They range from the futuristic appeal of the Contemporary Resort (the monorail travels right through the main building) to the Wild West feel of the Fort Wilderness Resort and campsite. Their landscaping, imagination and attention to detail are as good as the theme parks themselves. In all, there are more than 22,000 rooms throughout Disney's 43 square miles, while the 780-acre Fort Wilderness has 1,192 individual sites. However, all this grandiose holiday accommodation comes at a price. A standard room at the Grand Floridian Resort can cost up to $280 a night in high season, while a villa for six at

Disney's Village Resort would set you back $330, and even the more budget-priced Caribbean Beach Resort can be more than $100 a night. Eating out in the hotels and resorts is not cheap, either, and you won't find much in the way of fast-food outlets as you do along International Drive and Highway 192.

However, there is now a budget choic for holiday-makers in Walt Disney World itself, and it is aimed specifically at the British market — the brand new All Star Resorts (see below). This means the convenience of being so close to some of Orlando's biggest attractions ha been opened to a lot more holiday budgets, and it is worth a lot, especially in high season when the surrounding roads are packed.

Kids especially will love being a part c the Disney experience full-time, and there are also first-class child-minding and babysitting services available at mos Disney properties. Disney guests also ge to carry their own ID charge card with which you can charge meals, gifts, etc, tc your room (and have them delivered there). There is exclusive early entrance to selected theme parks on various days up to an hour before the general public, while some Disney resorts feature breakfast with Disney characters and dinner with Chip 'N' Dale. You also have the option of booking restaurants and dinner shows as soon as your reservation is confirmed, well ahead of other visitors Additional perks to Disney-accommodated guests include free parking at the big theme park car parks (a saving of $5 a time) and guaranteed admission even if the general public are being turned away in high season.

Around the Magic Kingdom you will find four of Disney's grandest properties the 15-storey **Contemporary Resort** boasts 1,050 rooms, a cavernous foyer and a recent $100 million renovation, as well as shops, restaurants, lounges, a rea sandy beach, a marina, two swimming pools, six tennis courts, an electronic games centre and a health club – and magnificent views. The accent is on fun, fun, fun, and it is definitely not the place for a quiet vacation! As with all Disney accommodation, rooms are large, scrupulously clean and extremely well furnished. Rates begin at $210 in high season. The **Polynesian Resort** is a real South Seas tropical fantasy brought to life with ultra-modern sophistication and comfort. Beautiful sandy beaches, lush vegetation and architecture cleverly disguise the fact that 853 rooms can be found here, built in film-set wooden longhouse style and all with balconies and wonderful views. Some excellent eating opportunities can also be discovered, along with canoe rentals, two popular kids' pools, a games room, shops and children's playground. Rates from $220 in high season. Disney's **Wilderness Lodge** opened in 1994 and is currently the 'in' place to be seen to stay. It is an imposing re-creation of a National Park lodge in amazing detail, down to the hot stream running through the massive wooden balcony-lined atrium lobby and out into the gardens, past the swimming pool (with hot and cold spas) and ending in Disney's very own version of the Old Faithful geyser, erupting every hour! It offers authentic backwoods charm with five-star luxury and is connected to the Magic Kingdom by boat, bus and monorail. It also has two full-service restaurants, a snack bar and a pool bar, and is one of the few places where you can get a Bison Burger! Rates begin at $169 in high season. The **Grand Floridian** completes the quartet of Magic Kingdom hotels, a hugely elaborate mock Victorian mansion with 900 rooms, an impressive domed and towered foyer and staff decked out in Edwardian dress. The rooms are luxurious, hence the mega price range, and it is worth a look even if you are staying somewhere else. It also has six restaurants, including Disney's top-of-the-range establishment Victoria and Albert's (where their set, six-course dinner with wine will set you back more than $100 per person!), four bars and the inevitable comprehensive array of sporting and relaxation facilities. Rates begin at $280 in high season and go as high as $540 for a suite! The Wilderness Lodge, Grand Floridian, Contemporary and Polynesian are all situated right on the monorail, the best and fastest system for getting into the Magic Kingdom and Epcot 96.

Epcot 96

Across at Epcot 96 you have the choice of five hotels, including the 'entertainment architecture' of The Swan and The Dolphin. These are either pastel-coloured concrete monstrosities or the best examples of how to make a hotel look fun, according to your point of view. **The Swan** is so named for the two unmistakable 45-foot statues atop the hotel, which has 758 rooms, three restaurants, two lounge bars, eight tennis courts (shared with The Dolphin), swimming pool, shops, health club and a white sand beach. If you appreciate room lamps shaped like pineapples, this is the place for you, but again it isn't cheap: high season rates start at $260 and 80% of its business tends to be convention-orientated. Sister hotel **The Dolphin** features a 27-storey pyramid with two giant dolphin statues on the top! A massive 1,509 rooms (the most of any one-building hotel in Orlando) indicate that here is another seriously busy hotel (especially with convention business) although the service is still first class. Seven restaurants, three bars, swimming pool and grotto fun-pool, fitness club, games room and some tasty shops (especially for chocolate lovers!) can be found here, with rates from $249. Both hotels are privately run but still have to conform to Disney's exacting standards for appearance, style and service. Transport to the theme parks and other amenities is provided by boat, tram and bus. The **Caribbean Beach** is one of the largest resort-type hotels anywhere in America, with 2,112 rooms and the accent on budget price and value for money. The rooms tend to be a bit smaller and plainer (although they will still comfortably house a family of four, and they all include mini-bars and coffee-makers), but the facilities in the form of restaurants, bars and outdoor activities (including a lakeside recreation area with themed waterfalls and slides) are as good as anywhere else in the resort. However, they can fill up quickly in high season and some people prefer to eat elsewhere. Transportation from the five Caribbean "villages" that make up the resort to the theme parks is by bus, and rates start at $99 peak season. Going up-market again, the refined, almost intimate, **Yacht Club** has 635 rooms designed with nautical themes, all set around an ornamental lake. For a hearty breakfast, the Yacht Club Gallery (one of three restaurants and two bars) also offers some of the most satisfying fare in

4

Walt Disney World. Sister hotel the **Beach Club** completes the Epcot line-up. With 580 spacious rooms set along a man-made white sand beach, you could easily be fooled into thinking you were on some tropical island paradise. You can also go boating or catch a water-shuttle service to Epcot 96, while other theme park transportation is provided by tram and bus. Water fun is provided at the shared Stormalong Bay, a heated two-and-a-half-acre recreation area with water slides and a sandy-floored lagoon. Standard rooms at both start at $230 during high season.

Budget accommodation

The recently opened **All Star Resorts** are Disney's first serious venture into capturing a big share of the budget accommodation market, particularly with us Brits, who typically tend to stay outside

The lobby of Wilderness Lodge

the Vacation Kingdom. Here, for just $69 or $79 a night year round, you can stay in one of the five sports-themed blocks (Surfing, Basketball, Tennis, Baseball and American Football) centred around a massive food court, two swimming pools, a games arcade and shops, or the music-themed version (Jazz, Rock, Broadway, Calypso and Country). Both centres, which have a total of 3,840 rooms, have pool bars, shops, laundry facilities and a pizza delivery service, and, while their

All Star Sports Resort guest room

bright, almost garish decor lacks the refined touches of other resorts, they are well-designed for budget-conscious families who still want to enjoy all the Disney conveniences. Transportation to other areas of Walt Disney World is still also provided free for All Star Resorts guests, by bus and tram.

Village Resort area

The other main accommodation centre within Walt Disney World is the Village Resort area, which is just off to the right as you drive in along Epcot Drive. Here you will find: **Dixie Landings**, a 2,048-room resort which has a steamboat as a reception area, a cotton mill as a restaurant and an old-fashioned general store (ie, the gift shop). Rooms are either *Gone With The Wind*-style mansionesque (surrounded by grand staircases and totally unnecessary columns) or rural Bayou backwoods (decorated with wooden and brass fittings). It also has Ol'Man Island, a three-and-a-half-acre playground, incorporating swimming pool, kids' area and a fishing hole! Transportation by boat and bus, and rates from $99. **Port Orleans** by comparison adopts the atmosphere of the French quarter of New Orleans for its 1,008 rooms. Turn-of-the-century style fittings and a Mardi Gras feel make this one of the most pleasantly imaginative hotels, with full-service dining at Bonfamilles restaurant plus the Sassagoula Floatworks Factory food court, two bars, a games room, shopping arcade and Doubloon Lagoon, a great fun-pool on which to unleash the kids. Again, rates from $99 at high season and transportation by bus to all the other entertainment facilities. **Disney's**

KEY TO INTERNATIONAL DRIVE ACCOMMODATIONS

1 = PEABODY ORLANDO	13 = GATEWAY INN
2 = ORLANDO MARRIOTT	14 = LAS PALMAS HOTEL
3 = RENAISSANCE	15 = CLARION PLAZA HOTEL
4 = HOWARD JOHNSON UNIVERSAL TOWER	16 = HOLIDAY INN EXPRESS
5 = DELTA ORLANDO	17 = ENCLAVE SUITES
6 = DAYS INN SAND LAKE ROAD	18 = PARC CORNICHE
7 = INTERNATIONAL INN	19 = RAMADA SUITES
8 = QUALITY INN INTERNATIONAL	20 = SUMMERFIELD SUITES HOTEL
9 = QUALITY INN PLAZA	21 = WESTGATE LAKES RESORT
10 = RAMADA INN PLAZA INTERNATIONAL	22 = THE CASTLE
11 = CRYSTAL TREE INN	23 = OMNI ROSEN HOTEL
12 = TRAVELODGE ORLANDO FLAGS	24 = HAWTHORN SUITES

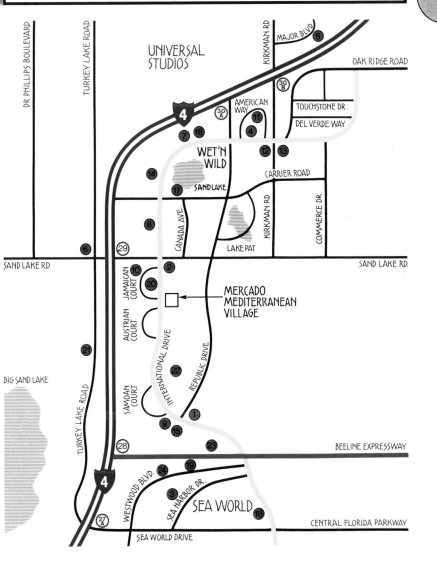

Village Resort is dotted around the Village Marketplace (see Shopping in Chapter Nine), consisting of 585 villa-type accommodations, most with their own kitchens, and housing from four to eight people. The villas are also well provided with pools, spas, laundry facilities, games arcades, bars and cafes within easy walking distance. For something out of the ordinary, try the Treehouse Villas, housed on stilts set in some pretty, secluded woods, with two bedrooms, two bathrooms, kitchen and breakfast bar. But note here that the villas are not located anywhere near the monorail system, so although there are shuttle buses, it is more important to have your own transport. Prices from $205 right up to $855 for a three-bedroomed Grand Vista Villa. **Disney's Vacation Club** is primarily a timeshare set-up of five-star proportions, but the one-, two- or three-bedroomed studios in a magnificent Key West setting can also be rented out on a nightly basis when not in use by club members. Additional facilities include swimming pools, tennis courts, games room, shops and fitness centre. Finally, Disney's **Fort Wilderness** offers an impressive array of camping facilities and chalet-style homes that can house up to six people. Two 'trading posts' supply fresh groceries, while there are two bars and cafés and a whole range of on-site activities, including the highly-popular and thrice-nightly Hoop-Dee-Doo Musical Revue, campfire programme, films, sports, games and a prime position from which to view the nightly Electrical Water Pageant. Buses and boats link the campsites with other Walt Disney World areas, with sites from $42 and homes at $200.

To make a reservation at any of Disney's properties, simply call 407 (if you're phoning from outside Orlando) 934 7639.

Village Hotel Plaza

In addition to the official Disney hotels, there are another seven 'guest' hotels inside Walt Disney World at the Disney Village Hotel Plaza. Again, these have the advantage of being on Disney's highly efficient transportation system, with the added perks of being able to make reservations for shows and restaurants before the general public, but they are almost without exception more expensive than hotels with similar facilities beyond the boundaries of Walt Disney World. Top of the list (for service, mod cons and price) is the 814-room **Hilton at Walt Disney World Village** (tel 407 827 4000, high season rates from $220), while also on the suitably expensive side are the **Grosvenor** (629 rooms, British Colonial decor, tel 407 828 4444), **Buena Vista Palace** (a bustling, 27-storey cluster of mirrored towers housing 1,028 rooms, many with a grandstand view of Epcot's Spaceship Earth, tel 407 827 2727) and the **Doubletree Guest Suites Resort** (229 family-sized suites offering excellent facilities, tel 407 934 1000). More modest (from $139 at peak periods) are the **TraveLodge Hotel** (325 rooms, good views over the Village, in-room coffee makers, two restaurants, cocktail lounge and 18th floor nightclub, tel 407 828 2424), **Royal Plaza** (high rise, 396 rooms from $147, heated pool, spa and three restaurants, tel 407 828 2828), and the **Courtyard by Marriott** (323 rooms in a 14-storey tower and six-storey annex featuring glass-walled lifts, from $135, tel 407 828 8888).

Lake Buena Vista

As you move further away from Walt Disney World the prices tend to moderate somewhat, although you can still spend a small fortune at the **Hyatt Regency Grand Cypress** in Lake Buena Vista, for example. This 1,500-acre resort offers three nine-hole and one 18-hole golf course (all designed by American golfing great Jack Nicklaus), a spectacular swimming pool complete with waterfalls and slide, 21-acre boating lake, tennis complex, health club and equestrian centre. Rates START at $200, but the 750 rooms and suites are magnificently appointed and equipped (it also has five restaurants, three lounges and a poolside bar, tel 407 239 1234). Nearby is **Marriott's Orlando World Centre**, an impressive landmark as you approach Walt Disney World, set as it is in 200 landscaped acres and surrounded by another golf course. An elaborate lobby, Chinese antiques and the sheer size of the hotel (1,503 rooms, seven restaurants, four pools and a health club) put it in the expensive range (rates from $184 per room, tel 407 239 4200), but it is very conveniently situated and it possesses one of the most stunningly picturesque pool areas, complete with waterfalls and palm trees, in Orlando. It does, however, get very busy, especially with convention business. Extra facilities include a separate wading pool for kids, an indoor pool, a sports pool (for water volleyball!), four whirpool spas, a golf school, tennis centre, five shops and a well-organised kids' programme. Phew! Lake Buena Vista is also home to the **Ramada Resort Maingate** at the Parkway (good value for money — from $75 high season — in a mid-price establishment, all the facilities and a handy situation, tel 407 396 7000). Good budget-style accommodation in this area can also be found at the **Comfort Inn** (640 rooms, motel style, tel 407 239 7300), **Radisson Inn Lake Buena Vista** (200 spacious rooms from $85, plus landscaped pool and spa, restaurant, pool-view cafe and children's playground, tel 407 239 8400), and the **Holiday Inn Sunspree Resort at Lake Buena Vista** (507 rooms from $99, tel 407 239 4500) and **Holiday Inn Maingate East** (670 rooms from $79, tel 407 396 4488) which are both excellent for kids, with a highly-rated supervised childcare programme, a good range of pools, restaurants and other facilities and all rooms feature mini-kitchenettes. Kids 12 and under eat free, as they do at the smart **Holiday Inn Maingate West** with its tropical courtyard, free-form heated pool and kiddie pool (287 rooms from $99, tel 407 396 1100). **The Sheraton Inn Lakeside**, also on west Highway 192, is surprisingly good value for a big-name group, especially with three pools, tennis courts, kids' playgrounds, mini-golf, paddleboats and two restaurants. Kids 10 and under also eat breakfast and dinner free with a paying adult and there is free transportation to Walt Disney World (651 rooms from $89, tel 407 396 2222). Likewise, the smaller **Hampton Inn Maingate**, again only one-and-a-half miles from Disney at the junctions of I4 and Highway 192, offers great value at just $88 in high season with a heated outdoor pool, free local phone calls, continental breakfast and shuttle service (164 rooms, tel 407 396 8484), as does

the **Hilton Gateway**, just west of I4, with a kids eat free programme, free morning coffee, two pools, a restaurant, deli and fitness centre (500 rooms from just $60, tel 407 239 5411). The **Hyatt Orlando** also looks as if it should be more expensive with its 922 rooms, three restaurants, four pools and kiddie pools, spas, playgrounds and other recreational facilities. Situated right on the junctions of I4 and Highway 192 it could not be more convenient, yet its year-round rates start at just $109 (tel 407 396 1234).

Kissimmee

Moving out along Highway 192 (the Irlo Bronson Memorial Highway) into Kissimmee, you will find the biggest choice of budget accommodation in Orlando. Facilities generally vary very little and what you see is what you get. All the big hotel chains can be found along this great tourist sprawl, and rates can be as low as $25 per room off-peak, or $35 for room with a kitchenette (what the Americans call an 'efficiency'). Be prepared to shop around for a good rate (discounts may be available at off-peak times), especially if you cruise along Highway 192 where so many hotels advertise their rates on large neon signs, and as a general rule prices drop the further you go from Walt Disney World. Don't be afraid to ask to see inside rooms before you settle on your holiday base. Take into consideration how much time you'll have to use extra facilities.

Chains

Among the leading chains are **Best Western** (all with pools, family orientated but large, in the budget $40–$80 range), **Days Inn** (rather characterless and without restaurants, but always good value — $50–$85 in most cases — and convenient and some rooms available with kitchenettes), **EconoLodge** (see under Best Western, but slightly more expensive), **Howard Johnson** (also a bit dearer, but with more spacious rooms and a free continental breakfast), **Quality Inn** (sound, popular chain, and from as little as $39), **Ramada** (rates can vary more widely between hotels in the $50–$100 range, some offer free continental breakfast) and **TraveLodge** (another identikit group, but also on the

4

KEY TO HIGHWAY 192 ACCOMMODATIONS

1 = RAMADA RESORT MAINGATE
2 = COMFORT INN MAINGATE
3 = RADISSON INN MAINGATE
4 = HOLIDAY INN SUNSPREE RESORT
5 = HOLIDAY INN MAINGATE EAST
6 = HOLIDAY INN MAINGATE WEST
7 = KINGS HOTEL
8 = CASA ROSA INN
9 = PARK INN INTERNATIONAL
10 = BROADWAY INN
11 = KNIGHTS INN MAINGATE
12 = SHERATON INN LAKESIDE
13 = HAMPTON INN MAINGATE
14 = HILTON GATEWAY
15 = HYATT ORLANDO
16 = DAYS SUITES
17 = LIFETIME OF VACATIONS RESORT
18 = VILLAGES AT MANGO KEY
19 = QUALITY SUITES
20 = HOMEWOOD SUITES
21 = BRYAN'S SPANISH COVE
22 = ISLE OF BALI
23 = ORBIT ONE
24 = PARKWAY INTERNATIONAL
25 = ORANGE LAKE RESORT
26 = FLORIDA GULF APARTMENTS
27 = ALEXANDER HOLIDAY HOMES (OFFICE)
28 = TROPICAL PALMS
29 = PHENIX PROPERTIES
30 = FLORIDA SELECT
31 = ADVANTAGE VACATION HOMES
32 = BRIGADOON HOLIDAY HOMES
33 = HOLIDAY VILLAS
34 = PREMIER VACATION HOMES
35 = CONCORD RESORTS
36 = WESTGATE VACATION VILLAS
37 = UNICORN INN

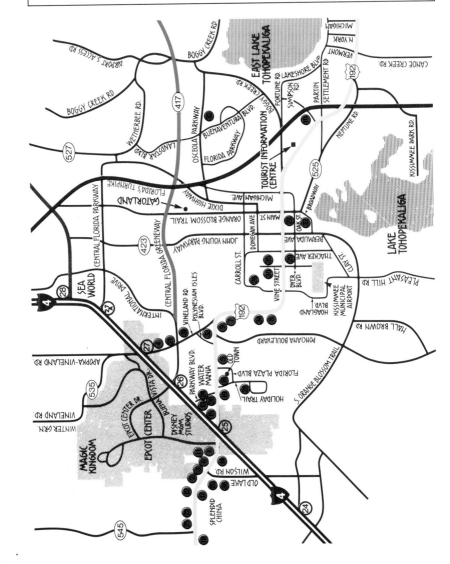

budget side). The **Fairfield Inns** are the budget-price version of the impressive Marriott chain, while the **Budgetel** group also rate highly for hotel security as well as lower prices. **The Holiday Inn** chain varies so widely these days, in both price and service, I have picked out only individuals worthy of note.

Independent organisations

In addition, there are literally dozens of smaller, independent outfits who offer special rates from time to time in order to compete with the big boys. Look out in particular for offers of 'Kids Eat Free' as this can save you quite a bit. Of the non-chain operators, **King's** (on west Highway 192) is prettily situated on the edge of a small boating and fishing lake and offers reasonable rates (around $50 per room, tel 407 396 4762), the **Casa Rosa Inn** offers simple, relatively peaceful Mediterranean-style hospitality (again on west Highway 192, tel 407 396

> BRIT TIP: When booking one of the chain hotels, make sure you have its full address — it is easy to end up at the wrong Holiday Inn or Howard Johnson!

2020), and the **Park Inn International** (same location, tel 407 396 1376) also has one of the better lake-front locations to go with its budget rates, and some of its rooms have kitchenettes. For pure budget price **The Broadway Inn** east on Highway 192 to Simpson Road is hard to beat (200 rooms from $35, tel 407 846 1530), as is the **Knights Inn Maingate**, just a mile west of Disney's main entrance on Highway 192 (120 rooms from $39, tel 407 396 4200).

International Drive

Furthest away from Walt Disney World, but handily situated for Universal Studios, Sea World and closer to downtown Orlando is the final main tourist area of International Drive. For overall location and value for money I-Drive is hard to beat. It is more thoughtfully laid out, some attractions are within walking distance, and the

hotels and motels tend to be slightly more attractive. Top of the range for quality is the **Peabody Orlando**, a luxurious, 891-room tower block with every possible facility you could wish for, including an Olympic-size pool, health club, four tennis courts with professional coaching available and some of the best restaurants in Orlando. However, rates

> BRIT TIP: For an attraction with a difference, don't miss the Peabody's twice-daily Duck March, which sees the hotel's trademark ducks take up residence from 11am–4pm in the huge lobby fountain! It's a fascinating sight and a great place for afternoon tea. Just sit and watch them roll out the red carpet for the resident mallards!

are also suitably impressive (in excess of $200 per room per night) and if there are any large conventions in town don't expect a quiet stay (tel 407 352 4000). The **Orlando Marriott** (1,054 rooms from $119, tel 407 351 2420) is similarly extravagant, with three swimming pools in its beautifully landscaped grounds (kids aged 11 and under also eat free with their parents), as is the magnificently appointed **Renaissance Resort** (on Sea Harbour Drive, 780 rooms from a mere $195, tel 407 351 5555), claiming the world's largest atrium lobby and with some enormous rooms and suites, an Olympic-size swimming pool, tennis courts, fitness centre including sauna and steam room, five restaurants and special kids' activities. Back on more budget lines, the **Howard Johnson Universal Tower** (302 rooms from $79, tel 407 351 2100) is a family-orientated establishment, superbly located for Universal Studios and Wet 'n Wild, as is the **Delta Orlando** (800 rooms from $99, tel 407 351 3340), which also benefits from being slightly off the main drag (on Major Boulevard). The **Days Inn** on Sand Lake Road is also worth seeking out (611 rooms, tel 407 351 1900) for its excellent all-round facilities and lakeside location (the Days Inn chain also offer free meals for kids under 12

4

when accompanied by their parents in their hotels that have restaurants), as well as the **International Inn** (315 rooms from $55, right opposite Wet 'n Wild and therefore pretty busy, tel 407 351 4444), the **Quality Inn International** (728 rooms, similar location, kids under 12 eat free, tel 407 351 1600), **Quality Inn Plaza** (a massive 1,020 rooms in multiple blocks with multiple pools and another kids-eat-free restaurant, high season prices from $55 but as low as $29, tel 407 345 8585), **The Crystal Tree Inn** (111 rooms, similar location, standard motel type, tel 407 352 8383) and **TraveLodge Orlando Flags** (270 rooms, again near Wet 'n Wild). **The Gateway Inn** (354 rooms at $80, tel 407 351 2000) offers free transport to Walt Disney World from just off International Drive on Kirkman Road, as well as giving you the choice of three pools, a restaurant, pool bar, lounge, café and mini-golf, while just around the corner on I-Drive is the tropically landscaped **Las Palmas Hotel**, a real bargain at $69 (262 rooms, tel 407 351 3900). If personal safety is paramount to you, the **Clarion Plaza Hotel** has a state-of-the-art security system, as well as a pool with jacuzzi and waterfall, two restaurants, a 24-hour deli and a nightclub (810 rooms from $125, tel 407 352 9700). The **Holiday Inn Express** is also worthy of note after its recent facelift, with a large heated pool, kiddie pool and games room, and it's slap in the middle of the action in I-Drive (217 rooms from $99, tel 407 351 4466).

New on I-Drive is the fanciful **Castle Hotel**, just behind Austin's and Café Tu Tu Tango restaurants. It is a nine-storey fantasy palace based loosely on the Magic Kingdom's castle and features tower and turret rooms, a grand outdoor heated pool with a 12-foot fountain, hot tub, pool bar and grill, and a children's play area. Its overall impression is a bit garish, but the rooms are all immaculately furnished and, at around $99–$125, a lot cheaper than many comparable hotels. Catering is also provided by the excellent Café Tu Tu Tango (216 rooms, tel 407 345 1511).

Off the beaten track

Getting slightly off the beaten track might bring you to the **Colony Plaza Hotel** on West Colonial Drive in west Orlando. Being away from the main drags has its appeal, plus there are two pools, tennis courts, a video games room, live entertainment in the Chit Chat Lounge and good shopping and other restaurants within easy walking distance (300 rooms at $70, tel 407 656 3333). Alternatively, the **Renaissance Hotel** just north of Orlando International Airport offers tremendous facilities, including an outdoor heated pool, fitness centre, sauna and steam rooms, spa pool and two restaurants, without the upmarket price tag and without being too far from the action (300 rooms from $110, tel 407 240 1000). Away in the selective suburb of Winter Park to the north of the city, the **Park Plaza Hotel** offers a smaller, more European style of hotel from just $80. It has an award-winning restaurant and is right in the middle of the exclusive Park Avenue shopping district (27 rooms, tel 407 647 1072).

Holiday homes

Finally, to round off this helter-skelter trip through places to stay, here is a quick look at a fast-growing area of accommodation in Orlando — that of suites hotels and holiday homes. These are extremely popular with Americans and beginning to catch on with us Brits as a neat way of larger family groups or friends staying together and cutting the cost of their stay both by doing much of their own cooking and the extra value of sharing. Typically, the homes, whether they come in the form of individual houses, collections of houses, resorts or condominiums (holiday apartment blocks), all usually have access to excellent facilities in the form of swimming pools and recreation areas, and are fully equipped with all mod cons like microwaves, TVs and washer-dryers. For these, you MUST be prepared to use a hire car to get around, but the savings for, say, a group of eight staying together are obvious. A three-bedroomed house sleeping eight can cost as little as $150 a night, or just $19 per person. Provided you are happy with the idea of doing your own cooking and washing-up, holiday homes definitely represent good value for money. Once again, the following can only be a representative selection of the properties on offer.

Basically, the choice is between what the Americans call suites — apartments built in hotel-like blocks around communal facilities but lacking some hotel features like bars and lounges – or out-and-out holiday homes, some in private residential areas and others in estate-type developments, most of which have their own pools and tend to work out slightly cheaper. Prices where listed are per WEEK in high season and will specify how many can share that particular apartment or house, but again rates can vary according to special deals and occasional price increases.

Budget suites

Suites hotels are a rapidly-expanding Orlando accommodation type, with the numerous versions of the **Embassy Suites** the prime example (and unmissable for their garish pink colouring). Typically a suites hotel gives you the extra benefit of your own mini-kitchen, including microwave and all cutlery and crockery, while many now provide a complimentary continental breakfast. Starting off with the suites in budget territory, the **Enclave Suites** on Carrier Drive, off Kirkman Road, offer deluxe studios that sleep four from $553/week and two-bed, two-bath studios sleeping six from $945 (tel 407 351 1155). They feature two outdoor and one indoor pool, a fitness room, jacuzzi, games room and restaurant. Kids eat free with their parents and there is complimentary continental breakfast and free local phone calls. **Days Suites**, next door to Old Town on Highway 192, has 604 one- and two-bedroomed suites, the largest of which can sleep six–10 people (tel 407 396 4700). Rates start at $623/week and kids under 12 eat free at their restaurant. Three pools, a cafeteria and barbecue area and kids' playground make for a full range of amenities. Next to Splendid China at the west end of Highway 192 is the **Lifetime of Vacations Resort**, a new motel/condominium complex with 50 units that sleep four and 50 that sleep six (tel 407 396 3000). High season rates start at $630, and their features include a heated pool, tennis, boating and fishing facilities, shuffleboard and a free barbecue every Wednesday. The brand

new **Club Esprit Apartment Suites** (tel 407 331 3132) to the north in the suburb of Altamonte Springs (next to the Altamonte Mall) is a superbly-furnished facility of one and two-bedroomed suites that also boasts a state-of-the-art fitness centre, 85-foot pool, floodlit tennis, jacuzzis, putting green and volleyball court. A week in high season is likely to cost $750 for a deluxe, two-bed apartment sleeping six.

For an equally well-equipped new resort the **Best Western Buena Vista Suites**, on International Drive adjacent to exit 27 of I4, also offers a taste of luxury. On top of a dazzling range of facilities, including a heated outdoor pool, jacuzzi and fitness centre, they offer a full, free breakfast and free transport to Disney's parks. Their two-room rates (that sleep 4–6) start at $763 in high season (tel 407 239 8588). The **Villages at Mango Key** are smart new town houses masquerading as a suites resort on Lindfields Boulevard, just off Highway 192 past Splendid China heading west (tel 407 397 2211). Their beautifully designed two-bedroom houses sleep six from $700 a week, while the three-beds sleep eight from $900, and there is a 10 per cent discount for second and third weeks. There is also a large, heated pool, jacuzzi, tennis courts and volleyball court. **Parc Corniche** condominium suite hotel is a similarly luxurious property on Parc Corniche Drive off International Drive, just south of Sea World (tel 407 239 7100). Surrounded by an 18-hole championship-quality golf course, it also has a heated pool, whirlpool and kiddie pool, playground, games room and full service restaurant and lounge, with a free continental breakfast and local phone calls. Rates for a one-bedroom suite start at $903 in high season and $1,225 for a two-bed suite. In a similar range are the **Quality Suites** at Maingate East, one mile east of I4 on Highway 192 (tel 407 396 8040). Their two-bedroomed suites can sleep up to 10 from $903/week and their magnificent courtyard area that houses two pools, a poolside bar, whirlpool spa and patio is the equal of any top-quality hotel. Kids under 10 eat free with their parents, and there is a free continental breakfast. The **Ramada Suites** at Tango Bay, near International

4

Drive, has 240 two-bed, two-bath suites that sleep up to six from $763–$903/week. There is a special Kidz Klub that is free to guests, plus free breakfast to add to their splendid facilities that consist of four jacuzzis, three pools, an exercise gym, video games room and paddleboats (tel 407 239 0707).

De luxe

Moving into the de luxe range you find the handily-located **Homewood Suites** on Parkway Boulevard next to Highway 192, just one-and-a-half miles from the main entrance of Walt Disney World. Their 156 suites sleep up to six from $973/week, but rates go as low as $483 out of season. Two pools and a jacuzzi, free breakfast and evening social functions are their main features, while each room has two colour TVs and a video player (tel 407 396 2229). **Hawthorne Suites** score highly for their location (on Westwood Boulevard, just behind Sea World), excellently furnished rooms and value for money that includes free breakfast daily, two TVs in every room, a free health club and little details like the provision of an iron and ironing board. Rates vary from $875 for a 1-bed suite sleeping four to $1,183 for a 2-bed sleeping six, and they have already proved popular with British guests (tel 407 351 6600). Galaxy Group Management have no less than four luxurious resort properties all within a few miles of Disney's attractions and boasting first-rate facilities. The **Isle of Bali** offers spacious two-bed, two-bath villas in a South Seas style, with the resort also offering swimming pool, spa bath, tennis courts and fishing and boating on their own lagoon. High season rates $1,015/week. **Bryan's Spanish Cove** features 116 lakefront villas sleeping six in a Treasure Island setting. Water activities abound, along with a very scenic swimming pool, kids' playground and games room. High season at $1,050/week. **Orbit One** has another 116 villas, again two-bed, two-bath (the master bathroom having a huge Roman tub!) in a picturesque landscaped garden setting less than two miles from Walt Disney World. Two large pools, one for kids, water slides, tennis, shuffleboard, putting green and a free

continental breakfast all add up to great amenities, with high season rates at $1,050. Top of the range are the 144 **Parkway International** villas in a mock-jungle setting and with safari decor (but five-star facilities). The villas are all stunningly furnished, and extra amenities include a nature trail, café, huge swimming pool, kids' pool and playground and free continental breakfast. For all Galaxy Group villas, call 407 239 5000.

Exclusive

If you're looking to stay away from the main tourist centres and fancy a round of golf or a few games of tennis as well, the **Mission Inn** could well be the place for you. This 625-acre resort is in a magnificent setting 35 minutes to the north west of Orlando, just off the Florida Turnpike, in Howey-in-the-Hills. Two top-notch golf courses, six tennis courts, a private marina, three restaurants and bars, a large pool and a lakeside pavillion are all set among Spanish colonial-style splendour, opulently furnished and ever so exclusive. Their rates reflect all this, at $1,295/week in high season (but down to $665 off peak), but they also offer a range of lodging and golf packages and seasonal specials (tel 904 324 3101).

Continuing the exclusive theme is the **Summerfield Suites Hotel** on International Drive (tel 407 352 2400). At $1,533/week high season it's not easy on your wallet, but the 146 one- and two-bedded rooms are magnificently furnished with every conceivable mod con. **Orange Lake Resort**, four-and-a-half miles west of Disney's main Highway 192 entrance, is another golfers' paradise, with 27 challenging holes and a driving range on top of the Olympic size pool, jacuzzis, saunas, 80-acre sandy-beach lake, watersports, children's playground, two restaurants, cinema and video games room. Rates are in keeping: up to $1,575/week for a two-bed, two-bath villa (tel 407 239 0000). The jewel in the crown, however, has to be the **Vistana Resort**, again in the Lake Buena Vista area (tel 407 239 3100). You almost never need set foot outside its confines as the Vistana possesses five pools, seven jacuzzis, 13 tennis courts, basketball, shuffleboard, fitness centres with steam and sauna rooms, an 18-hole mini-golf course, five kids' pools and playgrounds, video games rooms, general store and deli, two restaurants and bars and even a video library, as well as having its own, 24-hour security. Their sumptuous villas, in six different themed areas, sleep up to eight people, but wait for the price: up to $1,925/week!

Holiday homes

Turning to holiday homes, **Florida Gulf Apartments** have 60 homes scattered around the western Kissimmee area, ranging from $453/week for a two-bed property to $755/week for a four-bed with pool (tel 407 932 2000). All are generously furnished, are little more than five minutes from Walt Disney World and have use of community swimming pool, tennis courts and children's play areas, while many also have their own private pools. For great value and excellent properties, **Alexander Holiday Homes** (tel 407 933 6405), also in Kissimmee, have 160 detached two-, three- and four-bedded homes all with pools and immaculately furnished, within 15 minutes of Disney with rates from $453 to $573. From fully-fitted kitchens to walk-in wardrobes and private pools, these are a great way to enjoy a bit of Florida freedom on your holiday. Eight miles to the south, near Baseball City on Route 54, away from the main tourist hustle and bustle but still well located for all the main attractions, **Sunsplash Rentals** have 62 purpose-built houses again with every facility you could want and still at a sensible price from $550 a week. Private pools are standard and local phone calls are free (tel 407 424 6193).

Slap bang in the middle of Highway 192, and therefore centrally located for all Orlando's attractions, **Florida Now** have more than 50 spacious villas and private homes that also conform to the smart-but-budget-conscious variety (tel 407 397 2444). They take from four to eight people and rates vary from $475–$800/week. All are, of course, fully equipped, from microwave to bed linen, swimming pool to colour TV. **Tropical Palms**, on Holiday Trail just south of Highway 192 and close to the Old Town area, is a holiday camp with a difference, 100 pastel coloured villas and chalet-

bungalows spread out around a large heated swimming pool, outdoor café, laundry, playground and shuffleboard courts. The two-bedroomed villas can sleep up to eight people, while the smaller studio-type bungalows sleep four; both have charming open-air wooden patio decks. Rates from $483/week (tel 407 396 4595). **Florida Choice** have a terrific variety of homes with up to seven bedrooms (sleeping 16) around the Kissimmee area, the majority with private pools. Wonderful furnishings, convenient locations and 24-hour guest services make for a highly attractive proposition (tel 407 847 0284, or UK freephone 0800 897479) with high season rates from $485–715 ($1,500 for the huge, seven-bedroom option). **Ventura Resort Rentals** offer a similarly wide-ranging selection of villas and houses in both Orlando and Kissimmee, all with swimming pools and hot-tubs, and excellent facilities for golf, tennis, fishing and boating. One-bedroomed homes start at $595 going up to four-bed properties at $1,000 (tel 407 273 8770).

More luxurious

For an even more luxurious touch, **Florida Select** have 65 three- and four-bed houses, all with pools, just five miles west from Disney's main entrance on Highway 192 (tel 407 870 9871, or UK, 01782 394546). All have private pools, insect-proof patios and resident guest services, with their homes accommodating six–10 people and rates from $602/week in high season for a three-bed house, with the addition of long-stay and group discounts. In four locations around Orlando and Kissimmee, **Orlando Resorts** offer one-, two-, three- and four-bed villas and homes in convenient, spacious privacy. Not all have private pools, but there are central facilities that include pools, jacuzzis, tennis, fishing, boating and fitness centres as well as 24-hour security. Rates from $665/week in high season (tel 407 647 4480). **Brigadoon Holiday Homes** in Cypress Lakes, Kissimmee, have some extremely spacious three- and four-bed homes from $693/week (tel 407 240 0075, or UK 01702 79568). All homes have screened, solar-heated pools, cable TV and free local phone calls, and babysitting services are also available, with discounts for senior citizens and stays of more than two weeks. **Premier Vacation Homes** also go for the luxury end of the market with two-, three- and four-bedroom homes in the central area of Highway 192 (tel 407 396 2401). All homes have two full-sized bathrooms as well as fully-equipped kitchens, screened private pools and patios, while there is also a community centre with a large pool, tennis court and picnic and play areas. Rates go up to $700/week for a three-bed home and $840 for the four-bed variety. One of the largest operators, **Advantage Vacation Homes**, have 250 two-, three- and four-bedroom homes, most with private pools, in west Kissimmee, sleeping up to 10 people (tel 407 396 2262). Weekly rates are from $630–$1,400 and they offer golfing packages and senior citizen discounts.

Among the smartest operations in the Orlando area, **The Villas of Somerset** in Kissimmee and **Laguna Bay Villas** just south of Walt Disney World are worth investigating (rates from $553 up to $1,365/week, especially as their parent company, Holiday Villas, have a British office (tel 01623 649376) who will be only too happy to send you information. **Lifestyle Resorts** specialise in the Orlando area and also have an office over here (tel 0800 892568), as do **Concord Resorts** (0800 896650), who have some extremely attractive condominiums along the Irlo Bronson Memorial Highway and vacation homes to the east of Kissimmee (rates start at $973/week).

CFI Resorts

Finally, **CFI Resorts**, who operate the five-star Hotel Royal Plaza in Walt Disney World Village, also run four similarly top-quality villa resorts around Orlando. **Westgate Lakes Resort** is located just off I4 on Turkey Lake Road and is set among 97 acres of tropical splendour with lake frontage and watersports. Here 369 spacious one and two-storey villas sleep up to eight, and the first-class central facilities include a huge free-form swimming pool, jacuzzis, private beach, tennis courts, health club and children's playground and Kids Club programme, as well as three restaurants and bars and nearby golf. It doesn't come cheap, however: high season rates hit

$945 for a one-bed villa and $1,890 for a two-bed (tel 407 352 8051). **Westgate Vacation Villas**, in Kissimmee, are set among 187 acres around three lakes and offer free breakfast and cheese and wine parties with live entertainment. Villas are one-, two- or three-bedded and some have jacuzzis, while there are also tennis courts, eight pools, six kids' pools, a sauna, playground, fishing, paddleboats and a video games room, as well as snack bar, minimarket and gift shop. Rates peak at a whopping $2,100 a week, but the villas are the most luxurious you will find. **The Seasons** and **Club Orlando** are both situated just south of downtown Orlando and feature spacious one- and two-bedroom villas with all the attendant facilities and rates from $945–$1,365/ week in high season. For Westgate, Seasons and Club Orlando, tel 407 351 3351.

Once again, you can see there is no shortage of choice, and you will even find a few places offering bed and breakfast. However, these are a long way removed from a traditional British B&B with one notable and laudable exception. **The Unicorn Inn**, just off the main drag in downtown Kissimmee, opened in '95 run by a Yorkshire couple who have lavished a small fortune in turning a ramshackle building into a luxurious but homely bed and breakfast inn that really caters for the individual. Rates start at just $55 per night, and there are discounts for stays of one week or longer. Their location is ideal for walking around the prettier parts of town and you can be sure of a decent cup of tea for a change! Call Don or Fran for more information on this little gem on 407 846 1200.

Finally (and this time I really do mean it!), for any additional information on these ideas (or indeed any other tourist-rated topics), there are several tourist agencies who will be only too keen to help. First of all in Britain, there is an Orlando Tourist Information Office in London (tel 0171 243 8072), while in Orlando itself, the Convention and Visitors Bureau is located at 7208 Sand Lake Road, Suite 300, Orlando, Florida 32819 (tel 407 363 5800) and has its official Visitor Information Center in the Mercado Shopping Village (above).

Now, it's time to HIT THE THEME PARKS …

The Big Six Theme Parks

or spending the day with Mickey Mouse and Co

By now you should be prepared to deal with the main business of any visit to Orlando: Walt Disney World and the other main theme parks of Universal Studios, Sea World and Busch Gardens.

If you have only a week in the area this is where you should concentrate your energy and attention. Seven days is the bare minimum these days to comfortably enjoy the Big Six, and even then you may decide that the 90-minute drive down to Tampa for Busch Gardens is just a bridge too far. If you have less than a week you should concentrate on seeing as much of Walt Disney World as possible, with Universal studios as an option. However, Universal are about to embark on a major expansion programme which includes a second theme-park

BRIT TIP: Beware! This is where your holiday can start to get expensive. None of the Big Six will cost you less than $31 a day for adult admission, and over-nines are nearly always classed as ADULTS, so it is important you budget for your day out at each one using the At-A-Glance guides. Otherwise you can find yourself spending a LOT more than you imagined.

attraction as well as an entertainment complex and five resort-style

BRIT TIP: Beware the offers of cheap or free tickets for Disney as they are used as inducements to visit timeshare operations. And NEVER buy a Disney park ticket from a tout or unofficial source. The chances are it is stolen or non-transferable and you will have wasted your money.

hotels. Once these are up and running, two weeks rather than just one will become the BASIC requirement for a visit to central Florida's theme park city!

When it comes to price, be aware that, with the exception of Disney's parks, it is always possible to get a few dollars off your tickets to ALL the other attractions. Nearly all the local tourist publications will have money-off vouchers, while there are ticket outlets up and down Highway 192 and International Drive offering discounted tickets. Generally speaking, the holiday companies all offer good discounts to the main attractions as they buy in bulk (and Cosmos also offer a unique refund service for unused non-Disney tickets). But it is still occasionally possible to shop around and get better deals. Universal Studios have ticket booths that give several dollars off all tickets except Disney, while Know Before You Go have a similar operation at a number

ADVENTURELAND

1 JUNGLE CRUISE
2 SWISS FAMILY ROBINSON
3 PIRATES OF THE CARIBBEAN
4 THE ENCHANTED TIKI BIRDS

FRONTIERLAND

5 BIG THUNDER MOUNTAIN RAILROAD
6 COUNTRY BEAR JAMBOREE
7 DIAMOND HORSESHOE JAMBOREE
8 SPLASH MOUNTAIN
9 TOM SAWYER ISLAND

LIBERTY SQUARE

10 HALL OF PRESIDENTS
11 THE HAUNTED MANSION
12 LIBERTY SQUARE RIVERBOAT
13 MIKE FINK KEELBOATS

FANTASYLAND

14 CASTLE STAGE
15 LEGEND OF THE LION KING
16 PETER PAN'S FLIGHT
17 IT'S A SMALL WORLD
18 SNOW WHITE'S ADVENTURES
19 MR TOAD'S WILD RIDE
20 20,000 LEAGUES UNDER THE SEA

MICKEY'S STARLAND

21 GRANDMA DUCK'S FARM
22 MICKEY'S HOLLYWOOD THEATRE
23 MICKEY'S HOUSE & STARLAND SHOW

TOMORROWLAND

24 GRAND PRIX RACEWAY
25 SPACE MOUNTAIN
26 SKY-WAY
27 ASTRO ORBITER
28 ALIEN ENCOUNTER
29 TRANSPORTARIUM
30 CAROUSEL OF PROGRESS
31 TOMORROWLAND TRANSIT AUTHORITY
32 DREAM FLIGHT
33 WALT DISNEY WORLD RAILROAD
34 LAUNCH TO DISCOVERY ISLAND &
   FORT WILDERNESS

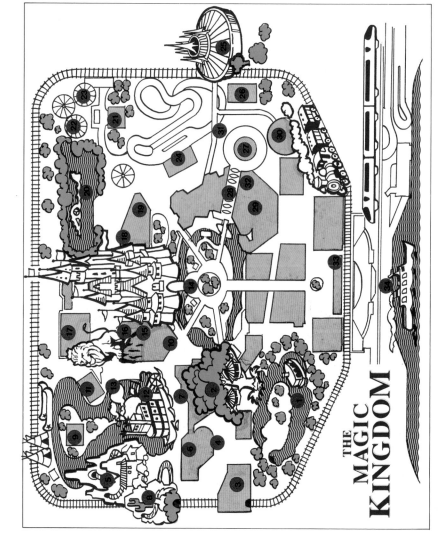

THE MAGIC KINGDOM

of offices and other outlets in the main tourist areas. Anheuser-Busch have perhaps the best discount offer for their parks of Busch Gardens, Sea World and Cypress Gardens with up to $6 off if you buy tickets in, say, Cypress Gardens for Sea World, or in Busch Gardens for Cypress Gardens.

Ratings

All the rides and shows are judged on a unique rating system that splits them into the Thrill Rides or Shows and the Scenic or Aaah ones (as in 'Aaah, isn't that nice!'). Thrill rides earn T ratings out of five (hence a TTTTT is as exciting as they get) and scenic rides get A ratings out of five (an AA ride is likely to be over-cute and missable). Obviously it is a matter of opinion to a certain extent, but you can be fairly sure that a T or A ride is not worth your time, a TT or AA is worth seeing only if there is no queue, a TTT or AAA should be seen if you have time, but you won't have missed anything essential if you don't, a TTTT or AAAA ride is a big-time attraction that should be high on your list of things to do, and finally a TTTTT or AAAAA attraction should not be missed out at any cost. The latter will have the longest queues and, hence, you will probably want to plan your visit around these rides. Some rides are also restricted to children over a certain height and are not advisable for people with back, neck or heart problems, or for pregnant women. Where this is the case I have just noted 'Restrictions, 3ft 6in', and so on. Where families have small children under the height restriction, but mum and dad still want to try the ride, you DON'T have to queue twice. When you get to the front of the queue, tell the operator you want to do a Baby Swap. This means mum can ride while dad looks after junior, and, on her return, dad can ride while mum

Guests at the Studio Gate

does the babysitting.

Irrespective of how much time you have to devote here, the starting point for any visit has to be Disney's Magic Kingdom, the park that best encompasses and embodies the spirit of utter delight that Disney bestows on all its visitors. It's the original Disney development that sparked the amazing tourist explosion of Orlando from the late 1970s. In comparative terms, the Magic Kingdom is closest to Disneyland Paris, Disneyland in Los Angeles and the Japanese version in Tokyo. Outside those three, it has no equal as an enchanting day out for all the family.

What I will now attempt to do is steer you through a typical day at the Magic Kingdom, with a guide to all the main rides, shows and places to eat, how to park, how to avoid the worst of the crowds (and the Magic Kingdom really DOES get busy) and how much you should expect to pay for your day out with Mickey Mouse and Co.

Magic Kingdom, open since 1971, takes up just 100 of Walt Disney World's 28,000 acres but attracts almost as many visitors as the other 27,900 put together! It has seven separate 'lands' like slices of a large cake centred on the most famous landmark of all Florida, Cinderella's Castle. There are 46 attractions packed in here, not to mention numerous shops and restaurants (although the eating opportunities are less impressive than Epcot 96

Magic Kingdom at-a-glance

Location	Off World Drive, Walt Disney World
Size	100 acres in 7 'lands'
Hours	9am–7pm off peak; 9am–10pm Washington's Birthday, spring school holidays; 9am–midnight high season (Easter, summer holidays, Thanksgiving and Christmas)
Admission	Under 3-free; 3–9, $30 (1-day ticket), $97 (4-day), $148 (5-day); adult (10+) $37, $124, $186.
Parking	$5
Lockers	Yes; under Main Street Railroad Station; 4 × 25c
Pushchairs/ Wheelchairs	$6 (Stroller Shop to right of main entrance) $6 or $30 (Main Ticket Centre or Stroller Shop)
Top Attractions	Splash Mountain, Space Mountain, Alien Encounter
Don't Miss	Mickey Mania Parade, SpectroMagic and evening fireworks (not off peak)
Hidden Costs	**Meals** Burger, chips and coke $5.80 Three-course dinner $24.45 (Liberty Tree Tavern)
	Kids meal $2.49
	T-shirts $14.95–$25.99
	Souvenirs $1.95–$25
	Sundries Mickey Mouse Hat (with ears!) $14.95

and Disney's MGM Studios). It's easy to get lost or overwhelmed by it all, especially as it does get so busy (even the fast-food restaurants have some serious queues in high season), so study the following notes on the various Lands and plan your visit around what most takes your fancy.

Location

It is located at the innermost end of the vacation kingdom, with its entrance toll plaza three-quarters of the way along World Drive, the main entrance road off of Highway 192. World Drive runs north–south through Walt Disney World, while the Interstate 4 entrance, Epcot Drive, runs basically east–west. As you drive into the World, you can tune your car radio to 810 AM and hear Disney's own radio station tell you all about the delights in store for your visit! Unless you are staying at one of Disney's hotels you will have to pay your $5 parking fee at the toll plaza and that brings you through to the Magic Kingdom car park (or parking lot), a truly enormous stretch of tarmac that can accommodate more than 10,000 cars! The majority of visitors arrive between 9.30 and 11.30am, so the car parks can become pretty jammed then, which is another very good reason to get here EARLY! If you are not here by 8am during peak periods you might want to wait until after 1pm, or even later in the day when the park is open late into the evenings (as late as midnight at the height of summer and at Christmas).

BRIT TIP: It is essential when you park to note on your parking ticket exactly what area you are parked in and the row number, eg. Mickey, Row 30. All the sections are named after Disney characters, and if you don't note where you are parked you could have difficulty relocating your hire car. They all look alike, remember! As an extra tip, try leaving something on the parcel shelf in the car, like an article of clothing, that you will recognise.

To give you another idea of the size of the operation, a system of motorised trams carries you from the car park to the Ticket and Transportation Centre at the heart of the Magic Kingdom's operation. Unless you already have your ticket (which will save you valuable time if you have), you will have to queue up at the ticket booths here to go any further. Once you have ticket in hand, you pass the booths to several turnstiles which give access to either the monorail or ferryboats, and it is only these methods of transport that will finally bring you to the doorstep of the Magic Kingdom itself. Of course, if you are staying on a Disney property, you can also catch the monorail directly or one of the trams or buses that make up Disney's free transport system. If you're at the head of the queue and can get straight on, the monorail (dead ahead of you) is slightly quicker in reaching the Magic

Kingdom. Otherwise, if you have to queue for the monorail, it is usually better to bear left and take the ferryboats which may be slightly slower but involve less queuing.

1. Main Street USA

Right, we've finally reached the park itself … but not quite. Hopefully you've paid heed to the need to arrive early and you're among the leading hordes aiming to swarm through the main entrance. The published opening times may say 9am, but the gates to Magic Kingdom are quite likely to open anything up to 45 minutes before then. This will bring you into **Main Street USA**, the first of the seven lands. Immediately on your right is the **Disneyana Collectibles**, a fascinating shop featuring original cartoon cels and prints. On your left is **City Hall**, from where you can pick up a park map and entertainment schedule of the day's events if you haven't been given them at the toll plaza and make reservations for the main restaurants. Ahead of you is **Town Square**, where you can take a one-way ride down Main Street on a horse-drawn bus or fire engine. The Street itself houses some of the best shopping in the Magic Kingdom as well as the **Cinema**, which shows continuous classic silent films, the **Penny Arcade** of old-time amusements and video games and the **Walt Disney Railroad**, the park's Western-themed steam train that runs the full circumference of the Magic Kingdom and is one of the better attractions when the queues are at their longest elsewhere. You can eat breakfast, lunch and dinner at Tony's Town Square Restaurant, a full service diner specialising in Italian meals, the Plaza Restaurant (lunch and dinner, sandwiches, salads and

5

sundaes), The Crystal Palace (breakfast, lunch and dinner, buffet-style food), the Main Street Bake Shop (delicious pastries, tea and coffee) or the Plaza Ice Cream Parlour.

> **BRIT TIP:** If you are determined to get the most from your day, make sure you have a good breakfast BEFORE you arrive to give you plenty of energy and save time once the park is open!

Unless you are a late arrival, give Main Street no more than a passing glance for the moment and head for the end of the street where you will find the real entrance to the park. This is where you will have to wait for the final opening hour to arrive, the famous 'Rope drop', and you should adopt one of three tactics here, each aimed at doing one or two of the most popular rides before the crowds build up and queues become substantial (queues of an hour for Splash Mountain are not unknown on the busiest days). One: if you fancy heading straight for the five-star log-flume ride Splash Mountain, keep left in front of the Crystal Palace and the majority of the crowd here will head for the same place. Two: if you have young children who can't wait to ride on Cinderella's Golden Carrousel or the other very popular rides of Fantasyland, stay in the middle and head directly through the castle. Three: if the excitement and thrills of the new Alien Encounter and the indoor roller-coaster Space Mountain appeal to you first, move to the right by the Plaza Restaurant and you'll get straight into Tomorrowland. Now you'll be in pole position for the initial opening

Main Street USA

rush to the main attractions (and it will be a rush — have your running spikes ready!).

2. Adventureland

If you head for the first option, to the left (effectively going clockwise around the park), you will first come to **Adventureland**. If you are heading for Splash Mountain, with the rest of the early-morning queue-beaters, you will pass the Swiss Family Treehouse on your left and bear right through an archway (with rest-rooms on your right) into Frontierland, where you bear left and Splash Mountain is dead ahead. Stopping to admire Adventureland, however, these are the attractions you will encounter.

Swiss Family Treehouse: this gigantic imitation Banyan tree is a clever replica of the treehouse from Disney's 1960 film *Swiss Family Robinson*. It's a walk-through attraction where the queues (rarely long) move steadily if not quickly, providing a fascinating glimpse at the ultimate treehouse, complete with kitchen, rope bridges and running water! AAA.

Jungle Cruise: it's not so much the scenic, geographically-suspect boat ride (where the Nile suddenly becomes the Amazon) that is so amusing here as the patter of your boat's captain, who spins a non-stop yarn about your jungle adventure that features wild animals, tropical plants, hidden temples and sudden waterfalls. Great detail but long queues, so visit either early morning or late afternoon (evening queues are shortest, but you'll miss some of the detail in the dark). AAA.

Pirates of the Caribbean: one of Disney's most impressive attractions that involves the use of their pioneering work in audio-animatronics, life-size figures that move, talk and, in this instance, lay siege to a Caribbean island! Your underground boat ride takes you through a typical pirate adventure and the wizardry of the special effects is truly amazing. This is worth several rides, although it may be a bit spooky for very young children. Queues are rarely very long here and almost non-existent late in the day and evening. AAAAA.

Tropical Serenade: by contrast, this is one of Disney's more ancient and now rather tired audio-animatronics ventures, with a Polynesian longhouse full of animated parrots, macaws and other singing and talking birds in a 17-minute musical revue. The main plus points are that queues are rarely very long and you do get to sit down in air-conditioned comfort. AA.

Additional entertainment is provided in Adventureland by a steel drum band, and the best of the shopping is the House of Treasure as you come out of the Pirates ride. For food, you have the choice of Aloha Isle, for yoghurt and ice-cream, El Pirata Y el Perico (Mexican snacks, hot dogs and salads), Sunshine Tree Terrace (for fruit snacks, yoghurt, tea and coffee) and The Oasis (more snacks and drinks).

3. Frontierland

Passing through Adventureland brings you to **Frontierland**, the target of many of the park's early birds. This Western-themed area is one of the busiest parts of the Magic Kingdom and is best avoided from late morning to late afternoon.

Splash Mountain: based on the 1946 classic Disney cartoon *Song Of The South*, this is a watery journey into the world of Brer Rabbit, Brer Fox and Brer Bear. The first part of the ride is all pretty, cartoon scenery and jolly fun with the main characters and a couple of minor downward swoops in your eight-passenger log-boat. The conclusion, a five-storey plummet at an angle of 45 degrees into a mist-shrouded

Frontierland – Splash Mountain

pool will convince you that you are falling off the edge of the world! A huge adrenalin rush, but very busy at nearly all times of day (try it first thing or during one of the main parades to avoid the worst of the queues). You will also get VERY wet! Restrictions, 3ft 6in. TTTTT.

Big Thunder Mountain Railroad: when Disney do a roller-coaster they make it one of the classiest, and here it is, a runaway mine train that swoops, tilts and plunges through a mock abandoned mine filled with clever props and spectacular scenery. You'll need to ride it at least twice to appreciate all the fine detail, but queues are again heavy, so go first thing (after Splash

5

Mountain) or late in the day. Restrictions, 3ft 4in. TTTT.

Country Bear Jamboree: now here's a novelty, a 16-minute musical revue presented by audio-animatronic bears! It's a great family fun show with plenty of novel touches (watch out for the talking Moose-head!). Again, you'll need to beat the crowds by going early morning or early evening. AAAA.

Diamond Horseshoe Saloon Revue: after all the audio-animatronic gadgetry here's an honest-to-goodness Western saloon show performed by real people! You no longer have to book, just turn up a little in advance, and if you fancy a slapstick song-and-dance routine featuring Can-Can girls, corny comedy and audience participation this is for you. Snacks and drinks are available before the show. AAA.

Frontierland Shootin' Arcade: apart from the Penny Arcade in Main Street, this is the only other attraction that will cost you a few extra cents, 25c in fact for five shots at a series of animated targets. TT.

Frontierland Stunt Show: your daily events schedule will tell you what times to watch out for this regular feature as the Good Guys shoot it out with the Bad Guys over the rooftops of Frontierland. AAA.

Tom Sawyer Island: take a raft over to this overgrown playground, complete with mysterious caves, grottos and mazes, rope bridges and Fort Sam Clemens, where you can fire air guns at passing boats. A good get-away in early afternoon when the crowds are at their highest, while Aunt Polly's Landing is a refuge within a refuge for snacks and soft drinks. TT.

Shops here sell (predictably) cowboy hats, guns and badges as well as Indian and Mexican handicrafts, while for food try Pecos Bill Café (salads, sandwiches and burgers), Westward Ho (soft drinks, snacks and yoghurt) or the Turkey Leg Wagon (tempting, smoke-grilled turkey legs).

4. Liberty Square

Continuing the clockwise tour of th Magic Kingdom brings you next into **Liberty Square**, Disney's homage to post-Independence America. A lot of the historical content here will go straight over the heads of British visitors, but it still has some great attractions.

Liberty Square Riverboat: cruise the 'rivers' of America on an authentic paddle steamer, be menaced by Indians and thrill to the tales of the Old West. This is also a good ride to take at the busiest times of the day, especially early afternoon. AAA.

Mike Fink Keelboats: A Davy Crockett journey along the same waters as the Riverboat, encoun-tering the same dangers and escaping the same crowds! AA.

The Haunted Mansion: a splendidly clever delve into the world of ghost train rides that is neither too scary for kids nor too twee for adults. Not so much a thrill ride as a scenic adventure, hence AAAA. Watch out for the neat touch at the end when your car picks up an extra 'passenger'! Longish queues during the main part of the day, however.

Hall of Presidents: this is the attraction that will mean least to us, a two-part show that is first a film about the history of the Constitution and then an audio-animatronic parade of all 42 American presidents Epcot's American Adventure does this better for overseas visitors. AA.

Shopping here is of a more antique-orientated nature, while eating opportunities offer the full service Liberty Tree Tavern (which serves hearty soups, steaks and traditional dishes like meatloaf and pot roast), Columbia Harbour

House (for counter-service fried chicken or shrimp and chips) or Sleepy Hollow (a picnic area serving snacks, drinks and some vegetarian meals).

5. Fantasyland

Exiting Liberty Square you walk past Cinderella's Castle and come into **Fantasyland**, the spiritual heart of the Magic Kingdom and the area with which young children are most fascinated. The attractions here are all designed with kids in mind, but some of the shops are quite sophisticated in their wares, while King Stefan's banquet is a must for a fun family meal.

It's A Small World: this could almost be Disney's theme ride, a family boatride through the different continents, each represented by hundreds of dancing, singing audio-animatronics dolls in delightful pageants of colourful set-pieces. It sounds horribly twee, but it creates a surprisingly striking effect, accompanied by Disney's annoyingly catchy theme song. Crowds are steady and peak in early afternoon. AAAA.

Dumbo the Flying Elephant: parents hate it, kids love it and all want to do this two-minute ride on the back of a flying elephant that gently swoops and circles in best Dumbo style, even if the ears do not flap. Do this one early or expect to queue. TTT.

BRIT TIP: When you are faced by more than one queue for an attraction, head for the left-hand one. Almost invariably this will move slightly quicker than that on the right (it's the psychological effect of driving on the right-hand side of the road, so they say).

20,000 Leagues Under The Sea: all aboard with Captain Nemo on the *Nautilus* for an underwater adventure that simulates a submarine dive. Older children will find it a bit tame, but its clever lighting effects work particularly well at night. Expect steady queues most of the day, however. TTT.

Minnie, Mickey, Goofy and Donald on 'Dumbo'

Mad Hatter's Tea Party: Again the kids will insist you take them on these spinning, oversized tea-cups that have their own 'steering wheel' to add to the whirling effect. Actually, they're just a heavily-disguised version of many similar fairground rides. Again, go early or expect serious crowds. TT.

Mr Toad's Wild Ride: Here's a good, fun runaway car ride for all the family as Mr Toad's jalopy takes you on a helter-skelter journey through fields, barns and his own ancestral manor, avoiding haystacks and other obstacles along the way. Very busy from mid-morning to late afternoon. TTT.

Snow White's Adventure: a completely revamped ride in 1995, but still similar to Mr Toad's, it tells the cartoon story of Snow White with a few ghost train effects that may scare very small children. Good fun, though, for parents and kids. Again, you will need to go early or late (or during the Mickey Mania Parade) to beat the queues. TTT.

Cinderella's Golden Carrousel this is the centre-piece of Fantasyland and shouldn't need any

5

more explanation other than it is a vintage carousel ride that the kids all adore. Particularly, there are long queues here during the main part of the day. TT.

Legend Of The Lion King: children will also love this cleverly-staged version of the recent Disney cartoon, using puppets, actors and special effects to tell the story of the young lion cub born to be King. It is a bit of a test of endurance, though, as queues are long and then there is a pre-show you have to stand through before taking your seat in the air-conditioned theatre. AAA.

Peter Pan's Flight: don't be fooled by the long queues at this one, it is a rather tame ride by Magic Kingdom standards, although it is still a big favourite with kids. Its novel effect of flying up, up and away with Peter Pan quickly wears off, but there is still a lot of clever detail as your 'sailing ship' journeys over the rooves of London and into Never Never Land. AAA.

Skyway: this one-way cable-car ride takes you to Tomorrowland and provides a terrific aerial view of the Magic Kingdom that is even more impressive at night. AAA.

In addition to the main rides, there are also different musical shows daily on the Castle Forecourt Stage in front of Cinderella's Castle and the Fantasy Faire behind Dumbo, while eating opportunities are at Pinocchio Village Haus (salads, burgers and hot dogs), The Little Big Top (beverages and shakes), Lumieres Kitchen (for children's meals) and the Enchanted Grove and Mrs Potts' Cupboard (for ice creams and sundaes). King Stefan's Banquet is THE place, however, for a Magic Kingdom meal, be it breakfast, lunch or dinner (and you need to make reservations for all three!). The majestic hall, waitresses in period costume and well-presented food make for a memorable dining experience, with

the food usually consisting of salads, seafood, roast beef, prime rib and chicken. Expect to pay around $27 for a three-course dinner.

Frontierland – Big Thunder Mountain Railroad

6. Mickey's Starland

Between 20,000 Leagues and the Mad Tea Party you will find the shrub-lined entrance to the Magic Kingdom's most recently added Land, **Mickey's Starland**, which was created to celebrate the Mouse's 60th birthday in 1988. It is easy to miss, but Starland does have its own station on the Railroad. Its primary appeal is to kids, but most parents can't help being carried away by the cartoon spirit of it all and the amusing detail in odd corners. It's main benefit is that it rarely gets very crowded and there are activities like the petting zoo which get you away from the queues for a change.

Grandma Duck's Farm: meet Minnie Moo (a white cow with spots shaped like Mickey's ears!) and her barnyard neighbours and get to touch chicks, sheep, calves, rabbits and goats in a spotlessly clean environment that very young kids just love. AA.

Mickey's House: here is a walk-through opportunity to see the world's most famous mouse at home (well, he's not actually THERE, but you can see 'unique personal memorabilia'!). AAA. It leads into **Mickey's Starland Show**: this live performance at regular intervals through the day features Bonkers,

Darkwing Duck and other characters from the various Disney TV shows. There is a pre-show tent featuring cartoons on a huge screen, and then Mickey invites his guests in to the live action, which is always a big hit with younger children. AAAA.

Mickey's Hollywood Theatre: after the show the youngsters can get to meet Mickey and get his autograph in his dressing room (if they're patient and queue up!). AAA.

In addition to the main set-pieces, Starland also has Minnie's Dollhouse, Mickey's Treehouse and the Mouskemaze for kids to explore, while there are various wagons serving ice-cream, popcorn, soft drinks and other snacks.

7. Tomorrowland

Continuing down from Fantasyland finally brings you into the last of the seven Lands, **Tomorrowland**, which has undergone an overdue facelift to smarten up its rather tired façades and spice up the attractions. It now boasts an almost cartoon-like space-age appearance guaranteed to appeal to youngsters, and has some of the Magic Kingdom's more original shops.

Space Mountain: this is one of the three most popular attractions with Splash Mountain and Alien Encounter, and its reputation is quite deserved. It is a fast, tight-turning roller-coaster completely in the dark save for occasional flashes as you whiz through 'the galaxy'. Don't do this one after you've just eaten! The only way to beat the almost non-stop crowds here is to go either first thing, late in the day or during one of the parades or the fireworks show. Restrictions, 3ft 8in. TTTT.

Grand Prix Raceway: despite the long queues, this is a rather tame ride on supposed race tracks that just put-puts along on rails with little real steering required. Restrictions 4ft 4in. TT.

Dreamflight: you will rarely find queues here and it is worth a trip if everywhere else is heaving. It is a rather uneven ride through the history of aviation in terms of the way it is presented, but it has its amusing moments. AAA.

Astro Orbiter: in all honesty this is just a jazzed up version of the flying Dumbos in Fantasyland, just a bit faster and higher and instead of an elephant you are 'piloting' a rocket. Large, slow-moving queues are another reason to give this one a miss. TT.

Carousel of Progress: this one will surprise, entertain and amuse all at the same time. It is a 100-year journey through the development of modern technology and how it affects our lives with audio-animatronics and a revolving theatre that reveals different stages in that development. Its 22-minute duration is also rarely threatened by crowds. AAA.

Tomorrowland Transit Authority: like the Astro Orbiter, this is an old attraction has been revamped during Tomorrowland's facelift. It provides an elevated view of the area, including a glimpse inside Space Mountain, in electro-magnetically-powered cars. If the queues are short, which they usually are, give it a go. AAA.

Alien Encounter: this new attraction draws some HUGE queues (go first thing if you can) to its clever, high-tech preamble and awesomely scary show, a 'teleportation' demonstration that goes seriously wrong and brings an Alien to life in the middle of the audience. The fear factor adds a new dimension to the Magic Kingdom, but it will be too strong for most kids (and anyone scared of the dark!). TTTT.

Metropolis Science Center: formerly the Transportarium, this 360° film show has become an amusing time travel 'experiment',

5

with comedian Robin Williams providing the voice of robot operator Timekeeper, who guides his assistant Nine Eye backwards and forwards in time. AAAA.

You can also catch the Skyway cable car here to Fantasyland, while the Galaxy Palace Theater hosts live musical productions featuring Disney characters and talent shows, at various times throughout the day. For food, Cosmic Ray's Starlight Cafe has burgers, chicken and salads, the Plaza Pavilion does pizza, subs and salads, Auntie Gravity's (ouch!) Galactic Goodies serves up frozen yoghurt and fruit juice and the Launching Pad offers hot-dogs, snacks and drinks.

Other events

Having come full circle around the Kingdom you are now back at Main Street USA, and you should return here in early afternoon if you want to get away from the crowds and have a better look at the impressive array of shops or take in the Main Street Cinema. Watch out for the Dapper Dans, a strolling barbershop quartet, who perform regularly.

In addition to the permanent attractions, the Magic Kingdom also has several other daily events which should not be missed. Watch out in particular for 'personal appearances' around the park of various Disney cartoon characters, who will happily pose for photographs. The imaginative detail of the architecture and gardens is not bettered anywhere else: such intricate touches as themed rubbish bins for each of the Lands and re-naming rest-rooms for 'Princes' and 'Princesses' marks this out as one of the great achievements in the entertainment world.

Watch out, too, for the mid-afternoon Mickey Mania parade, which traverses the park from Main Street up to the Castle Forecourt then left into Liberty Square and

Frontierland. Here all the characters of Disney's many films are brought to dramatic and colourful life in a terrific cavalcade that captivates children and uses up several rolls of film! And, if you think the park looks pretty good during the day, prepare to be amazed at how wonderful it looks at night when some of the lighting effects are truly astounding. When the park is open in the evenings (during the main holiday periods), there is also the twice-nightly SpectroMagic Parade (wait for the second one to beat the crowds), a mind-and eye-boggling light and sound extravaganza that has cornered the market in glitter and razzamatazz. It's difficult to do it justice in words, so make sure you see it! Evening hours are also highlighted by a truly spectacular firework show over the Castle which is sparked off every night by Tinkerbell (seeing is believing!). Be warned, however, that people start staking out the best spots to see the parades well in advance, up to an hour in some cases for the kerbs along Main Street. At Christmas and Easter there are also special Santa Claus and Easter Bunny parades.

With the crowds typically being so heavy here, it is well worth remembering that you CAN escape them by leaving the park in early afternoon (not forgetting to get a hand-stamp for re-admission and keeping your car park ticket which is valid all day) and returning to your hotel for a few hours by the pool or a dive into the water parks of Typhoon Lagoon or River Country. Disney's Discovery Island, a walk-through mini zoo and aviary, is also a great place to spend a quiet couple of hours.

pcot 96 at-a-glance

Location	Off Epcot Drive, Walt Disney World
Size	260 acres in Future World and World Showcase
Hours	9am–9pm off peak; 9am–10pm (Washington's Birthday, Easter, Summer holidays, Thanksgiving, Christmas)
Admission	Under 3-free; 3–9, $30 (1-day), $97 (4-day), $148 (5-day); adult (10+) $37, $124, $186.
Parking	$5
Lockers	Yes; to left underneath Spaceship Earth and International Gateway; 4 × 25c
Pushchairs/	$6 (to right underneath Spaceship Earth and International Gateway)
Wheelchairs	$6 (same location)
Top Attractions	Spaceship Earth, Body Wars, Honey I Shrunk The Audience, Maelstrom, Universe of Energy, American Adventure
Don't Miss	IllumiNations, dinner at any one of the many fine restaurants
Hidden Costs	**Meals** Burger, chips and coke $5.80 Three-course dinner $24.99 (Restaurant Marrakesh)
	Kids meal $2.49
	T-shirts $16.95–$36
	Souvenirs $1.95–$22
	Sundries Children's backpack $22

5

Epcot 96

maze and annoy your friends by vealing that Epcot stands for xperimental Prototype Community f Tomorrow once you have arvelled at the double-barrelled tertainment value of this 260-acre ture world playground. Actually, it not so much a vision of the future a look at the world of today, with very strong educational and vironmental message which ildren in particular are quick to ck up on.

At more than twice the size of the Magic Kingdom it is more likely to require a two-day visit (although small children will find it less entertaining than the Magic Kingdom) and your feet in particular will notice the difference!

Location

Epcot 96 is located on Epcot Drive and the parking fee is again $5 as you drive into its main entrance (there is also a separate entrance for guests of the Yacht and Beach Club Resorts and the Walt Disney World

FUTURE WORLD

1 SPACESHIP EARTH
2 INNOVENTIONS EAST
3 UNIVERSE OF ENERGY
4 WONDERS OF LIFE
5 HORIZONS
6 WORLD OF MOTION
7 ODYSSEY CENTER
8 JOURNEY INTO IMAGINATION
9 THE LAND
10 INNOVENTIONS WEST
11 THE LIVING SEAS

WORLD SHOWCASE LAGOON

12 MEXICO
13 NORWAY
14 CHINA
15 GERMANY
16 ITALY
17 THE AMERICAN ADVENTURE
18 JAPAN
19 MOROCCO
20 FRANCE
21 INTERNATIONAL GATEWAY
22 UNITED KINGDOM
23 CANADA

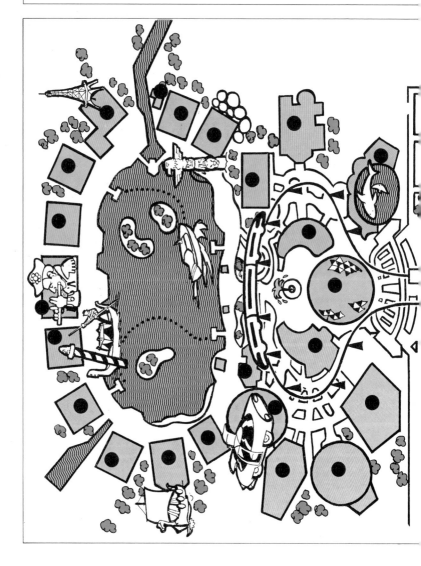

wan and Dolphin Hotels). It
pened in October 1982 and its
iant parking lot is big enough for
2,000 vehicles, so again a tram
akes you from your car to the main
ntrance (although if you are staying
t another of Disney's hotels you can
lso catch the monorail or bus
ervice to the front gate). Once you
ave your ticket, you wait by the
urnstiles for the opening moment
quite often accompanied by a
Disney character or two) and are
nen admitted to the central area of
Earth Station and Innoventions.

Epcot is divided into two distinct
arts arranged in a figure of eight
nd there are two tactics to avoid the
vorst of the early morning crowds.
The first or lower half of the '8'
onsists of **Future World**, seven
ifferent pavilions arranged around
Earth Station, Spaceship Earth (the
iant 'golfball' that dominates the
Epcot skyline) and Innoventions.
The second part, or the top of the
8', is **World Showcase**, a potted
ourney around the world via 11
nternationally-presented pavilions
hat feature a taste of their culture,
istory, shopping, entertainment
nd cuisine. Once you are through
he gates, start either by heading for
he Future World pavilions to your
eft (Universe of Energy, Wonders
f Life, Horizons and World of
Motion) and then continue up into
World Showcase. This way you will
isit some of the best rides in Epcot
head of the main crowds.
Alternatively, if the rides don't
ppeal quite so much as a visit to
uch diverse cultures as Japan and
Morocco, spend your first couple of
ours in the Innoventions centres
which are very popular from mid-
norning), then head into World
Showcase as soon as it opens at
1am and you will be ahead of the
rowds for several hours. If you time
our journey around the Showcase
which is a full 1.5-mile walk) to
rrive back in Future World by mid

afternoon, you will find the worst of
the milling throng will have passed
through.

The other thing you will want to
do early on is book a table for lunch
or dinner at one of Epcot's many
fine restaurants. The best

Monorail to Future World

reservations go fast, but there are
three different locations where you
can make your booking. These are
called Worldkey Information
Satellites and are clever audio-visual
terminals which give you access to
Disney hosts and hostesses who deal
with all the information about

Innoventions Plaza

Epcot. They will give you advice on
where and when to eat and take your
booking. The three Satellites are
located in Earth Station (not to be
confused with Spaceship Earth – it is
actually located underneath the
Spaceship and is the main information centre for Epcot), just to the
north of the two Innoventions
centres, and in front of the German
pavilion of World Showcase.

5

Future World

Here is what you will find in Future World.

Universe of Energy: there is just the one attraction here but it is a stunner as you are taken on a 45-minute show-and-ride that explores the creation of fuels from the age of dinosaurs to their modernday usages. The film elements convince you that you are in a conventional theatre, but then your seats suddenly rearrange themselves into 96-person solar-powered cars and you are off on a journey through the sights, sounds and even smells of the prehistoric era. The dinosaurs are very convincing! Queues are steady but not overwhelming throughout the day from mid-morning. AAAAA.

Wonders of Life

This is the newest of the World Showcase pavilions and also one of the most popular, hence you need to be here either early or late in the day. **Body Wars** is a terrific simulator ride through the human body as in the films *Fantastic Voyage* or the more recent *Inner Space*. It is quite a violent adventure, too, hence it is not recommended for people who suffer from motion sickness, anyone with neck or back injuries or pregnant women. TTTT. **Cranium Command** is a hilarious theatre show set in the brain of a 12-year-old boy and how he negotiates a typical day. It is both audio-animatronic and film-based. See how many famous TV and film stars you can name in the 'cast'. AAAA. **The Making of Me** is a sensitive film on the creation of human life and will therefore require parental discretion for children as it has its explicit moments, although not without humour. AAA. **AnaComical Players** and **Goofy About Health** are both theatre shows, one live the other animated, aimed at amusing and educating the youngsters, while the **Fitness Fairground**, with hands-or exhibits like exercise bikes, gives yov the chance to see just how far all the holiday fun has taken its toll on you body! You can also assess your golf/tennis/baseball swing in **Coach's Corner**, complete a health survey with the **Met Lifestyle Revue** and test your senses in the **Sensory Funhouse**. The Pure and Simple restaurant offers some delicious — and nutritious — alternatives to the usual burgers and chips.

Horizons

This is another one-ride pavilion that takes you through different visions of the future on both land, sea and space, including some that have already been overtaken by modern science. The 15-minute rid also features a simulated fast-movin; conclusion that can be mildly disconcerting for those who suffer from travel sickness. Queues fluctuate throughout the day, notably when the larger Universe of Energy has just disgorged its audience. It has also just been revamped, so expect some up-to-date touches. AAAA.

World of Motion

As Horizons re-opens its doors after refurbishment, so this pavilion, a 15-minute ride through the history of transport, closes down for its own facelift. It was just starting to look a bit dated, and you can be sure Disney's imagineers (Yes, their ride designers do get that special title!) will make it look like a brand new attraction.

The next door **Odyssey Center** i: not another pavilion but a restaurant and baby-care centre offering some of the park's best fast food in pleasant surroundings with Disney character shows several times a day.

Journey Into Imagination

The three different elements here lead on one from another, so start with the **Journey Into Imagination Ride** in the company of the inventive Dreamfinder and his baby dragon pal Figment. It's unfailingly and wonderfully silly with some hugely imaginative images that will either make you laugh out loud or groan. AAA. From the ride you go up into the **Image Works** which is essentially a series of hands-on exhibits for kids ranging from electronic paintbrushes and musical instruments to the Rainbow Corridor full of variously coloured neon tubes. Go back down the stairs and out of the building to your right and you come to the **Magic Eye Theatre** and the 3-D film *Honey I Shrunk The Audience* with Rick Moranis. If you have already seen *Muppets 3-D* at Disney MGM Studios you might have an idea what to expect. Special effects and moving seats add to the entertainment that makes you feel you have been miniaturised. And beware the sneezing dog! AAAAA. Outside, kids are always fascinated by the Jellyfish and Serpentine Fountains that send water squirting from pond to pond, and there is always one who tries to stand in the way and 'catch' one of the streams of water. Have your cameras and camcorders ready!

The Land

This pavilion features four elements that combine to make a highly entertaining but educational experience on food production and nutrition. **Living With The Land** is an informative 14-minute boat ride that is worth the usually long queue. This journey through various types of food production sounds a pretty dull idea, and it may not appeal much to younger children, but adults and school-age kids will certainly sit up and take notice of the three different 'biomes' or ecological communities, especially the greenhouse finale, you sail through. AAAA. Having ridden the ride you can also walk the walk on a guided tour through the greenhouse complex and learn even more about Disney's horticultural projects. It takes 45 minutes, but you have to book up in person at the desk just to the right of the Sunshine Season food court. **Food Rocks**, just to the right as you exit the ride is easy to overlook, but don't! This musical tribute to nutrition, presented by Food Rapper (what a great name!) and featuring Pita Gabriel (ouch!) is a hilarious 12-minute skit that will amuse kids and adults alike. Queues are almost non-existent here, too. AAAA. **The Circle of Life** is a 15-minute live-action/animated story that explains modern-day environmental concerns, easily digestible for kids. Queues not a problem here, either. AAA.

The Sunshine Season food court offers the chance to eat some of Disney's own produce, and again there are some healthy alternatives to the usual fast food fare, while the Garden Grill Restaurant is a slowly revolving platform that offers more traditional food, including pasta, seafood and delicious rotisserie chicken. A set lunch here is $10.50, while Mickey's kids meals are $3.99.

The Living Seas

This pavilion does for the sea what the Land Pavilion does for the land. The **Caribbean Coral Reef Ride** is a three-minute trip around the man-

5

made 5.7 million gallon aquarium that takes you to Sea Base Alpha, the main attraction. This two-level development takes visitors through six modules that present different stories of undersea exploration and marine life, including the chance to try on a deep-sea diving suit. Crowds build up substantially through the day so go either early or late. AAAA.

The pavilion also includes the highly-recommended Coral Reef restaurant that serves magnificent seafood as well as providing diners with a grandstand view of the massive aquarium. Dinner for two will cost around $60, which isn't cheap, but the food is first class.

Spaceship Earth

This ride spirals up the 18 storeys into the 'golfball', telling the story of communication from early cave drawings to modern satellite technology. This is easily the most popular ride in the park, largely because of its visibility and location, hence you need to do it either first thing or late afternoon when the crowds have moved on from Future World into World Showcase. The highlight is the depiction of Michelangelo's painting of the Sistine Chapel, which will be lost on small kids, but it's an entertaining 15-minute journey all along. AAAA.

Innoventions

These two centres of hands-on exhibits and computer games used to be Communicore East and West and underwent a complete overhaul recently to include a glimpse of Disney's latest investigations into virtual reality entertainment, **Disney Vision**, which gives you a chance to 'ride' the magic carpet from the recent animated film *Aladdin*. The kids will automatically gravitate to the free **Sega Game Centre** and

they may take a bit of moving along. Worth trying also is the Sega grand prix simulator which offers you the chance to 'race' other visitors (but for a few extra dollars. Naughty, Disney!) Alternatively it's just as

Video Game Chairs at the Hammacher Schlemmer exhibit.

entertaining to watch those involved. **Epcot Discovery Centre** is full of educational ideas and will answer all your questions about the park, while musical entertainment is provided periodically by the Future Corps Band. Food outlets include the counter service Electric Umbrella

Innoventions – Alec Tronic

Restaurant for lunch and dinner (sandwiches, burgers and salads), the Pasta Piazza Restaurant, which offers Disney character breakfasts as well as tempting pizzas and pasta, and the Fountain View Espresso and Bakery for tea, coffee and pastries. You'll also find the huge shopping plaza **Centorium** in Innoventions East, featuring stacks of quality Epcot and Disney memorabilia and souvenirs.

World Showcase

If you found Future World a huge experience, prepare to be amazed also by the more down-to-earth but equally imaginative pavilions around the World Showcase Lagoon. Each features a glimpse of the host country in dramatic settings. Several have either amusing rides or films that show off the tourist features of the countries, while in nearly every case the restaurants offering national fare are some of the best in Orlando.

Mexico

Starting at the bottom left of the circular tour of the lagoon and moving clockwise, your first encounter is the spectacular pyramid that houses **Mexico**. Here you will find the amusing boat ride along **El Rio del Tiempo**, the River of Time, which gives you a potted nine-minute journey through the people and history of the country. Queues here tend to be surprisingly long from mid-morning to late afternoon. AAA. The rest of the pavilion is given over to a range of shops in the **Plaza de los Amigos** that vary from pretty tacky to very sophisticated, the **Art of Mexico** exhibition, and the **San Angel Inn Restaurant**, a dimly-lit and romantically inclined full service diner offering traditional and very tempting Mexican fare. Outside, on the lagoon, is the **Cantina de San Angel**, a fast-food counter for tacos, chili and burgers, while, as with all the World Showcase pavilions, there is live entertainment and music at various times through the day (all advertised on the daily schedule).

BRIT TIP: The Cantina is a great spot from which to watch the nightly IllumiNations fireworks and laser show.

Norway

Next up is **Norway**, which features probably the best of the rides in World Showcase, the Viking-themed **Maelstrom**. This 10-minute longboat journey through the history and scenery of the Scandinavian country features a short waterfall drop and a North Sea storm, and attracts longish queues during the day, so again the best tactic is to go either early on or in the evening. TTT. **The Puffin's Roost** offers Norwegian shopping (clothing, trolls, toys and glasswork), while **To The Ends of the Earth** is a special exhibit in the reconstruction church of the two great early 20th-century expeditions to the North Pole of Captain Robert F Scott and Roald Amundsen. The pavilion also contains a clever reproduction of Oslo's Akershus fortress. Traditional music and dance is provided by the Trondheim trio and Fossekalen, while the **Restaurant Akershus** offers lunch and dinner buffets featuring hot and cold seafood, meats, cheeses and other Norwegian dishes and the **Kringla Bakeri** serves open sandwiches, pastries and drinks.

China

The spectacular architecture of **China** is well served by the pavilion's main attraction, the stunning **Wonders Of China**, a 20-minute, 360-degree film in the circular Temple of Heaven. Here you are surrounded by the sights and sounds of one of the most mysterious countries in the world in a special cinematic production, the technology of which alone will leave you breathless. If you were ever tempted to pay a visit to the country itself, this film will totally convince you. AAAA. Two restaurants, the **Nine Dragons** (table service, first class) and the **Lotus Blossom**

5

(counter service, fairly predictable spring rolls and stir-fries) offer tastes of the Orient, while the **Yong Feng Shangdian Shopping Gallery** is a virtual department store of Chinese wares and gifts. Don't miss the periodic shows of Oriental music and acrobatic acts on the plaza in front of the Temple.

Germany

Germany offers more in the way of shopping and eating than it does entertainment, although you will still find strolling players, courtyard musicians and a lively **Biergarten**, with its brass band. It also offers hearty portions of German sausage, saurkraut and rotisserie chicken. It boasts the highest number of shops of any Epcot pavilion, including chocolates, wines, china, crystal, toys and the inevitable cuckoo clocks (they're not just a Swiss speciality after all).

Italy

Similarly, **Italy** has pretty, authentic architecture (including a superb reproduction of St Mark's Square in Venice), lively music and amusing Italian folk stories, three tempting gift shops (enter Delizie Italiane's choice of chocolates, biscuits and candies in the open-air market at your peril!), and its feature restaurant, **L'Originale Alfredo di Roma Ristorante**. It's a touch expensive, but the atmosphere, decor and singing waiters (!) add extra zest to the meals, which include world famous fettucine, chicken, veal and seafood. Expect a three-course meal to cost you about $30.

America

At the top of the lagoon and dominating World Showcase is **The American Adventure**, not so much a pavilion as a celebration of the country's history and constitution. A colonial fife and drum band add authentic sounds to the 18th-century setting, overlooked by a faithful reproduction of Philadelphia's Liberty Hall. Inside the Hall you will find the spectacular **American Adventure Show**, a magnificent film and audio-animatronic production lasting half an hour which details the country's struggles and triumphs, its presidents, statesmen and heroes. It's a very glossy, patriotic performance, featuring outstanding audio-animatronic special effects, and, while some of it will leave foreign tourists fairly cold, it is difficult not to be impressed by the overall sense of pride and achievement inherent in so much American history. It doesn't pull any punches on the subject of Native American issues, either. AAAA. Outside, handcarts offer touches of American nostalgia and antiques, while the **Liberty Inn** offers some fairly predictable fast-food fare for lunch and dinner. The **America Gardens Theatre** facing the lagoon presents regular musical performances from worldwide artists which varies seasonally.

Japan

Next up on the clockwise tour is **Japan**, where you will be introduced to typically Japanese gardens and architecture, including another breathtaking replica in the form of the 8th-century **Horyuji Temple**, some magnificent art exhibits, musical performances and live entertainment like kite-making and the unlikely skill of shaping rice toffee into amazing, lifelike forms. For a different dining experience, the **Teppanyaki Dining Rooms** offer a full, table-service introduction to Japanese cuisine while **Yakitori House** is the fast-food equivalent, and a very satisfying and reasonably-priced one, too.

Morocco

Morocco, as you would expect, is a real shopping experience, with artfully-crafted bazaars, alleyways and stalls selling a well-priced array of carpets, leather goods, clothing, brass ornaments, pottery and antiques (seek out that Magic Lamp!). All of the building materials were faithfully imported and hand-built to give Morocco an outstanding degree of authenticity, even by the World Showcase's high standards, and will keep you gazing at its clever detail around the winding alleyways to the **Nejjarine Fountain** and gardens. **Restaurant Marrakesh** offers a full Moroccan dining experience, complete with traditional musicians and a belly dancer. It's slightly pricey ($49.95 for the Moroccan feast for two) but the atmosphere is always lively and VERY different!

France

France is predictably overlooked by a replica Eiffel Tower, but the smart streets, buildings and the sheer cleanliness of it all is a long way removed from modern-day Paris! This is a pre-World War I France, with official buskers, comedy street theatre and mime acts adding to the rather dreamy atmosphere. Don't miss the **Impressions de France**, another stunning big-film production that serves up all the grandest sights of France to the accompaniment of the music of Offenbach, Debussy, Saint-Saens and Satie. Crowds get quite heavy from mid-morning to early evening but it is a stunning performance (although kids might feel a little left out). AAAA. If you are looking for a major gastronomic experience this is also the pavilion for you as there is the choice of four restaurants, of which **Chefs De France** and **Bistro de Paris** are both major discoveries.

The former is an award-winning, full-service and therefore expensive establishment featuring top quality French cuisine created by French chefs on a daily basis, while the latter offers more intimate bistro dining, still with an individual touch and plenty of style. Alternatively, **Au Petit Café** and the **Boulangerie Patisserie** are sidewalk cafés offering more modest fare at a more modest price.

United Kingdom

Coming next to the **United Kingdom** will be something of a disappointment to British visitors. Sad to say, but this is the dullest of all the 11 international pavilions, certainly with very little to entertain those of us who have been inside a traditional pub before or shopped for Royal Doulton or Pringle goods. That really is the sum total on offer here. The **Rose and Crown** is a fairly authentic pub, but you can certainly get better food and drink (steak and kidney pie $11.50, cottage pie $10.50 and a pint of Bass, Harp Lager or Guinness for a whopping $4.50) at these prices. Entertainment includes stiltdancing puppeteers and a traditional herb garden and maze, while other shops are The Tea Caddy, The Magic of Wales, Lords and Ladies (perfumes, tobacco and family trees) and The Toy Soldier (traditional kids' games and toys).

Canada

Canada completes the World Showcase circle, with its main features being **Victoria Gardens**, based on the rightly world famous Butchart gardens on Vancouver Island, some spectacular Rocky Mountain scenery, a replica French gothic mansion, the Hotel du Canada, and another stunning 360 degree film, **O Canada!** As with China and France, this beautifully showcases the country's sights and

5

scenery, and serves as a terrific, 17-minute advertisement for the Canadian Tourist Board. It gets busiest from late morning to late afternoon. AAA. **Le Cellier** restaurant is a modestly-priced cafeteria-style eating house offering seafood, chicken, soup and salads for lunch and dinner. Try their fresh poached salmon (Canada can boast a number of novel varieties of salmon) or bread custard with, of course, maple syrup.

> BRIT TIP: If World Showcase is too crowded, step out of the way for an hour through the International Gateway (between the UK and French pavilions) and have a more relaxed meal at The Yacht or Beach Club Hotel resorts.

If you plan a two-day visit to Epcot 96 it also makes sense to spend the first day in World Showcase, arriving early and heading there while most of the rest of the morning crowds linger in Future World, booking your evening meal around 5.30pm, and then lingering around the lagoon for the evening's main attraction, **IllumiNations**, which is half an hour before closing time every day. If you think you've seen fireworks and lasers before, think again. Here the whole lagoon and surrounding pavilions come to light and life in a mind-boggling display of pyrotechnics that will be indelibly etched on your memory for a long time to come. Try to put a price on how much money has just gone up in smoke before your eyes — it runs into thousands of dollars EVERY night! For your second visit try arriving in late afternoon and then doing Future World in more leisurely fashion than is the case in mid-morning to mid-afternoon. You will find queues at most of the pavilions almost non-existent for rides like Universe of

Energy, Body Wars, Horizons and Living With The Land, although Spaceship Earth stays busy nearly all day (except for the evening, when everyone is out around the lagoon for IllumiNations). You CAN do Epcot in a day — if you arrive early, put in some speedy legwork between the attractions and give some of the peripheral detail a miss. But, of all the parks, it is a shame to hurry this one.

In the shops (almost 70 of them around the whole of Epcot 96), try to save your browsing for the busiest times of day when most people will be packing out the rides. The Innoventions Centres are also busiest from mid-morning to late afternoon, and relatively uncrowded in the evening.

For the ultimate in Disney's educational experiences (and this is a fairly well-kept secret), you can sign up for two behind-the-scenes tours of Epcot 96. **Hidden Treasures of World Showcase** is a closer look at the architecture, art and entertainment of the 11 pavilions, while **Gardens of the World** offers an insight into the horticultural side of the park. Both are open to all guests aged 16 or over and last four hours — but they cost an extra $20 each and you need to book up often three weeks in advance on 407 345 5860.

Finally, take time out to smell the roses — literally. Epcot 96 possesses some magnificent gardens, many of which look positively manicured they are so well kept, and it is easy to bypass some horticultural delights in your eagerness to dash from one pavilion to another, notably the more than 10,000 rose bushes! Take notice, too, of how the park lights up at night. Sit in the Cantina de San Angel with a margarita and marvel at the astonishing feats of imagination that have gone into creating this theme park wonderland.

1. ALADDIN'S ROYAL CARAVAN PARADE
2. SUPERSTAR TELEVISION
3. INDIANA JONES EPIC STUNT SPECTACULAR
4. CHEVY CHASE & MARTIN SHORT IN THE MONSTER SOUND SHOW – SOUND WORKS
5. STAR TOURS RIDE
6. TEENAGE MUTANT NINJA TURTLES
7. JIM HENSON'S MUPPET "VISION 4D"
8. "HONEY I SHRUNK THE KIDS" MOVIE SET ADVENTURE
9. CATASTROPHE CANYON "SPECIAL EFFECTS" TOUR
10. THE STUDIO SHOWCASE COSTUMES & PROPS
11. INSIDE THE MAGIC: M.G.M. STUDIOS AT WORK
12. THE GREAT MOVIE RIDE ALL TIME BEST MOVIES EVER MADE
13. VOYAGE OF THE LITTLE MERMAID "ARIEL'S WONDERFUL STORY
14. BACKSTAGE STUDIO TOUR
15. THE MAGIC OF DISNEY ANIMATION
16. THE TWILIGHT ZONE TOWER OF TERROR
17. BEAUTY & THE BEAST THEATRE OF THE STARS

5

Disney MGM Studios at-a-glance

Location	Off Buena Vista Drive or World Drive, Walt Disney World
Size	110 acres (more than half as studio backlot)
Hours	9am–7pm off peak; 9am–10pm high season (Easter, Summer holidays, Thanksgiving, Christmas)
Admission	Under 3-free; 3–9, $30 (1-day), $97 (4-day), $148 (5-day); adult (10+) $37, $124, $186.
Parking	$5
Lockers	Yes; next to Oscar's Service Station, to right of main entrance; 4 × 25c
Pushchairs/ Wheelchairs	$6 (from Oscar's Service Station) $6 or $30 (same location)
Top Attractions	Twilight Zone Tower of Terror, Star Tours, Great Movie Ride, Muppet Vision 3-D
Don't Miss	Aladdin's Royal Caravan, evening fireworks (high season only), Indiana Jones Stunt Spectacular.
Hidden Costs	**Meals** Burger, chips and coke $5.65 Three-course dinner $18.95 (Sci-Fi Dine-In Theater)
	Kids meal $2.49
	T-shirts $14.99–$29.99
	Souvenirs $1.99–$17.95
	Sundries Mickey Mouse glass mug $6.95

Welcome to Hollywood! Well, Disney's version of it, at least. When it first opened in May 1989, Michael Eisner, Chairman of the Walt Disney Company, insisted it was 'the Hollywood that never was and always will be'. Sounds double Dutch? Don't worry, all will be revealed in your day-long tour of this real-life combination of theme park and working TV and film studio. It's the most common question about MGM, and yes, there really are genuine film and TV productions going on even while you're riding around the park peering into the different backstage areas.

Slightly bigger than the Magic Kingdom at 110 acres but substantially smaller than Epcot 96's 260, Disney MGM Studios is a different experience yet again with its combination of rides, spectacular shows (including the unmissable Indiana Jones Stunt Show), street entertainment, film sets and the by now familiar array of smart gift shops. Like the Magic Kingdom, the food on offer here won't win many awards, but some of the restaurants (notably the Sci-Fi Diner and 50s Prime Time Café) do have superbly imaginative settings that will keep everyone amused for the duration of the meal. MGM also has rather more to keep the attention of smaller children than the education-orientated Epcot 96, but you can still easily see all it has to offer in a day, and if you make an early start you can safely say you have 'done' it by 5pm unless the crowds are really heavy.

Location

The entrance arrangements will be fairly familiar if you have already visited either the Magic Kingdom or Epcot. The Studios are located on Buena Vista Drive (which runs between World Drive and Epcot Center Drive) and the parking fee is $5. Look out for the landmark 130-foot water tower adorned with Mickey Mouse ears and dubbed — wait for it — the **Earffel Tower**! Again, make a note of where you park before you catch your tram to the main gates, where you must wait for the official opening hour. However, if the queues build up quickly, the gates will again open early, so be ready to jump the gun and get a running start!

Once through the gates you are into Hollywood Boulevard, which is a street of mainly gift shops, and you have to decide which of the three main ride attractions to head for first as these are the ones where the queues will be heavy nearly all day. Try to ignore the lure of the shops as it is better to browse in the early afternoon when the queues build up at the rides. Incidentally, if you thought Disney had elevated queuing to an art form in their other two parks, wait until you see the clever ways they are arranged here! Just when you think you have got to the ride itself there is another twist to the queue that you hadn't seen or an extra element to the ride which holds you up. The latter are called 'holding pens' and are merely an ingenious way of making it seem like you are being entertained instead of

queuing. Look out for them in particular at the Great Movie Ride and Muppet Vision. An up-to-the-minute check on queue times at all the main attractions is kept on a special bulletin board on Holleywood Boulevard, just past its junction with Sunset Boulevard. You also have the chance to get free tickets to be in the audience for current TV show productions, and these are dished out on a first-come, first-served basis at the **Production Information Window** immediately to the right inside the main entrance gates. (Although these are American shows, remember, and may not mean very much to us).

Hollywood Boulevard

MGM is also laid out in rather more confusing fashion than its two main counterparts, which all have neatly packaged Lands or pavilions, so you need to consult your maps frequently to make sure you are going in the right direction. It is easier to get sidetracked here than in any of the other main theme parks.

Three main rides

Having said that, the opening-gate crowds will all surge in one of three directions which will give you a

5

pretty good idea of where you want to go. By far the biggest attraction in MGM is the brand new **Twilight Zone Tower of Terror**, a magnificent haunted hotel ride that culminates in a 13-storey drop in a lift! It's not for the faint-hearted, but it is a huge thrill, and consequently the queues build up here like nowhere else, up to two hours at peak periods. Consequently, if the Tower appeals to you, do it FIRST! Head up Hollywood Boulevard then turn right into Sunset Boulevard and it is at the end of the street, looming ominously over the rest of the park. The second major attraction, the space-flight simulator **Star Tours**, is at the opposite side of the park. Go up Hollywood Boulevard, and turn left and past Superstar Television and the Monster Sound Show. When it first opened this was the bee's knees for adventure rides and it is still, for my money, one of the cleverest rides you will encounter. If you dash straight out of Star Tours, you can head straight back to the top of Hollywood Boulevard for the third main attraction, the **Great Movie Ride**, where queues again touch an hour at peak times. Here you ride through a potted history of classic films into some elaborately re-created scenes.

Here's a full run-down of all the attractions in more detail, working around the park in a clockwise direction.

Great Movie Ride

The Great Movie Ride: this faces you as you walk in along Hollywood Boulevard and is a good place to start if the crowds are not too serious. An all-star audio-animatronics cast re-create a number of box office smashes, including Jimmy Cagney's Public Enemy, Julie Andrews in Mary Poppins, Gene Kelly in Singing In The Rain and many more masterful set pieces as you ride through on your conducted tour. Small children may find the menace of the Alien a bit too strong, but otherwise it has fairly

universal appeal and features some live twists it would be a shame to spoil by revealing. AAAA.

The Twilight Zone Tower of Terror

Superstar Television: this 30-minute audience participation show features American TV shows like *General Hospital, Cheers, The Golden Girls* and *The Johnny Carson Show*. About a dozen 'volunteers' are chosen from the front of the queue before you enter the 1,000-seat theatre, and they will all feature in re-creating scenes from the various TV programmes. With the assistance of Disney's own 'production director' it can often be a hilarious show, and queues are rarely very long. AAA.

The Monster Sound Show: comedians Chevy Chase and Martin Short star in a specially-made and extremely funny short film to illustrate the use of special sound effects, which various members of the audience are then hand-picked to help re-create. Like Superstar TV, it relies on plenty of gusto from the audience and is kept going at a suitably fast pace by the 'director'. There is also a post-show section called **SoundWorks** which provides everyone with a hands-on chance to try out various sound effects. AAAA.

Indiana Jones Epic Stunt Spectacular: consult your Show Times schedule for the various times during the day when this rip-roaring stunt cavalcade hits the stage. A specially-made movie set creates three different backdrops for Indiana Jones' stuntmen and women to put on a dazzling array of clever stunts, scenes and special effects from the Harrison Ford film epics. Again there is an audience participation element and some amusing sub-plots I won't reveal. Queues for the near-45-minute show begin to form up to half an hour before showtime so be prepared for a wait here, but the auditorium holds more than 2,000 so everyone usually gets in. TTTTT.

Star Tours

Star Tours: anyone remotely amused by the *Star Wars* film trilogy will enjoy just queuing up for this ride, a breathtaking seven-minute spin in a Star Speeder. The elaborate walk-in area is full of Star Wars gadgets and gizmos that will completely take your attention away from the fact you often have to wait in line here for up to an hour. From arguing robots C3PO and R2D2 to your robotic 'pilot', everything has a brilliant sense of space travel, and the ride won't disappoint you! Restrictions, no children under three. TTTTT.

Jim Henson's Muppet Vision: the 3-D is crossed out here and 4-D substituted in its place, so be warned some very strange things are about to happen! A 10-minute holding pen pre-show takes you in to the specially-built Muppet Theatre for a 20-minute experience with all of the Muppets, 3-D special effects and much more. When Fozzie Bear points his 3-D squirty flower at you, prepare to get wet! It's a gem, and children in particular will love it. Typically, queues are substantial through the main parts of the day, but Disney's queuing expertise always makes them seem shorter than they actually are. AAAAA.

Honey, I Shrunk The Kids Movie Set Adventure: this adventure playground for kids gives youngsters the chance to tackle gigantic blades of grass that turn out to be slides, crawl through caves, investigate giant mushrooms and more. However, some may turn round and say 'Yeah. A giant ant. So what?' and head back for the rides. There can be long queues here, too, so arrive early if the kids demand it (and bring plenty of film). TTT. (Kids only).

Inside The Magic: this Special Effects and Production Tour is a near hour-long walk-through series of explanations and demonstrations into various ingenious film techniques. Watch a brave audience 'volunteer' get torpedoed and deluged with gallons of water, see kids ride the bumblebee scene from *Honey I Shrunk The Kids*, marvel at how a special two-and-a-half minute Bette Midler film took five days to make and learn the secrets of post-production and other special effects. Queues are long but steady-moving. AAAA.

Voyage Of The Little Mermaid: this 15-minute live performance is primarily for children who have seen and enjoyed the Disney cartoon. Like Legend of the Lion King in the Magic Kingdom it brings together live actors, animation and puppetry to re-create the highlights of the film. Parents will still enjoy the special effects, but queues tend to be surprisingly long so go either early or late. Those in the first row may also get a little wet! AAA.

Backstage Studio Tour: here's a directly competing attraction that knocks spots off the Universal Studios version. Whereas Universal's rather tame studio tour merely shows you the outside of their production stages and the backlots, Disney's more imaginative tram tour drives right through some production areas, shows you famous 'houses' from film and TV and culminates in **Catastrophe Canyon**, a huge special effects set that tries to drown you and blow you up all at the same time! You exit the tour into the **Studio Showcase** of costumes, props and set-pieces from recent films like *Who Framed Roger Rabbit*, and are then handily-placed for the Inside the Magic tour. Queues tend to be long and steady throughout the day, but there is plenty to watch while you're waiting. AAA (plus TTTT!).

The Magic of Disney Animation: a hugely amusing and entertaining half-hour tour through various stages of cartoon creation. It's really up to you how you pace the walk-through tour, but don't miss Robin Williams in a special cartoon creation, *Back To Neverland*, with Walter Cronkite and the fascinating view of some of Disney's animators at work. It concludes with a film performance of some of the highlights of Disney's many animated classics, and you will be

5

amazed at how much you have learned about the whole process in the course of your tour (although small children might be a bit lost by it all). Queues are rarely serious here, so it's a good one for the afternoon. AAAA.

Tower of Terror

The Twilight Zone Tower of Terror: the tallest landmark in Walt Disney World invites you to experience another dimension in this mysterious Hollywood hotel that time forgot. The exterior is intriguing, the interior is fascinating, the ride is scintillating and the queues are mind-blowing! The only unfortunate aspect of this really thrilling new attraction, which is so much more than just the advertised 13-storey free-fall, is the fact the majority of queuing time is outside in the sun, and when it is hot you are almost melting by the time you reach the air-conditioned inner sanctum of the spooky hotel. Typically, just when you think you have got through to the ride itself, there is another queue, but the inner detail is so clever you can spend the time inspecting how incredibly realistic it all is — before you enter the Twilight Zone itself. You have been warned! Restrictions, 3ft 6 in. TTTTT.

Beauty and the Beast: a live performance of the highlights of this recent Disney classic will entertain the whole family for half an hour in the nearby Theatre of the Stars. Check the daily schedule for showtimes. AAA.

Parades

New to MGM Studios is the **Spirit of Pocahontas**, a clever 28-minute musical and animated/puppetry show that highlights the key elements of Disney's latest film. It is staged five times a day in the Backlot Theater and features Native American performers as well as another highly elaborate setting. Have your cameras handy here for the **Backlot**, a collection of clever façades that give the appearance of city scenery, which you can wander around on foot. In the best Disney tradition, there is also a twice-daily parade of **Aladdin's Royal Caravan** which shouldn't be missed for a real close-up meeting with some memorable cartoon characters. Kids adore it. AAAA. During the park's peak periods, there is also an evening

fireworks show to rival the Magic Kingdom's (but not Epcot's). Best viewing point is along Hollywood Boulevard.

Food

While the choice of food may not be wide-ranging, there is always plenty of it and at a reasonable price. **The Holly-wood Brown Derby** offers a full-service restaurant in fine Hollywood style (reservations necessary — special Early Evening Value meals from 4–6pm at $15.75), while **Mama Melrose's Ristorante** is a similar table-service Italian option. The **Sci-Fi Dine-In Theater** is a big hit with kids as you dine in a mock drive-in cinema, complete with cars as your 'table', waitresses on roller-skates and a big film screen showing corny old black-and-white science fiction clips. You know you've outstayed your welcome when the film clips start to repeat themselves! By the same principle, the **50s Prime Time Café** is a hilarious dining experience as you sit in mock stage sets from American 50s TV sitcoms and eat meals 'just like Mom used to make'. Watch out for the waiters, who all claim to be your brother and warn you to take your elbows off the table, etc! Reservations are necessary, also. Otherwise, your choice of fast-food eateries consist of the **Commissary** ($7.50 for a hot chicken sandwich and a beer), **Backlot Express, Hollywood & Vine, Rosie's Red-Hot Dogs** or the **Soundstage Restaurant** ($2.80 for coffee and biscuits) and **Catwalk Bar** for various counter-service options, from sandwiches and salads to pizza, pasta and

> BRIT TIP: I always recommend the Sci-Fi Diner or 50s Prime Time Café just to make your main meal here that little bit different. There are plenty of ice cream, drinks, popcorn and hot-dog stalls around the park to keep you going as well!

fajitas. Children's Value Meals are available at all of these for $2.49.

There are also — count them — 26 gift and speciality shops to be investigated, 12 of them along Hollywood Boulevard which are worth checking out in early afternoon when the crowds have all passed through here and before the evening crowds pile back in! Look out for **Sid Caheunga's One-Of-A-Kind** (just to the right of the main entrance gates as you look out) which stocks rare movie and TV items, including many celebrity auto-graphs, the **Legends of Hollywood** (on Sunset Boulevard) for a rather different range of souvenirs and **It's A Wonderful Shop** (in the Backlot) for Christmas gifts and collectibles. Otherwise all the main rides and film attractions have their own shops selling the predictable souvenirs with their own themes.

It's finally time to leave Walt Disney World behind and venture out into the rest of Orlando's great choice of attractions. And they don't come much bigger or more ambitious than Universal Studios.

With a total area of 444 acres, parking space for 7,100 cars, six main rides, 12 shows, animated characters throughout the park, 26 shops, a huge backlot and 16 restaurants, all set in six separately-themed areas, this is a major competitor to Disney and one which is very successful in its own right. Universal Studios opened its Florida park in June 1990 (it has had its

5

Universal Studios at-a-glance

Location	1000 Universal Studios Plaza, off Kirkman Road and Turkey Lake Road (Junction 30B off I4)
Size	444 acres in 6 themed areas
Hours	9am–7pm off peak; 9am–10pm high season (Washington's Birthday, Easter, Summer holidays, Thanksgiving, Christmas)
Admission	Under 3-free; 3–9, $30 (1-day), $44 (2-day); adult (10+) $37, $55.
Parking	$5
Lockers	Yes; opposite Guest Relations in Front Lot; 2 × 25c
Pushchairs/ Wheelchairs	$6 (next to First Union Bank) to right of main entrance $6 and $30 (same location)
Top Attractions	Jaws, Back To The Future, ET, Earthquake, Kongfrontation
Don't Miss	Dynamite Nights Spectacular, dining at Hard Rock Café
Hidden Costs	**Meals** Burger, chips and coke $6.20 Three-course dinner $19.15 (Hard Rock Café)
	Kids meal $4.45
	T-shirts $14.95–$29.95
	Souvenirs $2.25–$49.95
	Sundries Studios video $19.95

1 KONG FRONTATION
2 GHOSTBUSTERS
3 THE ADVENTURES OF ROCKY & BULLWINKLE
4 MURDER, SHE WROTE MYSTERY THEATRE
5 BACKSTAGE LOT
6 HITCHCOCK'S 3-D THEATRE
7 NICKELODEON STUDIO TOUR
8 PRODUCTION STUDIO TRAM TOUR
9 THE FUNTASTIC WORLD OF HANNA-BARBERA
10 LUCY: A TRIBUTE
11 JURASSIC PARK
12 EARTHQUAKE – THE BIG ONE
13 JAWS
14 BEETLEJUICE'S GRAVEYARD REVUE
15 THE WILD, WILD WEST STUNT SHOW
16 DYNAMITE NIGHTS STUNTACULAR
17 BACK TO THE FUTURE . . . THE RIDE
18 ANIMAL ACTORS SHOW
19 FIEVEL'S PLAYLAMP
20 E.T. ADVENTURE
21 THE GORY, GRUESOME & GROTESQUE HORROR MAKE-UP SHOW
22 AT & T AT THE MOVIES
23 A DAY IN THE PARK WITH BARNEY

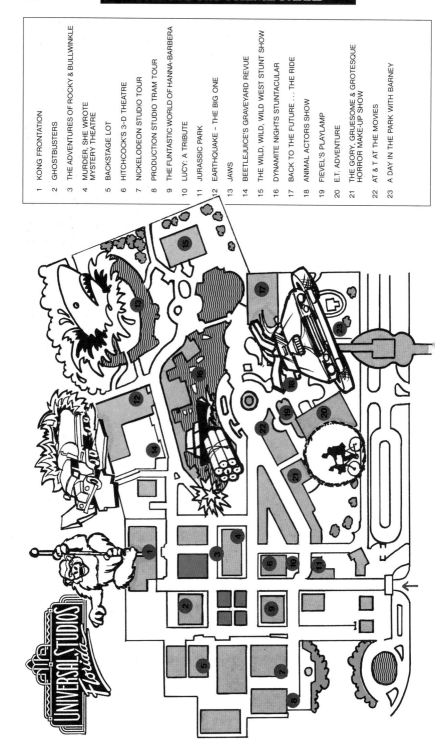

original Los Angeles site open to the public since before World War II!) and has quickly become a major player in the theme park stakes, with significant plans for expansion in the next few years, including a new, theme-park attraction and a water park. If you have already been to the L.A. Studios, this is better!

The obvious question to ask here is do you need to go to both Disney's MGM Studios as well as Universal, and the answer is an emphatic YES! Universal is a very different kettle of fish to MGM, with a more in-your-face style of entertainment that goes down well with older kids and younger adults. Younger children are also well catered for in Fievel's Playland and the new A Day In The Park With Barney show. Be aware also, Universal can require more than a full day in high season. As with Disney's parks, the strategies for a successful visit are the same. Arrive EARLY (ie up to 45 minutes before the official opening time), do the main rides first, avoid main meal times if you want to eat, and step out for a few hours in the afternoon if the crowds get too much (remembering to get a hand stamp for re-admission and keeping your parking ticket for re-use).

Highlights are the five-star simulator ride Back To The Future (state of the art technology here), the new Jaws ride, the Funtastic World of Hanna-Barbera (another simulator, slightly toned down for young children) and the other two blockbuster rides of King Kong and Earthquake. Queues at all of these top an hour at peak periods, and even the smaller attractions get very busy.

Location

Universal is sub-divided into six main areas, set around a huge, man-made lagoon, but there are no great distinguishing features between many of them so keep your map handy to steer yourself around. The park is located just off Kirkman Road, near the intersection of I4 and the Florida Turnpike. If you are travelling on I4, take exit 30B (going

Universal Studios

[North] east, it is on the LEFT, so watch out) on to Kirkman and head north for two blocks before turning left into the main entrance. Parking will cost you $5 and there are trams to take you to the front gates. Once through with the madding crowd, your best bet is to turn right on to Rodeo Drive, along Hollywood Boulevard and Sunset Boulevard and into Expo Center for Back to the Future ... The Ride. From there, head straight across the bridge to Jaws, then go back along the Embarcadero for Earthquake and Kongfrontation. This will get most of the main rides under your belt early on before the crowds really build up, and you can then take it a bit easier by putting your feet up for a while at one of the several shows.

Here's a full blow-by-blow guide to Universal Studios.

The Front Lot

Coming straight through the gates brings you into **The Front Lot**, which is basically the administrative centre, with a couple of large gift stores (have a look at these in mid-afternoon) plus The Fudge Shoppe and the Beverly Hills Boulangerie (sandwiches, pastries and tea and coffee — $5.95 for a beef sandwich, $3.10 for a beer).

Production Central

Ahead and to the left is **Production Central**, and this brings you into the main business of the park.

Hitchcock's 3-D Theatre: this tribute to the film-making genius of the late Alfred Hitchcock is a touch over-long for most children at 40 minutes, although it has three separate elements to keep you guessing at 'What Happens next?' The 3-D effects from his horror film *The Birds* come to the rescue of the first section, which is basically just a series of clips from his 53 films for Universal Studios. Next up is a re-creation of the famous shower scene from *Psycho*, with an audience 'volunteer' and a neat twist at the end, and finally some more special effects from *The 39 Steps* are explained with film techniques. Queues build up very quickly here after opening time, so save it for late in the day. It also advises parental discretion for young children, but few seem put off by the horror elements, which are fairly tame by modern standards. TTT.

Nickelodeon Studios: a lot of this American kids' TV series will be lost on us Brits (although it's now on satellite TV in Britain) as visitors are taken behind the scenes into the production set. All kids will be able to identify, however, with the chance to get gunged in green slime by the Gakmeister! And they'll love the rest rooms which feature green slime 'soap' and sirens when you flush the loo! Long queues build up quickly, though. AAA.

Production Tram Tour: after the MGM Studios tour this seems a bit dull and lacking in zest as the tram simply takes you around the backlot area and your guide tells you who does what inside each of the barn-like sound stages. Give it a miss

if queues are long. AA.

The Funtastic World of Hanna-Barbera: coming back from the tram tour brings you to one of the top-line simulator rides that is always a big hit with kids. It involves a cartoon chase of the funniest order, with your seats becoming jet-propelled in the bid to catch Dastardly and Muttley and save the day for the Jetsons, Scooby-Doo and an all-star cartoon cast. Humongous queues, so go either first thing or late. Restrictions, 3ft 4 in, but some fixed seats for those with heart, back or neck problems and pregnant women. TTTT.

The Nickelodeon slime treatment

The **Bone Yard** is now a rather depleted area of the backlot reserved for famous old props after they were discarded by the films in which they starred. Next to it is Jurassic Park — the photo opportunity. Have your picture taken next to a roaring, 40-foot Tyrannosaurus Rex for just $4.50!

Behind the Bone Yard and easy to miss — but don't — is the special Backstage movie lot which usually features some of the clever scenery from the latest blockbuster Universal film. It changes from season to season, but recent highlights have been Backstage with the Flintstones and Casper on Location. AAA.

Murder She Wrote Mystery Theatre: here's a chance to become the executive producer of the TV show starring Angela Lansbury as you are guided through the post-production process and have to save the episode from disaster. Lots of fun, with audience participation over its 40-minute duration. It's a good sit-down opportunity when your feet have begun to protest, especially as the queues begin to die off in the afternoon. AAA.

The Adventures of Rocky and Bullwinkle: primarily for kids is this 15-minute live show with the cartoon heroes as they battle their arch-rivals Natasha and Boris (check your daily programme for showtimes). Lots of corny gags, explosions and cartoon frippery. AAA.

The main eating outlet here is the **Studio Stars Restaurant**, which features an all-you-can-eat buffet (adults $10.95, kids $5.95, reservations accepted) plus a full à la carte menu with tempting seafood (grilled salmon $12.95), pizza, pasta and sandwiches (Gourmet burger $7.60). Shopping opportunities include the Hanna-Barbera Store, Jurassic Park Kiosk, Bates Motel Gift Shop and the MCA Recording Studios, where you can cut your own record!

New York

From Production Central you head on to **New York** and some great scene-setting in the architecture and detail of the buildings and streets. It's far too clean to be authentic, but the façades are first class and worth a closer look.

Ghostbusters: this promises rather more than it delivers, especially for the large crowds it pulls during the main part of the day, but it still produces some spectacular special effects. There is a 10-minute standing-room only pre-show, which invites you to become a Ghostbusters franchisee (and introduces a couple of members of the audience to ectoplasmic slime!) before the full theatre show where things, naturally, go slightly awry and the Ghostbusters have to wage a full-scale battle with spooks galore. Avoid the first two rows if you can to get the best overall view. Big climax, but still a little hollow compared to some of the other attractions. AAA.

Screen Test Home Movie Adventure: this would be a glorious opportunity to star in your own episode of *Star Trek*, or relive your day with King Kong and take home the resultant video if it weren't for the fact the American video system is different to ours (it has to be PAL compatible for use on European video equipment), so there is little point in spending much time on this. AA.

Kongfrontation: Universal's engineers have really gone to town on this attraction, a full-scale encounter with the giant ape on a replica of the Roosevelt Island tram. The startlingly real special effects (King Kong even has banana breath!) and clever spiel of your tram driver all add up to a breath-taking experience that will convince you that you have met King Kong and lived to tell the tale! It's only a five-minute ride and queues regularly top an hour, so going early is the best plan of campaign. TTTT.

The Blues Brothers: fans of the film will not want to miss this live show as Jake and Elwood Blues (well, pretty good doubles, anyway) put on a stormin' performance on New York's Delancey Street four or five times a day. They cruise up in their Bluesmobile and go through a selection of the film's hits before heading off into the sunset, stopping only to sign a few autographs.

5

Six tons of howling fury awaits visitors in Kongfrontation

Terrific entertainment. AAAA.

For your dining convenience (or so it says here), you have the choice of two contrasting restaurants. **Finnegan's Bar and Grill** offers the likes of shepherd's pie, fish and chips ($9.25), corned beef and cabbage along with more traditional New York fare like prime rib (from 4pm only $9.95), burgers, fries and beer as well as live Irish-tinged entertainment and Happy Hour from 5–7pm (half-price beer and wine). **Louie's Italian Restaurant** has counter-service pizza and pasta ($3–7), Italian ice cream and the delicious tiramisu (the Italian version of trifle only jazzier). For shops you have the choice of Ghostbusters Paranormal Merchandise, Safari Outfitters Ltd (and the chance to have your picture taken in the grip of King Kong!) and Second Hand Rose, a thrift shop featuring old collectibles, antiques and clothing. New York also boasts a particularly noisy, and therefore kid-friendly, amusement arcade and the Fotozine stall, where you can have your picture put on the front of a well-known magazine (surely no-one does that any more?).

San Francisco/Amity

Crossing Canal Street brings you all the way across America to **San Francisco/Amity** and two of the biggest queues in the park.

Earthquake — The Big One: this three-part adventure has them lining up from first thing in the morning until almost last thing at night. Go behind the scenes first of all to two special stage sets where, with audience help, some of the special effects of the blockbuster film, starring Charlton Heston, are explained in detail. Then you enter the Bay Area Rapid Transit

Eathquake – The Big one

underground and arrive in the middle of a full-scale earthquake that will shake you to your boots. Tremble as the walls and ceilings collapse, trains collide, cars fall in on you and fire erupts all around, followed by a seeming tidal wave of water. It's not for the faint-hearted (or small children), while those who have bad backs or necks, or are pregnant, are advised not to ride. TTTT.

Jaws: the technological wizardry alone will leave you gasping on this relatively new attraction, where

The Great White Shark

queues of more than an hour are commonplace. The man-made lagoon holds five million gallons of water; nearly 2,000 miles of wire run throughout the seven-acre site, which required 10,000 cubic yards of concrete and 7,500 tons of steel; and

the 32-foot monster shark attacks with a thrust equal to a Boeing 727 jet engine! Yes, this is no ordinary ride (at more than $45m to build it couldn't be) and its six-minute duration will seem a lot longer as your hapless tour boat guide tries to steer you through an ever-more spectacular series of stunts, explosions and watery menace from the Great White. Yes, of course it's only a model, but I defy you not to be impressed — and just a little terrified — by this fabulous ride. TTTTT.

Beetlejuice's Graveyard Revue

Beetlejuice's Graveyard Revue: Disney's MGM Studios has Beauty and the Beast and the Little Mermaid, Universal goes for Dracula, Frankenstein, the Wolfman, the Phantom of the Opera and Frankenstein's Bride in this 18-minute musical extravaganza. It eschews completely the twee prettiness of Disney's attractions yet still comes up with a fun family show, with versions of hits like Wild Thing and Great Balls Of Fire all in a spectacular stage setting. AAAA.

Back to the Future – The Ride

The Wild, Wild, Wild West Stunt Show: corny gags, fistfights, explosions, high-level falls and dramatic shootouts all add up to 15 minutes of rootin', tootin' Wild West adventure, Universal Studios style. Hilarious finale and some very loud bangs (not good for very small children) are accompanied by large crowds, but the auditorium seats almost 2,000 so there is usually no serious queuing here (provided you arrive 15 minutes early). AAAA.

San Francisco also has the best choice of eating establishments in the park, with **Lombard's Landing** the pick of the bunch (reservations accepted). Great seafood, pasta and sandwiches are accompanied by a good view out over the main lagoon (three-course meal from $15.60), and there is a separate pastry shop for desserts and coffee. **Richter's Burger Co** offers a few interesting burger variations ($2.75–6.50), while the **Midway Grill** serves smoked sausages and Italian sausage hoagies ($5–6). For a quick snack, **Chez Alcatraz** has shrimp cocktails, clam chowder and speciality hot sandwiches, **Boardwalk Snacks** does corn dogs, chicken fingers, candy floss and frozen yoghurt and there is a Haagen Dazs ice cream counter.

For shopping, try Quint's Nautical Treasures for seaside souvenirs and Shaiken's Souvenirs for more up-market mementoes. The added attraction of this area is a boardwalk of fairground games (which will cost you an extra few dollars to take part), including a Guess Your Weight stall which usually attracts a good crowd if only for the fun patter of the man in charge.

Expo Center

Crossing the footbridge from Amity brings you into **Expo Center** and Universal's other five-star thrill attraction.

Back To The Future … The Ride: simulators just do not come any more realistic than this journey through space and time in Dr Emmit Brown's time-travelling De Lorean. The queues are immense, but a lot of the queuing time is taken up by some brilliantly attention-grabbing pre-ride information on the many TV screens above your head. Once you reach the front of the queue, there is still more information to digest and clever surroundings to convince you of the scientific nature of it all. Then it's into your time-travelling car and off in hot pursuit of baddie Biff, who has stolen another time-car. The huge, wraparound screen and violent movements of your vehicle bring the realism of the ride to a peak, and it all adds up to a huge experience, well worth the wait. Restrictions, 3ft 4in. TTTTT.

Animal Actors Stage: prepare to be amazed now by the feats of acting giants like Lassie, Mr Ed, Beethoven and Benji as they put on their very own show to upstage all those pesky humans. It's a big theatre, too, and there is never much of a wait, so roll up and see those dogs put their trainers through the hoops! This is also a good one to avoid the afternooon crowds. AAAA.

Fievel's Playland: strictly for kids but also a big hit with parents for taking them off their hands for a good half hour or so, this playground based on the miniaturised world of the cartoon mouse offers youngsters the chance to bounce under a 1,000 gallon hat, talk to a 20-foot Tiger the Cat, climb a 30-food spider's web and shoot the rapids (a 200-foot water slide) in Fievel's sardine can. TTTT (young 'uns only!).

A Day In The Park With Barney: this was new in 1995 and is again strictly for the younger set (ages two to five). The purple dinosaur from the hugely popular kids TV show (so I am told by my friends who have kids of the necessary age!) is brought to life on stage in a 65,000 square foot arena that features a pre-show before the main event, which lasts about 12 minutes, plus an interactive post-show area. The show and its jokes are guaranteed to make mum and dad cringe, but the youngsters seem to love it and they are the best judges in this instance. PS: Check out the state-of-the-art rest-rooms here! AAA.

Fievel's Playland

E.T. Adventure: this is as glorious as scenic rides come, with a picturesque queuing area made up like the pine woods from the film and then a spectacular leap on the trademark flying bicycles to save E.T.'s home planet. Steven Spielberg (Universal's creative consultant) has added some extra special effects and characters, and the whole experience is a huge hit with young to teenage kids and their parents. Queues here occasionally touch two hours at peak periods, so be aware you want to do this one either early or late. AAAAA.

For food here there is only one choice — the **Hard Rock Café**.

This guitar-shaped restaurant of the internationally famous chain is right next door to Expo Center (past Fievel's Playland and the picture opportunity Bates Motel house), and you need to get a hand stamp to exit the park as it is not part of Universal Studios itself. Hard Rock devotees will make an immediate pilgrimage here, and if you fancy a loud, raucous, rock 'n' roll dining experience yourself, surrounded by the world's largest collection of rock memorabilia, then make sure you get to lunch or dinner EARLY as the queues at mealtimes take some believing. Otherwise, you have the choice of the **International Food Bazaar** (a food court-style indoor diner) offering Greek, Italian, Chinese, German and American dishes ($3–7) in air-conditioned comfort or **Animal Crackers**, which offers hot dogs, chicken fingers, smoked sausage hoagies and frozen yoghurt. Shop at Back To The Future Gifts, Animal House or E.T.'s Toy Closet and Photo Spot.

Hollywood

Finally, your circular tour of Universal brings you back towards the main entrance via **Hollywood** (where else?). Visit AT and T At The Movies for a number of hands-on exhibits taking you through the history and future of film-making, and check out the Jurassic Park behind-the-scenes exhibit (although this small room containing some of the props, costumes, models and original sketches for the hugely successful film is pretty ordinary compared to most of the attractions. Perhaps that's not too surprising when there are plans in store to incorporate some Jurassic Park ideas into the new theme park). Main attraction is the **Gory, Gruesome and Grotesque Horror Make-Up Show** (not recommended for young 'uns) which demonstrates some of

5

the often highly amusing ways in which films have attempted to terrorise us. It's a 20-minute show, queues are rarely long and the secrets of the special effects are well worth learning. AAA.

The last attraction (or first, depending on which way you go round the park) is **Lucy: A Tribute**, which will mean little to all but devoted fans of the late Lucille Ball and her 60s TV comedy *The Lucy Show*. Classic shows, home movies, costumes and scripts are all paraded for close viewing, but youngsters will find it rather tedious. AA.

If you haven't eaten by now there is a choice of two contrasting but highly enjoyable eateries, **Mel's Drive-In**, a re-creation from the film American Graffiti, serving all manner of burgers, hot-dogs and milkshakes to the accompaniment of the Hollywood Hi Tones a capella quartet who sing 50s tunes several times a day outside, and **Café La Bamba**, a counter-service Mexican diner offering tacos, burgers, barbecue chicken and steak ($2–7.25), with margaritas and beer (Happy Hour from 3–6pm). There is also **Schwab's Pharmacy** for old-fashioned milkshakes, sundaes, ice cream cones and chili dogs (ugh, what a mixture!). Shop for hats in the Brown Derby, for monster masks and other horror touches in Hollywood Make-Up and Masks, for movie memorabilia (especially with a Lucille Ball flavour) at Silver Screen Collectibles and for some of the smartest but most expensive clothing, hats and sunglasses at It's A Wrap.

Photo opportunities

In addition to all the set-piece action, watch out for photo and autograph opportunities with cartoon characters like Scooby Doo, Fred Flintstone, Woody Woodpecker and Yogi Bear and filmstar lookalikes of Charlie Chaplin, W.C. Fields, Marilyn Monroe and Groucho Marx. There are also three locations that offer you the chance to practise your trick photography on pre-set special effects stands. Watch out for them in New York, Hollywood and San Francisco/Amity. Don't be surprised, either, if part of the park is suddenly closed off for filming — this is a working film studios after all.

If you would like to enjoy a character breakfast with some of your favourite cartoon stars, call 407 354 6339 in advance to make a reservation or go first thing to the Guest Relations office (on the right through the main gates). Adults cost $13.50, kids $8.75. It is staged in different locations and is not always available, so it is advisable to call in advance. Universal's restaurants also offer a special Children's Menu for under-10s, with burger and chips, chicken fingers and chips or ham and cheese toastie and chips all at $4.45 and soft drinks at 95 cents.

Finally, and this is a big finally, don't leave before the Studios' nightly *tour de force*, the **Dynamite Nights Stunt Spectacular** on the main lagoon, 15 minutes before the park closes. Here you'll see some top film stunt men put through their paces on speed boats and jet-skis as a Miami Vice-type drugs bust swings into operation and the bad guys try to shoot it out with some eye-popping results. Half the lagoon seems to get blown up right in front of you, and what they can't do with these high-speed boats isn't worth mentioning. But be warned: the best vantage points around the lagoon get staked out up to an HOUR early and the designated splash zones are well marked for good reason and you can get SERIOUSLY wet! Don't miss it. TTTT.

1 MANATEES: THE LAST GENERATION
2 SPECIAL EVENTS PAVILION
3 PENGUIN ENCOUNTER
4 PACIFIC POINT PRESERVE
5 SEA LION & OTTER STADIUM
6 TERRORS OF THE DEEP
7 NAUTILUS THEATRE
8 CLYDESDALE HAMLET
9 ANHEUSER-BUSCH HOSPITALITY CENTER
10 SHAMU'S HAPPY HARBOR
11 WILD ARCTIC
12 ATLANTIS WATER SKI STADIUM
13 HAWAIIAN RHYTHMS
14 SEA WORLD THEATRE
15 TROPICAL REEF
16 WHALE & DOLPHIN STADIUM
17 SHAMU STADIUM
18 INFORMATION

5

Sea World at-a-glance

Location	7007 Sea World Drive, off Central Florida Parkway (Junctions 27A and 28 off I4)
Size	More than 200 acres, incorporating 20 shows
Hours	9am–7pm off peak; 9am–10pm high season (Easter, Summer holidays, Thanksgiving, Christmas)
Admission	Under 3-free; 3–9, $31.80; adults (10+) $37.95.
Parking	$5
Lockers	Yes, by main entrance; 4 × 25c
Pushchairs/ Wheelchairs	$5 (from Information Centre, to left of main entrance) $5 and $25 (same location)
Top Attractions	Shamu Stadium, Terrors Of The Deep, Penguin Encounter, Wild Arctic
Don't Miss	Mermaids, Myths & Monsters show; Manatees: The Last Generation; Behind-the-Scenes Tours
Hidden Costs	**Meals** Burger, chips and coke $6.04 Three-course meal $15.95 (Bimini Bay Café)
	Kids meal $3.59
	T-shirts $14.99–$29.95
	Souvenirs $1.59–$58.95
	Sundries Sea World Umbrella $12.99

Just four short years ago Sea World was the ideal place in which to become gently acquainted with the idea of running yourself ragged in the cause of enjoyment in central Florida. It was quiet, low-key and happy to live in the Second Division of the entertainment world. Not any more.

A dramatic and highly successful development programme by corporate owners the Anheuser-Busch Company has given Sea World the big-park treatment and it is now one of the most refreshing and vibrant of the Big Six, demanding a full day's attention.

Happily, the queues and crowds here have yet to reach the monster proportions of elsewhere, so this is a park where you can still proceed at a relatively leisurely pace, see what you want to see without too much shoulder-jostling and yet feel you have been superbly entertained (even if meal-times do get crowded in the various restaurants around the park).

Sea World is also still a good starting point if this is your first visit to Orlando as it will give you the hang of negotiating the vast areas, navigating by the various maps and learning to plan your visit around the different showtimes which all the parks offer. There is also a strong educational and environmental message to much of what you see, so much so that I defy you not to become emotionally involved with the Manatees: The Last Generation?

exhibit, which features a number of letters from similarly concerned British visitors on its exit rampway. To underline the educational points, there are also two behind-the-scenes tours you can take (book up as soon as you enter) which provide an even deeper insight into Sea World's marine conservation, rescue and research programme, as well as their entertainment resources. You can either take the 90-minute **Animal Lover's Adventure** to see where rescued animals are rehabilitated or the 45-minute **Animal Training Discoveries**, which lets you in on some of the secrets of their training and research facilities. You have to pay an extra $6 ($5 for children) for these tours, but they are well worth it and, if you take one of them early on, they will increase your enjoyment and appreciation of the rest of the park. Watch out, also, for periodical special ticket deals, like Second Day Free or Second Day for just $5.

Baby Shamu with his mother

Location

Sea World is located off Central Florida parkway, between I4 (exit 27A going [North] east or 28 heading [South] west) and International Drive, and the parking fee is $5. It is still a good idea to arrive a bit before the officially-scheduled opening time so you're in good position to book one of the back-stage tours at a time convenient to you or scamper off to one of the few attractions that does

attract crowds, like the Penguin Encounter and Dolphin Community Pool during high season and at feeding times.

The biggest attraction for the hordes, however, is the most ambitious venture in Sea World's 22-year history, **Wild Arctic**, an interactive ride-and-view experience which is easily one of the most breath-taking exhibits in the whole of Orlando.

It has replaced the old Mission: Bermuda Triangle simulator ride and goes much further into providing a realistic environment which is both educational and thrilling! It consists of two elements, an exciting (simulator) jet helicopter journey into the Arctic wilderness which arrives at a cleverly re-created research base, Base Station Wild Arctic, where the 'passengers' are disgorged into a frozen wonderland to meet some denizens of the North, like real polar bears, Beluga whales and walruses. Not to be missed. TTTT plus AAAAA!

The rest of the park covers in excess of 200 acres, with 10 shows (11 with the nightly Polynesian Luau dinner show which costs an extra $29.63, £20.09 for kids eight to 12 and $10.55 for three to sevens, and for which you don't necessarily have to visit the rest of the park), 10 large-scale continuous viewing attractions and nine smaller ones, plus relaxing gardens, a kids' play

5

BRIT TIP: For all the main shows, make sure you arrive at least 20 minutes early during peak periods to grab one of the better seats and avoid the last-minute rush.

area and a particularly smart range of shops (which is a noticeable feature of the Anheuser-Busch parks). Their hire push-chairs (strollers) are also the most amusing — shaped like baby dolphins so you push them along by the tail! Be warned, though, the size of the park will take you by surprise and requires a lot of to-ing and fro-ing to catch the various shows, which can be very wearing in the hot and humid summer months. Keep a close grip on your map and entertainment schedule and try to establish your own programme that gives you regular time-outs to sit and enjoy some of the quieter spots. You do get a suggested schedule on your park map as you arrive, but this doesn't take into account where the crowds are likely to go or the optional back-stage tours.

Main features

The park's main features are as follows.

Shamu Stadium: Sea World has long since outgrown its tag as just the place to see killer whales, but the Shamu show is still one of its most amazing experiences. See the killer whales and their trainers pull off some spectacular stunts, as well as explaining all about these majestic creatures. There are two distinct shows, one during the day (lasting 25 minutes) and a more relaxed, informal one at night (20 minutes). Both are worth seeing, and are easily the most popular events in Sea World so do make an effort to arrive early. Also, be warned: the first five to 14 rows of the stadium will get VERY wet. When a killer whale leaps into the air in front of you, it displaces a LOT of water on landing! AAAAA.

Sea Lion & Otter Stadium: this is home to Hotel Clyde and Seamore, the resident sea lions who, with their pals the otter and walrus

Wild Arctic

(plus a couple of humans to be the fall-guys!), put on a hilarious 25-minute performance of watery stunt and gags. Arrive early for some first-class audience mickey-taking from the resident (human) bellhop. AAAA.

Marine research

Whale and Dolphin Stadium: more breathtaking marine mammal stunts and tricks, with the accent once again on informing and educating the audience in a gentle manner of the current state of research into these creatures and the dangers they face. The show is 20 minutes long and is rarely over-subscribed, but once again the first few rows face a soaking! AAAA.

BRIT TIP: The weather may occasionally mean some of the outdoor entertainment is cancelled, but don't let it stop you enjoying yourself. Buy one of the cheap, plastic ponchos that will appear for sale in the shops at the first sign of rain ($3.99, but cheaper if you've had the foresight to buy one at a supermarket like Wal-Mart) and make the most of the drastically reduced queues as people head for cover!

tlantis Water Ski Stadium: the
ll-new Baywatch Ski Show features
0 minutes of top-quality ski-ing
tunts, daredevil acts and comedy
routines all served up in the style of
he hit TV programme. It may be
ancelled in bad weather, so in the
immer months try to see it early
n. AAA.

Sea World Theater: this actor-
ctivated film and stage show
Window To The Sea highlights all
he marine research Sea World helps
nd promotes. It lasts 20 minutes
nd may be a bit technical for young
hildren but is very informative in
ea World's clever, entertaining
ay. AAA.

Nautilus Theater: completely
evamped to stage the new Big
plash Bash, a musical song and
ance show with various aquatic
hemes. It lasts a full half-hour and
lthough the first 10 minutes are
retty ordinary revue material, it
omes to life with the fall of Atlantis
nd some spectacular staging and
iser effects, building to a big finale.
Children may get restless until the
pecial effects take over. AAA.

Hawaiian Rhythms: an amusing
ong and dance pastiche of
Polynesian culture on Sea World's
each stage, lasting 25 minutes but
vith little shade from the fierce sun
n summer. Beware the audience
nember chosen to go on stage — it's
n embarrassing experience! AAA.

Clydesdale Hamlet: these
nassive stables are home to the
nheuser-Busch trademark
Clydesdale dray horses. They make
reat photo opportunities when they
re fully-harnessed for one of their
egular tours of the park, and there
s a life-size statue outside on which
o sit the kids to take their picture.
A.

**Anheuser-Busch Hospitality
Center**: adjoining Clydesdale
Hamlet, this offers you the chance to
ample the company's most famous
roduct, beer (in fact, the world's
No 1 bottled beer, Budweiser, and

its cousins). Sadly, it's only one
sample per over-21 visitor, but it still
makes a nice gesture, and you can
take your free sample and sit on a
very pleasant outdoor terrace which
makes for a relaxing break from all
the usual theme park hustle and
bustle. AAA. **The Deli** restaurant
here is also an attractive proposition,
serving fresh-carved turkey and beef,
German sausage, saurkraut, fresh-
baked breads and delicious desserts.

The world of the manatee

Endangered

Manatees: The Last Generation?:
here is an exhibit that will really tug
at your heart-strings as the tragic
plight of this endangered species of
Florida's waterways is illustrated.
Watch these lazy-looking creatures
(half walrus, half hippo?) lounge
around their man-made lagoon from
above, then walk down the ramp to
the special circular theatre where a
five-minute film with amazing 3-D
effects will reveal the full dangers
facing the harmless manatee. Then
pass into the underwater viewing
section, with hands-on TV screens
offering more information about
them. It's a magnificently-staged
exhibit and a few tears at the
animals' uncertain future are not
unknown. It is also right behind the
Whale and Dolphin Stadium, so
DON'T go just after one of the
shows there. AAAAA.

Pacific Point Preserve: another
Sea World first, this carefully re-
created rocky coast habitat shows off

the park's seals and sea lions at their most natural. A hidden wave-making machine adds the perfect touch of reality, while park attendants are on hand at regular intervals to provide informative talks on the animals.

Waiting for a wave at Pacific Point Preserve

You can also buy small packs of smelt from two stalls to throw to the ever-hungry sea beasts. AAAA.

Shamu's Happy Harbour: three acres of cleverly designed adventure playground await youngsters of all ages here, with all things climbable or crawlable. Activities include a four-storey net climb, two tented 'ball rooms' to wade through, and a giant 'trampoline' tent. It does get busy in mid-afternoon, but the kids seem to love it at any time. TTT (kids only!).

Terrors

Terrors Of The Deep: the world's largest collection of downright dangerous sea creatures can be found here, brought vividly and dramatically to life by the walk-through tubes that surround you with prowling sharks, barracudas and moray eels. It's an eerie experience (and perhaps too intense for very small children), but brilliantly presented and, again, very informative. Queues do build up here at peak times, though. AAAAA or TTTTT. Take your pick!

Tropical Reef: after the dramas and amusements elsewhere, this may seem a little tame, but stick with it. Literally thousands of colourful fish inhabit the centrepiece 160,000-gallon tropical reef, while 17 smaller tanks show off other intriguing species. AAA.

Penguin Encounter: always a hit with all the family (and hence one of the more crowded exhibits at peak periods) are the eternally comical penguins in this brilliantly presented (if decidedly chilly) showpiece. You have the choice of going close and using the moving walkway along the whole of the display or standing back and watching from a non-moving position, while both positions afford views of how the 17 different species are so breathtaking under water. Watch out for the daily snowfalls inside the display which the penguins seem to love! Feeding time is also the most popular time for visitors, so arrive early if you want a prime position. AAAA.

Water Fantasy: back in the Sea World Theatre this alternates with the Window To The Sea show in the afternoon and is an engaging 20-minute presentation of a multitude of musical fountains that perform all manner of clever dances. It's a good one to take in if the crowds are a bit too much elsewhere or if you need to cool down. AAA.

Fireworks

Shamu: Close-Up: this new exhibit can be found at the opposite side of Shamu Stadium, affording a much closer and more natural look at the killer whales while at their leisure. Attendants are on hand to answer all your Shamu questions. AAA.

Breathtaking

Mermaids, Myths & Monsters: this nightly conclusion to Sea World's attractions is a truly breathtaking affair, featuring lasers, fireworks and one of the neatest illusions I've seen for a long time involving the use of film projection on to the steady spray of water fountains. You will truly believe King Neptune arises from the lagoon in front of you, accompanied by a myriad of other mythical sea creatures. TTTT.

In addition to all the main set-pieces there are several smaller ones which can be equally rewarding for their more personal touch. Touch is certainly the right word at **Stingray Lagoon** where it is possible to feed and stroke these menacing-looking creatures that are actually quite harmless. The **Dolphin Community Pool** offers a similar experience with dolphins, and is very popular around feeding time. The **Flamingo**, **Pelican** and **Spoonbill Exhibits** offer, amongst other things, the answer to the eternal question 'Dad, why has that pink duck got only one leg?' The **Tide Pool** is another hands-on experience with starfish and sea anemones, and, for an extra $3, you can ascend the **Sky Tower** for a lofty overview of the park (and the lower portion of International Drive). Watch out, too, for the best photo opportunity of the day as a big, cuddly Shamu greets kids just inside the main entrance. For the kids who can't do without a daily video games fix, there is a new **Midway**

Games Area of amusements and fun challenges just to the left of Shamu's Happy Harbour.

There are also 10 different places to eat, with the **Buccaneer Smokehouse** (Barbecued, mesquite-grilled chicken, ribs and beef), **The Deli** (mentioned, above, in the Anheuser-Busch Hospitality Center), **Bimini Bay Café** (for a relaxing, full-service lunch or dinner, about $30 for two) and **Mango Joe's Café** (delicious grilled fajitas, $6.49, speciality salads and sandwiches — Club Sandwich $5.49, fries $1.29) the best of the bunch. As in the other main parks, try to eat before midday or after 1.30pm for a crowd-free lunch, and before 5.30pm and after 8pm if you want a leisurely dinner.

Your wallet will also be in severe peril in any of the 27 shops and photo-opportunity kiosks. Make sure you visit at least **Shamu's Emporium** (where a cuddly Shamu will cost you anything from $5.99 to $18.99, or a Shamu towel will set you back $15.99), **Manatee Cove** (more cuddlies, from $5.99–$17.99), **Friends Of The Wild** (dedicated to animal lovers everywhere) and **The Label Stable** for Anheuser-Busch gifts and merchandise (some of it very smart). Your purchases can also be forwarded to Package Pickup in Shamu's Emporium for you to collect on your way out, provided you leave at least an hour for this service to work.

5

Shamu: close up!

1 **CONGO**

2 CONGO. "RIVER RAPIDS"

3 CONGO. "KUMBA" ROLLER COASTER

4 **TIMBUKTU**

5 TIMBUKTU. "SCORPION" ROLLER COASTER

6 **STANLEYVILLE**

7 STANLEYVILLE FALLS LOG FLUME

8 TANGANYIKA TIDAL WAVE

9 BIRD GARDENS

10 **MOROCCO**

11 MYOMBE RESERVE

12 CROWN COLONY

13 SKYRIDE - MONORAIL - QUESTOR

14 **SERENGETI PLAIN**

15 ANHEUSER-BUSCH BREWERY

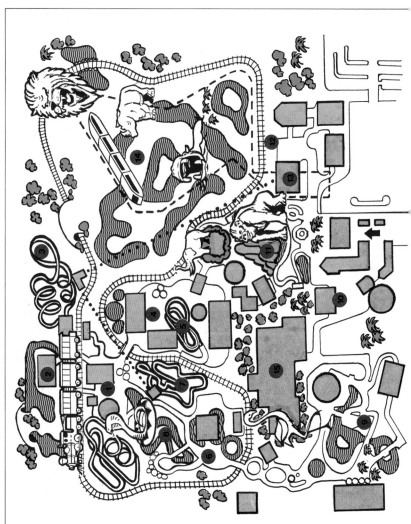

Busch Gardens at-a-glance

Location	Busch Boulevard, Tampa; 75-90 minutes drive from Orlando
Size	335 acres in eight themed areas
Hours	9.30am–6pm off peak; 9am–8pm high season (Easter, Summer holidays, Thanksgiving, Christmas)
Admission	Under 3-free; 3–9, $28.20; adults (10+) $34.60
Parking	$3
Lockers	Yes; in Morocco, Congo and Stanleyville; 2 × 25c
Pushchairs/ Wheelchairs	$5 and $18 (Stroller and Wheelchair Rental in Morocco) $5 and $31 (same location)
Top Attractions	Kumba, Questor, Congo River Rapids, Stanleyville Falls, Tanganyike Tidal Wave, Myombe Reserve
Don't Miss	Hollywood Live On Ice, Elephant Wash, Mystic Sheikhs band
Hidden Costs	**Meals** Burger, chips and coke $5.94. Three-course meal $21.50 (Crown Colony House)
	Kids meal N/A
	T-shirts $12.95–$19.95
	Souvenirs $2.99–$24.95
	Sundries Colour caricature drawings $14.95

5

Question: when is a zoo not a zoo? Answer: when it is also a theme park like 335-acre Busch Gardens in nearby Tampa.

Busch Gardens, the second of the three Anheuser-Busch parks in the area, started life as a mini-menagerie for the wildlife collection of the brewery-owning Busch family. In 1959, they opened a small hospitality centre next to the brewery and things have kind of mushroomed ever since. Now, it is a major, multi-faceted family attraction, the biggest on Florida's west coast and little more than an hour from Orlando, fully justifying its place in the Big Six.

It is rated among the top four zoos

The world's largest roller coaster loop

in America, with more than 3,300 animals representing 330 species of mammals, birds, reptiles, amphibians and spiders. But that's just the start. It boasts a safari-like section of Africa spread over 80 acres of grassy veldt, with a special monorail viewing attraction. Interspersed among the animals are 28 bona fide theme park rides, including the mind-numbing new rollercoaster Kumba, which guarantees a new experience for coaster addicts, and yet another in the series of simulator rides, Questor, a *Journey To The Centre Of The Earth*-type machine. There are shows, comedians, musicians, strolling players and a brand new family extravaganza in the impressive Moroccan Palace Theatre, Hollywood Live On Ice.

The overall theme is Africa, hence the park is subdivided into areas like Nairobi and The Congo, and the dining and shopping opportunities are the equal of any of the other big theme parks. It doesn't quite have the pizzaz of an Epcot or Universal, and the staff are a bit more laid back (not quite so many 'Have a nice days' or eager-to-please smiles), while the attention to detail is not as overwhelming as the other five. In a way, it is like the big brother of the Chessington World of Adventures in Surrey, although admittedly on a much grander scale (and in a better climate!). But it has guaranteed, five-star family appeal, especially with its selection of rides just for kids, and the sheer size of the place demands that this is also a full-day attraction.

Location

Busch Gardens is the hardest place to locate on the sketchy local maps and the signposting is not as sharp as it could be, but from Orlando the directions are pretty simple. Head (South) west on I4 for almost an hour (it is 55 miles from I4's junction with Highway 192) until you hit the intersecting motorway I75. Take I75 north for three-and-a-half-miles until you see the exit for Fowler Avenue (Highway 582). Continue west on Fowler Avenue for another three-and-half-miles, and, just past the University of South

Florida on your right, turn LEFT into McKinley Drive. A mile down McKinley drive and Busch Gardens' entrance will be on your right, where it is $3 to park.

You may think you have left the crowds behind in Orlando, but, unfortunately, in high season you'd be wrong. It is still advisable to be here in time for the 9am opening, if only to be first in line to ride Kumba, which is easily the most popular attraction and draws queues of up to an hour during the main holiday periods. The Congo River Rapids, Stanley Falls log flume ride and Tanganyika Tidal Wave (all opportunities to get very wet!) are also prime rides, as is Questor and the other two rollercoasters, Python and Scorpion. However, the queues do take longer to build up here, so for the first couple of hours you can enjoy generally queue-free riding, which comes as a major bonus at any time of year.

The Mystic Sheikhs

Busch Gardens is divided into eight separate sections, with the main rides all furthest away from the main entrance, so the best tactic at opening time is to dash straight through to The Congo at the far

le for Kumba, the Congo River
pids and Python, with nearby
anleyville offering the chance to
the other two water rides early
. The latter is always advisable as
gives you the maximum amount of
ne to dry out afterwards! Here is
e full lay of the land, travelling in
anti-clockwise direction.

Morocco

oming through the main gates brings
u first into **Morocco**, home of all the
ain guest services and a lot of the best
ops. Epcot's Moroccan pavilion sets
e scene rather better, but the
chitecture is still impressive and this
rsion won't overtax your wallet quite
much as Disney does! For a quick
al try the **Zagora Café**, especially at
eakfast when the marching, dancing,
ght-piece brass band called the **Mystic
eikhs** swing into action to entertain
e early morning crowds. Alternatively,
e **Boujad Bakery** will serve you coffee
d pastries, including Mexican churros,
ich are like long, thin doughnuts.
atch out, too, for the strolling **Men
f Note**, a four-piece a capella group,
d the **Steel Drum Band** at various
nes during the day. The **Sultan's Tent**
ves you your first animal encounter in
e form of a resident snake charmer,
ile turning the corner brings you face
face with the alligator pen. Morocco is
o home to two of the biggest shows in
sch Gardens. The **Marrakesh
heater** offers various variety shows
at change from time to time (Heart of
e Country is a salute to country music
d dance, while Latin Heat features
uth American entertainment; check
ur daily Entertainment Guide for full
tails), while the **Moroccan Palace
heater** houses the new award-winning
ow Hollywood Live On Ice. Even if
e thought of an ice show doesn't
mediately appeal to you, think again,
cause this is a surprising and highly
tertaining 30-minute spectacular that
nsists of a tribute to musicals, horror
ms, silent movies and James Bond
rformed by an all-star ice-dance cast in
zzling costumes and lavish settings.
AA. You can even be part of the daily
at and variety programme, the Harris
d Co show, a live TV broadcast from

the **Tangiers Theater** in which park
guests are the audience.

Crown Colony

Crown Colony sits in the bottom right-
hand corner of Busch Gardens and has
five distinct components. Here, you can
take the **Monorail ride** (AAAA) around
the 80-acre Serengeti Plain (see below)
or the **Skyride** cablecar (AAA) on a one-
way trip to The Congo. The station for
both is in the same building, with various
lemurs, monkeys and birds staring out of
their cages at these strange humans all in
long lines. Who's watching who, you
wonder. The **Clydesdale Hamlet** is also
here, but if you've seen the massive dray
horses and their stables at Sea World,
the set-up is identical. **Questor** is Busch
Gardens' answer to Wild Arctic (Sea
World), Body Wars (Epcot 96), Star
Tours (Disney MGM Studios) and Back
To The Future (Universal Studios), but

A black rhino on the Serengeti Plain

somehow seems to avoid the high-profile
nature of the other simulator rides and
gets somewhat overlooked. It is directly
opposite the Skyride and Monorail
Station, in the far corner past the
Clydesdale Hamlet, and the queues are
far less daunting than its other-park
rivals. However, at peak times you may
have to wait for half an hour or so, so an
early morning or late afternoon visit is
advisable to share this journey with a
crazy inventor in search of a fabled
crystal of magical powers. Needless to
say, his Questor travelling machine is
less than totally reliable as it plunges
underground, through rivers, over
waterfalls and even takes to the air.
Restrictions, 3ft 6in. TTTT. The
**Crown Colony Restaurant and
Hospitality Center** is a large Victorian-
styled building overlooking the Serengeti

Plain and affording either counter-service salads, sandwiches or pizzas (downstairs) or a full-service restaurant upstairs with magnificent views of the animals roaming the Plain. For a memorable lunch, book here early in the day.

Serengeti

The **Serengeti Plain** itself is home to buffalo, antelope, zebra, giraffe, camels, lions, baboons, hippos, rhinos and many exotic birds and can be viewed either fairly close-up on the Monorail or at a more relaxed distance for part of the journey on the Busch Gardens **Trans-Veldt Railroad**, a full-size, open-car steam train that chugs slowly from its main station in Nairobi all the way round to Congo, Stanleyville and back (AAA). You get a different view of the Plain from both forms of transport, so make a point of doing both during your day. Queues for the Monorail build up steadily through the main part of the day from late morning onwards.

Nairobi

Nairobi is also home to the awesome Myombe Reserve, one of the largest and most realistic habitats for the threatened highland gorillas and chimpanzees of central Africa. This three-acre walk-through has a superb tropical setting where the temperature is kept artificially high and convincing with the aid of lush

Silverback gorilla in the Great Ape Domain

forest landscaping and hidden water mist sprays. Take your time to wander through, especially as there are good, seated vantage points, and be patient to catch these magnificent creatures going about their daily routine. It is also highly informative,with attendants usually on hand to answer any questions. AAAAA.

At **JR's Gorilla Hut** you can buy your own cuddly baby gorilla ($11.95), while you can get a snack or soft drink at the **Myombe Outpost** (orange juice $1.50 and $2.50). This is also the place to see the Gardens' Asian elephants (check the advertised times for the **Elephant Wash** which is always worth watching) and the **Nairobi Animal Nursery**, which house all manner of rehabilitating and hand-reared creatures that can be seen close-up. Continuing round the Nursery brings you to the oddly out of place **Showjumping Hall of Fame**, which wi mean little to all but ardent equestrians, the **Reptile House** and the inevitable **Petting Zoo**, for kids to stroke goats, sheep and baby deer. **The Curiosity Caverns**, just to the left of the Nursery, are easy to miss but don't if you want to catch a glimpse of various nocturnal and rarely seen creatures in a clever cave-lik setting.

Timbuktu

Passing through Nairobi brings you int the more ride-dominated area of the park, starting with **Timbuktu**. Here in North African desert setting you will find many of the elements of a tradition fun fair, with a couple of brain-scrambling rides and two top-class shows.

Scorpion, a 50mph rollercoaster, features a 62-foot drop and a full 360 degree loop that is guaranteed to dial D for dizzy for a while afterwards. The rid lasts just 120 seconds, but it seems longer! The queues also build up here from late morning to mid-afternoon, an you have to be at least 4ft tall to board. TTTT. **The Phoenix** is a positively evi invention, sitting its passengers in a gigantic, boat-shaped swing that eventually performs a full 360 degree rotation in dramatic, slow-motion style. Don't eat just before this one! TTTT. **Sandstorm** is a fairly routine whirligig contraption that spins and levitates at fairly high speed (hold on to your stomach!). TTT. The **Crazy Camel** is an odd sort of ride resembling a giant sombrero that spins and tilts its riders into a state of dizziness, although not quite with the same level of success as Sandstorm. TT. Then there are a series of scaled-down **Kiddie Rides** that alway eem popular with the under-10s (and ive mum and dad a break for a few inutes as well). The **Carousel Caravan** ffers the chance to ride a genuine Mary oppins-type carousel, while there is also he inevitable **Electronic Arcade** and a **Games Area** of side shows and stalls that equire a few extra dollars to play. The **esthaus** is a combined German Bierfest nd entertainment hall, offering a ixture of German and Italian food from iant corned beef and turkey sandwiches o pasta, pizza and salads. It's a jolly, ather raucous establishment, with the avarian Colony Band and Dancers erforming two traditional German folk hows at different times of the day, but pcot's German pavilion definitely has he edge for authenticity. The final lement of Timbuktu is the **Dolphin Theatre**, complete with its aluminium culpture outside that is a homage to the alue of recycling. The Dolphins Of The)eep show borrows heavily from Sea Vorld's dolphin offering, but still comes p with some terrific leaps, stunts and ricks. AAAA.

Kumba the rollercoaster

Congo

'ou're really into serious ride territory as ou come into **The Congo**, with the nmistakable giant turquoise structure of **Kumba** (which is a handy landmark as ou approach the park). First of all it's he largest and fastest rollercoaster in the outh-east United States and, at 60mph, t features three unique elements: a iving loop which plunges the riders a ull 110 feet; a camelback, with a full 360 egree spiral that induces a feeling of veightlessness for three seconds; and a 08-foot vertical loop, the world's argest. For good measure, it dives nderground at one point! It looks

terrifying close up, but it is absolutely exhilarating, even for non-coaster fans. It is probably the smoothest rollercoaster you can ride, and the three-minute duration is just long enough to fully appreciate the wind-generated sound that gives the ride its African name, as Kumba means 'Roar', and roar it certainly does along its 4,000-foot track. The height restriction here is an ungenerous 4ft 4in. TTTTT. The **Congo River Rapids** look pretty tame

Congo River Rapids

after that, but don't be fooled. These giant rubber tyres will bounce you down some of the most convincing rapids outside of the Rockies, and you will end up with a fair soaking for good measure. TTTT. The **Ubanga-Banga Bumper Cars** are just that, typical fairground dodgems (TT), and you won't miss anything by passing them by for the more daring **Python**, the third of Busch Gardens' rollercoasters, with this one featuring a double spiral corkscrew at 50mph from a drop of some 70 feet. Height restriction here is 4ft, and the whole ride lasts just 70 seconds, but it's a blast. TTTT. Nearby, the **Monstrous Mamba** is almost a carbon copy of Timbuktu's Sandstorm, but just with a different name and paint job, while there are more **Kiddie Rides** to stop the smaller visitors feeling left out. There are four different refreshment stalls here, in addition to the larger **Vivi**

5

Storehouse Restaurant which offers a typical mix of burgers, sandwiches and roast beef fare.

Stanleyville

You pass over **Claw Island**, home of the park's spectacular rare white Bengal tigers, to get to **Stanleyville**, which all rather merges into one area from the Congo. Here there are more watery rides, with the popular **Stanley Falls log flume ride** (which is almost identical to the ones at Chessington, Thorpe Park and Alton Towers), which guarantees a good soaking at the final drop (TTT) and the distinctly cleverer **Tanganyika Tidal Wave**, which takes you on a scenic ride along 'uncharted' African waters before tipping you down a two-stage drop which really does set you down with tidal wave force. TTTT.

> BRIT TIP: Don't stand on the bridge into the neighbouring **Orchid Canyon** unless you want to catch the full weight of the Tidal Wave!

Stanleyville Theatre is a good place to relax and put your feet up for a while as you are entertained by a number of circus-style acts in the World Talent Showcase, or try the smaller **Zambezi Theatre** for the Congo Comedy Corps, who will demand full audience participation in their zany antics. For a hearty, if somewhat messy, meal, visit the Stanleyville Smokehouse — their woodsmoked ribs platter at $6.59 is a good value and a real lip-smacking delight. As you leave Stanleyville behind, say hello to the warthogs and orang-utans (who are rarely active during the heat of the day) in the large pens either side of the Train Station.

Bird Gardens

Your anti-clockwise route now brings you to the final and most peaceful area, the **Bird Gardens**. Here it is possible to unwind from the usual theme park hurley-burly, especially as there are two excellent, well-themed play areas for kids that give parents the chance to put their

feet up for a bit. The exhibits and shows are all family-orientated, too, with the World of Birds presented in the **Bird Show Theater**, the story of the Littlest Zebra in the **Animal Tales Theater**

Myombe Reserve

(purely for younger kids) and the **Hospitality House Stage** offering ragtime jazz at regular intervals. Take a slow walk round to appreciate the lush, tropical foliage, and special displays such as the walk-through **Aviary**, the **Birds of the Pacific, Flamingo Island, Eagle Canyon** and the emus (guaranteed a Rod Hull-free zone). The highlight of the Bird Gardens, confusingly enough, is the **Koala Display**, in the south-west corner

Kiami and Adele in the koala habitat

where these natives of Australia happily sit and seemingly do nothing all day while drawing large crowds for doing so. A free taste of the Anheuser-Busch products is also on offer in the **Hospitality House**, and you can complete your tour of Busch Gardens with a self-guided walk through the park's real *raison d'être*, the **Brewery**. Audio, film and poster displays take you through the full process of beer-making and you get to peer through the glass walls at the millions of bottles being produced before your very eyes. Thirsty stuff!

Your circular route brings you back into Morocco to finish the day with a spot of shopping in the area's bazaars. Middle Eastern brass, pottery and carpets will all try to tempt you into opening your wallet yet again, while there is also a full range of Anheuser-Busch products and gift ideas if you haven't already succumbed to the array of gift-shops and cuddly-toy emporiums around the rest of the park.

And ...

In addition to all the aforementioned activities, you can enhance your visit to Busch Gardens by taking one of a number of different tours or educational classes around the park. The three-hour **Behind The Scenes** tour can be booked daily for an extra $8 in much the same way as the Sea World backstage tours operate. There is also a **Senior Safari** offering a close-up look at the animals

and the zoo facilities for more mature adults, and a **Photo Safari** around the Serengeti Plain on an open truck especially designed for keen photographers. Then there is **A Is For Animals** (for toddlers and parents), **Junior Zookeeper** (for four to five-year-olds), **Night Hike** (nine to 12-year-olds) and **Really Reptiles** (to introduce reptiles and amphibians to six to eight-year-olds). All these programmes are extra to the normal admission charge and run at different times; for full details call the park's Education Department in advance on 813 987 5555. Charges vary according to the time and number of people interested.

And that's it. The Big Six in all their glory and detail. And if that doesn't reveal the full importance of planning a strategy for your Orlando visit, then I don't know what will. Especially as we're now about to plunge into an even wider-ranging area of attractions, activities, sports and recreation that will demand just as big a portion of your holiday as the main theme parks themselves ...

5

Sea World

KEY TO ORLANDO – MINOR ATTRACTIONS

A	=	WINTER PARK	S	=	GRAND CYPRESS EQUESTRIAN CENTER
B	=	STOWAWAY ADVENTURES	T	=	POINCIANA RIDING STABLES
C	=	TOHO AIRBOAT EXCURSIONS	U	=	ROCK ON ICE
D	=	OLD FASHIONED AIRBOAT RIDES	V	=	ORLANDO ARENA
E	=	KISSIMMEE AIRPORT	W	=	CITRUS BOWL STADIUM
F	=	WARBIRD AIR MUSEUM	X	=	OSCEOLA COUNTY STADIUM
G	=	EUROPA FUNKRUZ	Y	=	BASEBALL CITY
H	=	RIVERSHIP ROMANCE	Z	=	SEMINOLE GREYHOUND PARK
I	=	GRENELEAFE GOLF AND TENNIS RESORT	A1	=	MELBOURNE GREYHOUND PARK
J	=	POINCIANA GOLF AND RACQUET RESORT	B1	=	ARABIAN NIGHTS
K	=	METROWEST COUNTRY CLUB	C1	=	KARTWORLD
L	=	MARRIOTT'S ORLANDO WORLD CENTER	D1	=	AMERICAN GLADIATORS
M	=	LAKE CANE TENNIS CENTER	E1	=	CAPONE'S
N	=	ORANGE LAKE COUNTRY CLUB	F1	=	MARK II DINNER THEATER
O	=	SANLANDO PARK	G1	=	MEDIEVAL TIMES
P	=	JUNGLELAND	H1	=	KING HENRY'S FEAST
Q	=	SPLASH 'N SKI	I1	=	WILD BILL'S
R	=	KATIE'S WEKIVA RIVER LANDING	J1	=	SLEUTH'S

The Other Attractions
or one giant step for tourist kind

If you think you have seen everything Orlando has to offer by sticking simply to the Big Six, in the words of the song,'You ain't seen nothin' yet'. It would be relatively easy to turn the Six into Seven by adding The Kennedy Space Center, or Spaceport USA as it is also known, to the list of must-see parks because although it's not strictly a theme park, it is adding new attractions all the time and is fast becoming a full day's excursion from Orlando to the east or 'space' coast.

Then there are Cypress Gardens and Silver Springs to give you a taste of the more natural things Florida has to offer, the new Kissimmee attraction Splendid China for a completely different park experience, the mind-boggling Gatorland, with its multitude of alligators and gator shows (and great value, too), Disney's mini-zoo Discovery Island and the one-off family centres like Mystery Fun House and Ripley's Believe It Or Not.

Then you have to consider the water fun parks of Wet 'N Wild, Water Mania, Typhoon Lagoon, River Country and Blizzard Beach, as well as the opportunity to get off the beaten track at places like restful Winter Park, the St John's River and several well-organised nature excursions, not to mention the chance to take a helicopter or balloon ride (very popular in Florida) or go on an air-boat over the marshes of one of the lakes or rivers.

By night you have a whole new dazzling array of opportunities from the two huge entertainment complexes of Church Street Station (in downtown Orlando) and Pleasure Island (another Disney venture), through the myriad of popular dinner shows that offer you the chance to cheer on medieval knights or solve a crime mystery while you eat, to the more standard nightclubs and bars.

You can also indulge most of your favourite sporting pastimes either as a player or spectator, including baseball, tennis, golf (central Florida has almost 200 immaculate courses), mini-golf, go-karting, basketball, ice skating, ten-pin bowling and even bungee-jumping. Or you can just declare a time-out and head for one of Florida's many inviting beaches that are not more than an hour's drive from Orlando.

The choice, as they say, is yours, but it is an immense selection. Here is a full run-down of all the other attractions that you may want to try to fit in during your Orlando stay.

Kennedy Space Center

The real beauty of visiting the home of America's space programme is that it doesn't necessarily cost you any money. Parking and many of the films and exhibits are completely free, and you can spend several hours wandering around the complex and adjoining **Rocket Garden**, learning all about the past, present and future of space exploration. You can inspect a full-size, replica **Space Shuttle**, see real moonrock and spacecraft, take in the **Satellites and You** show which uses some great audio-visual effects to reveal how satellites affect our lives, get to grips with a whole range of hands-on educational exhibits and have your picture taken with a fully-suited Spaceman! You should also stop by the **Astronauts Memorial**, a stark, sombre but very moving tribute to the men and women who have died in the course of the space programme.

Space Shuttle Launch

Missions

For most people, that just whets the appetite and you can then choose from several paid-for attractions that include tours of the Space Center and three special film presentations in the giant IMAX cinemas. New owners Delaware North Park Services are also scheduled to spend around $60 million over the next two years in upgrading the Spaceport to provide more flexible tours, which will be themed and called Missions, create a new Saturn V Rocket attraction and a space shuttle-themed kids' playground and add more hands-on and interactive exhibits. There will also be special, 8-passenger VIP tours. It is already a thrilling day out for anyone even remotely interested in science fiction and fact, although a lot of it may be a bit too detailed for young children, but it promises to deliver a lot more excitement in 1996 and 97. The giant IMAX films — 55-foot screens which give you the impression of sitting right on top of the action — offer the choices of the 37-minute **The Dream Is Alive**, which puts you inside a space shuttle mission, **The Blue Planet**, an awesome view

of Earth from space which lasts 42 minutes, and the new **Destiny In Space**, a 40-minute programme narrated by Mr Spock himself, Leonard Nimoy, which highlights the challenges of space exploration

> BRIT TIP: If you are planning to do any of the tours or see one of the IMAX films, head straight for the **Ticket Pavilion**, in the centre of the complex, when you arrive to book up. The ticket staff will be able to prepare your own schedule according to what you want to see, marrying up the tours with the film times.

and presents astounding film footage of the shuttle in space. All three cost $4 each for adults and $2 a time for kids, and you can happily see all three without any of it being repeated or overlapping. However, you are pushed for time, either The Dream Is Alive or Destiny In Space should be seen at the very least.

In addition to all the attractions, the complex also boasts a first-class gift shop, two counter-service cafeterias and two snackports.

To get to the Kennedy Space Center, take the Beeline Expressway out of Orlando (Highway 528, and it's a toll road, remember, so you'll need $3 or $4 in cash) for about 45 minutes then bear left on the SR 407 (DON'T follow the signs to Cape Canaveral or Cocoa Beach at this point) and turn right at the T-junction on to SR 405. You may be confused by various distance markers that list the Space Center as variously 1, 3 and 7 miles away from this point, and they are all right! Its a matter of where you take the Space Center to be as it actually occupies 84,000 acres. Spaceport USA is located six miles along SR 405 on the right-hand side and is well signposted. On your return journey it is easy to miss the left-hander back on to SR 407 but don't worry if you do. Stay on SR 50 and it brings you back into downtown Orlando.

Busiest days at Spaceport USA are typically Wednesday and Thursday, with Monday, Tuesday and weekends the quietest times. Opening hours are 9am to dusk every day except Christmas Day, and the centre gets busiest around lunchtime. The centre currently deals with 3 million visitors a year – as many as Sea World and Busch Gardens – and their new plans estimate a 2 million increase! The first tours and IMAX presentations start at 9.45am, and the final tour of the day is two hours before dark. **Total attraction rating: AAAA.**

The greatest attraction of all, however, is an actual space shuttle launch, of which there are about seven or eight a year and FREE tickets are available on a first-come, first-served basis to be on site when they lift off (along with about 250,000 other people!). You should call 1-800 572 4636 to book your tickets seven days in advance, which then must be collected in person the day before the launch. Alternatively, nearby Titusville is a good spot to watch a launch, as well as the beaches to the north. To be on hand for a shuttle launch is a truly awe-inspiring experience. As this book went to press, the provisional launches for 1995 were scheduled for March 2, June 8, June 22, July 20, September 21, October 26 and November 30, weather permitting!

U.S. Astronaut Hall of Fame

While the Kennedy Space Center tells you all about the machinery of putting men in space, the neighbouring Astronaut Hall of Fame (on SR 405, just before the main entrance to the Space Center) gives you the full low-down on the men involved. This museum to the space programmes of the Mercury, Gemini and Apollo missions houses some fascinating memorabilia, interactive exhibits and engaging explanations of the people behind the spacesuits. Prepare to be amazed at how incredibly small the cockpits of the early manned spaceflights were and amused by personal touches like Buzz Aldrin's High School report! Your entrance fee also includes a ride on the **Shuttle To Tomorrow**. You might expect a simulator ride, but in fact it is rather simpler, with the cargo bay of a replica shuttle converted into a passenger deck for an audio-visual experience of future travel, with headphones providing stereo surround-sound for take-off and landing. Recently they have added a zero-gravity simulator and a projection room that will take a video of you as if you are space-walking, plus a From Test Pilot to Astronaut exhibit that features a special 3-D film and revolving seats! Again, it is more for the older children and adults, but it is a handy two-hour introduction to the space programme if you start here and then head for the Kennedy Space Center.

Admission is $9.95 for adults and $5.95 for kids (3 to 12), with opening hours from 9am–5pm (9–7pm in summer), seven days a week. **Total attraction rating: AAA.**

There is also the usual gift-shop, with refreshments provided by the Milky Way Café, a fairly basic canteen-style eaterie geared more for the kids of the weekly U.S. Space Camp. The residential **Space Camp** may be of interest to you if you have children of 10–14 who would like to train to be junior astronauts for five days. It's not a cheap programme — $475–$600 depending on age, inclusive of full board for the five

BRIT TIP: Every Friday morning is graduation day, so avoid the Hall of Fame then unless you want to be surrounded by dozens of highly enthusiastic 'space cadets' and their parents.

days — but it is a magnificent educational recreation for kids, and the Camp is happy to take visitors from the UK. You have to book up about two months in advance of your visit, but then just bring your youngsters along on Sunday afternoon and they are taken off your hands until Friday morning (now is that an attractive proposition for harassed parents?). They are arranged into groups and then go through activities like flight and space-walk simulators, simulated space missions, studying rocket propulsion, space technology and other scientific experiments, all under the most careful supervision.

If your youngster is mad keen on

Cypress Gardens

being an astronaut, sign him or her up for Space Camp!

Cypress Gardens

Turning from the futuristic to the more natural, Cypress Gardens offers more than 200 acres of immaculate botanical gardens, spectacular flower festivals, world famous water-ski shows and plenty

Southern charm

of good ol' southern hospitality. It was, in fact, the first 'theme park' in Florida, pre-dating Walt Disney World by some 35 years, and, under the ownership of the shrewd Anheuser-Busch company, it has gradually and carefully expanded in recent years to maintain a very pleasant alternative to the usual park experience.

It is about a 45-minute drive from Kissimmee, down I4, turning off at Exit 23 and south on to Highway 27 and then right on SR 540 just past Haines City. Cypress Gardens is about five miles along SR 540 on the left-hand side.

After the major tourist hustle of Orlando, the Gardens are an island of peace and tranquillity, even in the hotter months as there are plenty of places to get out of the sun and away from the crowds. Plan on spending the best part of a day here, too, as there is plenty to keep everyone amused. Start with a boat tour round the canals of the **Botanical Gardens**, then stroll round the gardens themselves, taking note of the immense **Banyan Tree** (unlike the Magic Kingdom's Swiss Family Treehouse, this one is real!), the photogenic **Southern Belles** in their colourful period outfits and the beautiful **Gazebo**, which hosts around 200 weddings a year! Visit the Oriental and French gardens, then retrace your steps and take in the spectacular new **Waterski Show**, Totally Mardi Gras, which features world-class skiers and world-famous routines (odd fact: Cypress Gardens' trademark ski show is the world's longest-running single attraction, operating every single day since 1942!). Have your picture taken in front of the scenic **Mediterranean Waterfall**, then marvel at the delights of the centrepiece garden attraction, which varies according to the season: the **Spring Flower Festival** runs from March 1–May 31, the **Victorian Garden Party** from June 1–September 30, the **Chrysanthemum Festival** from November 1–30 and the **Poinsettia Festival** from December 1–January 8. For my money, the elaborate

Cypress Gardens Greatest American Ski Team

Victorian Garden Party, featuring clever topiary 'statues', is the highlight of four hugely imaginative

Spring Flower Festival

programmes.

Continuing through the park brings you to the **Plantation Gardens**, which offers the practical side of gardening with tips on 'how to grow' herbs, vegetables, roses and other flowers and a twice-weekly seminar with the head gardener. Also here is the new **Wings Of Wonder** exhibit, a huge butterfly house where more than 1,000 butterflies hatch from glass cabinets and flutter around in tropical splendour. Stop off for afternoon

6

tea or a free Anheuser-Busch product sample at the beautifully restored mansion that is the **Hospitality Center** and listen to live music on the terrace. **The Island in the Sky** will then lift you up 15 storeys on its circular revolving platform for a grandstand view of the park. **Cypress Junction** houses America's biggest model train exhibition, while next door is **Carousel Cove**, a selection of games, rides and other activities to keep the youngsters amused for a while. There are also three show arenas, offering contrasting live entertainment all day. The large **Crossroads Arena** stages the Varieté International act of Russian and Ukrainian circus stars, lasting about half an hour, **Cypress Theatre** houses the Feathered Follies 20-minute exotic bird show and the **Gardens Theatre** offers the 15-minute Seasons of Cypress show.

There are 17 shops and gift stores to tempt you into buying yet more souvenirs, from the **House Of Names** (find out your family name derivation and heraldry), to **Sweet Creations** (home-made fudge and

Wings of wonder

real citrus juice, marmalades and jellies) and **Plantation Emporium** (Victorian gifts and fashions), plus the usual T-shirts, sweat-shirts and Anheuser-Busch name products. The **Village Fare** food court offers a good choice of different eating, from freshly-carved roast beef to pizza and salads, as does the **Cypress Deli**, while **Landings Chicken & Biscuit** serves fried chicken, barbecue platters and salads and the **Crossroads Restaurant** is full-service dining in air-conditioned comfort. Again, there's no shortage of choice, quality is high and value for money is particularly good.

Cypress Gardens is open from 9.30am to 5.30pm 365 days a year, except for November 24–January 7, when it stays open until 10pm for the **Garden of Lights** display. Admission is $26.95 for adults, $22.88 for Seniors (over 55) and $16.45 for kids aged three–nine. **Total attraction rating: AAAA.**

BRIT TIP: Remember you can SAVE $6 off Sea World and Busch Gardens tickets if you buy them here, or $7 off Cypress Gardens admission if bought at the other two parks.

Silver Springs

Continuing the theme of more natural attractions brings you to Silver Springs, just under two hours' drive to the north of Orlando. This 350-acre nature park (don't worry, you won't have to walk round all of it) surrounds the headwaters of the crystal-clear Silver River. Glass-bottomed boats take you for a close-up view of the artesian springs (the largest in the world) that bubble up here, along with plenty of marine wildlife. Expect close encounters with alligators, turtles, racoons and plenty of waterfowl, while the park also contains a collection of more exotic animals, like giraffes, camels and zebras that can be viewed from either land or water. Three animal shows, a five-acre tropical wildlife exhibit, a petting zoo and a new white alligator exhibit complete the rest of the attractions. Once again, you will feel as if you have left the crowds far behind. To ruin a few more illusions of the film industry, this was also the setting for the famous 1930s and 40s films of the

Silver Springs glass-bottomed boat

minute ride which goes down well with all the family and gives a first-class view of the seven different springs and a host of marine life. The first glass-bottomed boat sailed here in 1878 and millions of visitors have now peered into the depths of the Silver River and marvelled at the non-stop flow of the springs, which pump 550 million gallons of water into the river every day. Similarly, the **Lost River Voyage** is another 20-minute boat trip down one of the unspoilt stretches of the Silver River including a visit to the park's animal hospital where the local park ranger introduces you to all his current charges. The third boat trip on offer, the **Jungle Cruise**, is effectively a water safari along the Fort King Waterway, where animals from six continents are arranged in natural settings along the riverbanks. As an alternative to messing about on the river, the **Jeep Safari** is a 15-minute ride in the back of an open trailer through a natural forest habitat that is home to more animals from other corners of the world, such as marmosets, tapirs, antelope and vultures. The feeling of a safari is underlined by the much closer proximity to the animals on this particular journey. As you leave the Jeep Safari, the kids will enjoy a visit to **Doolittle's Petting Zoo** where the main attractions are Khama and Kimba, products of the park's successful giraffe breeding programme, as well as goats, deer and llamas. A specially constructed enclosure displays the park's rare **White Alligator**, one of

Jeep Safari ride

Tarzan series starring Johnny Weissmuller. This was where they staged all the spectacular scenes of Tarzan's great swimming exploits including his regular wrestling battles with alligators, and once you have appreciated the amazing tropical nature of the undergrowth you will understand why they decided to save on the cost of shipping the film crew all the way to Africa.

Silver Springs is located on SR 40 just through the town of Ocala, 72 miles to the north of Orlando. Take the Florida Turnpike north (it's a toll road, remember) until it turns into I75 and 28 miles further north you turn off and head east on SR 40. Another 10 miles brings you to Silver Springs, just past the Wild Waters water-park on your right.

Silver Springs' main attraction is its **Glass Bottomed Boats**, a 20-

6

only 18 in the world, and then there are the three **Cypress Island Animal Shows**, each one lasting 15 minutes and featuring an entertaining — and occasionally hair-raising — look at the worlds of reptiles, household pets and creepy crawlies. The hair-raising occurs only if you are the unlucky victim chosen to display a large tarantula, giant cockroach or scorpion. As you exit the animal shows take 15 minutes to wander the **Board Walk** and see the largest crocodile in captivity, the 16-foot, 2,000lb Sobek, as well as a collection of alligators, turtles and Galapagos tortoises. **The Osceola Gardens** provide a peaceful haven to sit and watch the world go by for a while, and the only odd note is struck by the somewhat out of place **A Touch of Garlits Museum**, which houses vintage American cars and racing cars. The usual collection of shops and eateries are fairly ordinary here, in contrast with the slick appeal of Orlando's parks, although **The Deli** offers some pleasant sandwich alternatives for lunch. In all, you would probably want to spend a good half day here with the possibility of a few hours in the neighbouring six-acre water park of **Wild Waters** which offers slides like the new Thunderbolt, the twin-tunnelled Tornado, the 220-foot long Silver Bullet and the helter-skelter Osceola's Revenge, as well as a 400-foot tube ride on the turbo charged Hurricane, a huge Wave Pool, a supervised play area for kids and a nine-hole mini-golf course.

Like Cypress Gardens there is no car parking charge, but admission fees are $26.95 for adults and $18.95 for children (three–10 years). Opening hours are 9.00am to 5.30pm year round.

A Silver Springs/Wild Waters day ticket is available at $30.95 for adults and $22.95 for kids (three–10). **Attraction rating: AAA 1/2.**

Splendid China

New in 1994 and still expanding and modifying its various displays and exhibits, Splendid China is unique to central Florida and a completely different type of attraction. Here, you won't find rides and other flights of fancy, but you will be taken on a fascinating journey through one of the biggest and most mysterious and breathtaking countries of the world.

A half-mile long replica of the Great Wall of China

This elaborate 76-acre park offers a range of intricate, miniaturised features like the Great Wall of China, the Forbidden City and the Stone Forest, some fascinating full-size exhibits, thrilling acrobats and martial arts experts, and, naturally enough, some great food. Recent additions include 5-person golf cart tours around the park and an enlarged playground for young children. Realistically, it will not hold the attention of small kids for long, and in high summer there is little escape from the relentless heat, but these are minor problems Splendid China is fully engaged in solving. An expansion programme has already added another 350 acres to its potential, and an Asian Trade Centre and Market is one idea under development. Where it scores impressively as an attraction is in its amazing eye for detail, its total air of authenticity (genuine Chinese crafts-men were brought in to hand-build every miniature) and its peaceful atmosphere — quite an achievement in the tourist bustle of Orlando!

Splendid China is located at the western end of the main tourist drag of Highway 192, three miles west of its junction with I4 and opposite the big Key W Kool Restaurant. Three to four hours is the minimum time requirement here, and you can easily spend half a day taking in all the different shows and one of the excellent restaurants. Here's how its 10,000-mile journey through 5,000 years of history works. The four elements of the park are essentially:

1) The Exhibits. More than 60 painstakingly re-created scale models of China's greatest buildings, statues and landmarks. **The Great Wall** is one of the most striking, at half a mile long and up to five-and-a-half feet high, it is constructed of more than six million tiny bricks, all faithfully put into place by hand. Other highlights include Beijing's **Imperial Palace** and the **Forbidden City**, the 26-storey **Grand Buddha of Leshan** (reduce to a 'mere' 36 feet tall), and the **Mausoleum of Genghis Khan**. The stairs by the side of the **Mausoleum of Dr Sun Yat Sen** afford a wonderful high-rise overview of the park, while the famous **TerraCotta Warriors** exhibit offers a chance to get in the air-conditioned cool for a minute or two. Splendid China is fully three-quarters the size of The Magic Kingdom, so it demands a fair amount of leg work to fully appreciate all the exhibits (noting how the specially imported Chinese grass is manicured around the smallest figures!), therefore it is not the time to discard your walking shoes.

2) The Shows. There are six centres for the performing arts which showcase the talents of some of China's top musicians, artists, acrobats and martial arts exponents. The **Temple of Light Amphitheater** is the main centre, featuring national song and dance exhibitions of around 30 minutes a

China in miniature

time. **Harmony Hall** features a short film about the creation of Splendid China and its sister park near Hong Kong, which is a good starting point for any visit, as well as staging some of the scintillating acrobatic displays. Outside, the **Suzhou Gardens** are home to various musical and martial arts specialities, while the **Pagoda Gardens** also stage acrobatic shows. The **Panda Playground**, where the kids can get rid of some excess energy, doubles up as the venue for some more daring acrobats, and the **Wind and Rain Court** holds other traditional acts, like the daring knife-climbing ceremony. New acts are featured all the time and there are various festivals, like martial arts, through the year.

3) The Restaurants. The park sets great store by the quality of its food, whether it be in its sumptuous five-star restaurant or its cafeteria-style buffet. The jewel in the crown is the elegant **Suzhou Pearl** overseen by the internationally renowned chef, Wu Chen, and featuring a full range of authentic gourmet Chinese cuisine, including Cantonese, Mandarin, Mongolian, Peking, Szechuan and Hunan. Chef Wu also has a hand in the budget-priced **Seven Flavors**, a cafeteria-style diner offering American food as well as a range of tempting Chinese dishes. The **Pagoda Garden**, in the furthest corner of the park, is a straight-forward American deli-style

6

establishment offering burgers and sandwiches while the **Wind and Rain Court Restaurant** has the greatest range of Chinese dishes outside the Suzhou Pearl. **The Great Wall Terrace** serves a mixture of authentic Chinese and traditional Western meals.

4) The Shops. Unlike all the other theme parks, Splendid China's shopping opportunities are all located in the same area so you can peruse their wares on returning to the Suzhou Gardens near the main entrance. The 11 gift shops are also one up on their counterparts by stocking a more up-market and distinctive range of goods, from Bonsai trees to furniture, jewellery to T-shirts, silk and satin clothing to children's toys, and antique curios to contemporary artefacts. In many instances you can also watch the local craftsmen and women at work producing the various wares.

The mixture of Chinese and Floridian staff add to the friendly atmosphere that the park generates, but ultimately it is a difficult concept to describe so the best advice is to see it for yourself. Adult admission is $22.01, children (5–12) are $12.99 while children four and under are free. Opening hours are 9.30am to 7.30pm seven days a week. **Attraction rating: AAAA.**

Gatorland

For another taste of the 'real' Florida this is as authentic as it gets when it comes to the wildlife, and consequently it is hugely popular with children of all ages. When the wildlife consists of several thousand menacing alligators and crocodiles in various natural habitats and three fascinating shows, you know you're in for a different experience. Gatorland was founded in 1949 and is one of the few family-owned attractions left in Florida, hence it possesses a home-spun charm which few of its big-money competitors can match.

BRIT TIP: If you have an evening flight home, Gatorland is a handy place to visit on your final day. Conveniently located, it is the ideal place to soak up a couple of 'spare' hours.

Entrance is through a giant set of alligator jaws which should fully prepare you for the sights within. Start by taking the **Gatorland Express Railroad** around the park to get an idea of its 50-acre expanse. Wander around the **Alligator**

Breeding Marsh Walkway, with its three-storey-high observation tower, and get a close-up view of these great reptiles who seem to hang around the 2,000-foot walkway in the hope someone might 'drop in' for lunch. Breeding pens, baby alligator nurseries and rearing ponds are also situated throughout the park to give you an idea of the full growth cycle of the Florida alligator and enhance the overall feeling that it is the visitor who is behind bars and not the animals themselves. In addition to the world's largest collection of gators and crocodiles, the park also contains monkeys, snakes, deer, goats, talking birds and a black bear as well as a serene flamingo lagoon complete with water plants and graceful palms. However, the alligators are the main attraction and it is the two gator shows which really draw the crowds (although you will never find yourself on the end of a queue here). The 800-seat **Wrestling Stadium** sets the scene for some real Cracker-style alligator feats (a Cracker is the local term for a Florida cowboy) as Gatorland's resident 'wranglers' catch themselves a six-foot gator and proceed to point out the animal's various survival features, with the aid of some stunts that will have you seriously questioning your cowboy's sanity. The **Gator Jumparoo** is another eye-opening spectacle as some of the park's biggest creatures, some more than 15 feet long, use their tails to 'jump' out of the water and be hand-fed tasty morsels like whole chickens! In between, you can take in the **Snakes of Florida** show which demonstrates that these reptiles, although dangerous, are not slimy and nasty after all, but in fact dry-skinned, and shy (and that Florida is home to more venomous varieties than you would imagine).

Obviously, face-to-face encounters with these living dinosaurs is not everyone's cup of tea, but it's an experience you're unlikely to repeat anywhere else. In addition to the attractions, you can also dine on smoked alligator ribs and deep-fried gator nuggets at **Pearl's Smokehouse**. The park is also home to hundreds of nesting herons and egrets, providing a fascinating close-up view of the nests from February to July, while a smart new $1 million renovation of the gift shop and admission area should be complete in 1996.

More than 5,000 alligators and crocodiles at Gatorland

Gatorland also scores in its great value for money for three–four hours entertainment, with adult tickets at $10.95, children under 10 $7.95 and under threes being free. Gatorland is located on the South Orange Blossom Trail, two miles south of its junction with the Central Florida Greeneway and three miles north of Highway 192. Opening hours are 8.00am to dusk daily. **Attraction rating: AAAA.**

Discovery Island

Still with the nature zoo theme, Walt Disney World's Discovery Island is a rather more refined look at some tropical wildlife, with three animal shows and more than 100 species of animals and 250 of plants. This is a real island in Bay Lake and one of Walt Disney World's harder-to-find spots. You won't find it signposted on any of the main routes into the vacation kingdom, but aim for the Fort Wilderness Resort and you will find the (free) parking area

6

for Discovery Island and River Country at the aptly-named Gateway Depot. Leave your car there and catch one of Disney's free shuttle buses to The Fort Wilderness Campground, from where you walk the last 100 yards to the Discovery Island Jetty (if you are staying in the Disney hotels around the Magic Kingdom, there are also regular boats to the island). You can also stop off by the bus-stop to let the children play with the animals of the Fort's **petting farm**, or even visit the stables and take a **trail ride** around the 800 wooded acres on horseback (book at Pioneer Hall or, in advance, on 407 824 2832). Compared to the extravagant nature of Disney's theme parks, this attraction is totally spartan, but there are still plenty of clever touches that mark it out as a cut above your average zoological park. It will take you about an hour to walk around the 11-acre sanctuary on the extensive boardwalks and paths which ring the island. Around the circuit you will find the **Alligator Pool, Tortoise Beach, Pelican Bay, Toucan Corner, Cranes Roost, Monkey Point** and **Flamingo Lagoon** where exotic reptiles and birds all thrive in this tropical haven. Kids will also enjoy the **Island Animal Hospital**, while the three shows are all family orientated and will add the best part of another hour to your visit. **Feathered Friends** features tame cockatoos, macaws and parrots, **Birds Of Prey** is an informative demonstration with the likes of the southern bald eagle and various owls, hawks and vultures, and **Reptile Relations** is another chance to meet Florida's number one scaly exhibit, the alligator, and some of his friends.

Admission is $10.00 for adults and $5.50 for kids aged three–nine (under threes free). Discovery Island admission is included free for seven days with a five-day World Hopper Pass. Children ages eight to 14 can also be booked on the four-hour guided tour Discovery Island Kid Venture for $30 in June, July and August. Opening hours are 9am to dusk every day. **Attraction rating: AAA.**

Mystery Fun House

This three-part adventure playground is primarily for kids and will happily occupy Junior for up to three hours. The three elements are the Mystery Fun House itself, the new Jurassic Putt Golf Park, and Starbase Omega, an elaborate laser battle game that mum and dad seem to get just as much of a kick out of as the kids.

Start with the **Mystery Fun House** and work your way through the mirror maze into the Egyptian Tomb. Another 13 chambers of surprises await you, including a fire-breathing dragon in the Topsy-Turvy Tilt Room, the mysteries of the Forbidden Temple, the dangers of the Chamber of Horrors (why do kids seem to revel in the gruesome delights of death and torture?), and concluding in the Grand Ballroom with its circus theme. Next, take in the high-tech **Starbase Omega**. You'll be fully kitted out with electronic power-vest and laser blaster, briefed for your 'mission' (usually a battle with all the visitors divided into two teams) and then unleashed on the combat zone via the Millennium 333 transporter. The unique 'space gravity surface', dry ice and rousing music add to the fun and this 21st-century version of cops and robbers is guaranteed to bring out the kid in everyone. The new **Mini-Golf** set-up offers a few variations on the standard crazy golf courses with which Orlando is overstocked. The Jurassic Putt theme means you have to test your skill against a number of dinosaur obstacles, including an 18-foot Brachiosaurus and a sabre-toothed tiger. If all that is not enough to keep your youngsters entertained the Mystery Fun House also has Orlando's largest video games arcade, an ice cream parlour, several gift shops, a shooting gallery, an 'old-tyme' photo booth, and a restaurant that features the periodic Whiz-Bang Revue. The Mystery Fun House also offers a number of birthday party packages from $10.50 per person ($11.75 with pizza or hot dogs); for details call 407 351 3356. Visits to the Mystery Fun House can also be made on the special Fun House Trolley which operates along the main tourist length of International Drive and is free if you ride all the way to the Fun House. Otherwise you can pay $1.50 for the round trip back to your hotel.

The Mystery Fun House is located on Major Boulevard, just off Kirkman Road as you approach Universal Studios. It is open 365 days a year from 10am to 10pm and a combination ticket for all three features costs $13.85. If you want to do them individually, it is $7.95 for the Mystery Fun House, $6.95 for Starbase Omega, and $4.95 for the Mystery Mini-Golf. **Attraction rating: TTTT.**

Ripley's Believe It Or Not

You can't miss this particular attraction, next door to the Mercado Shopping Centre on International Drive, as its extraordinary tilted appearance makes it seem as though it was designed by an architect with an aversion to the horizontal. However, once inside you will soon find yourself back on the level and for an hour or two you can wander through this museum dedicated to the weird and wonderful.

Robert L Ripley was an eccentric explorer and collector of enormous energy who, for 40 years, travelled worldwide in his bid to assemble a collection of the greatest oddities known to man. If you've ever been to the Guinness World of Records in London you'll have an idea what to expect, although Ripley's goes somewhat further into the realms of the bizarre. The Orlando branch of this now worldwide museum chain features 8,900 square feet of displays that include authentic artefacts, video presentations, illusions, interactive exhibits and music. The elaborate re-creation of an Egyptian tomb showcases an Egyptian mummy and three rare mummified animals, while the collection of miniatures include the world's smallest violin and a single grain of rice handpainted with a tropical sunset. Larger-scale exhibits include a portion of the Berlin Wall, a two-thirds scale 1907 Rolls Royce built entirely out of matchsticks and a version of the 'Mona Lisa' textured completely from toast! It's all good amusing fun, if not overwhelmingly educational, and it should keep all the family entertained — especially if you challenge each other to brave the twisting, turning Lava Tunnel.

Admission is $8.95 for adults and $5.95 for children age four to 11 and it is open from 9am to 11pm daily, with extended hours during the peak season. **Attraction rating: AAA.**

Fantasy Of Flight

Brand new to central Florida is this $30million aviation museum attraction which is an absolute must even for anyone not usually interested in the history of flight or the glamour of the Golden Age of flying. Just 25 minutes down I4 towards Tampa (take Junction 21, Polk City, go north on SR 559 for half a mile then turn left into the main entrance), Fantasy of Flight is a three-part adventure featuring the world's largest private collection of vintage aircraft, a series of expertly re-created "immersion experiences" into memorable moments in aviation

6

history (like a World War II bomber mission with a real Flying Fortress!), and eight incredibly realistic fighter simulators that take you through a WWII aerial battle. The whole experience is crafted in 1930s Art Deco style, including a full-service Diner and original gift shop, and there is strong British appeal with the War depictions and many of the exhibits, like the last air-worthy Sunderland Flying Boat. Admission is $8.95 for adults, $7.95 for Seniors (60-plus) and $6.95 for kids (5–12, under 5s free), while the fighter simulators are $5.95 extra. It is open from 9am-8pm in peak holiday periods and 9am-5pm at other times. Fantasy of Flight is the brainchild of American entrepreneur and aviation whiz Kermit Weeks and I have yet to encounter an attraction put together with more genuine love and care. For more information call 941 984-3500.

The Water Parks

If anyone has been down the slides and flumes at the local leisure centre, they will have an inkling of what Orlando's five big water parks are all about. Predictably, Disney weigh in with three of the most elaborate examples, but the independently run Wet 'n Wild and Water Mania are equally adept at providing hours of watery fun with slides and wave pools in an amazing variety of styles that owe a lot to the imagination of the theme park ride creators. They never opt for a simple up-and-down slide when they can twist you round, turn you upside down, send you into free-fall and fire you through dark tunnels all in the course of dumping you in pools of various sizes.

All five parks require at least half a day of splashing, sliding and riding to get full value from their rather high admission charges, but if you

prefer to get your kicks in watery rather than land-borne fashion, these are definitely for you and you will want to try at least a couple of them. In all of them you can set yourself up as you would for a day at

Splash down at Water Mania

the beach, staking out a convenient spot of sand, grass or similar area. Lockers are always provided for your valuables and you can even hire towels.

Typhoon Lagoon

Until Disney's Blizzard Beach opened, the elaborate Typhoon

> BRIT TIP: Ladies, down some of the whizziest slides it is advisable to wear a one-piece swimsuit rather than a bikini. Your modesty could be at stake here!

Lagoon was the biggest and finest example of Florida's water parks. In high season, it is also the busiest, so be prepared to run into more queues and congestion in all the main areas. The 56 acres of Typhoon Lagoon are spread out and around the two-

BRIT TIP: While these parks are a great way of cooling down in the hottest parts of the day, it is easy to forget that this is also the best way to pick up a five-star case of sunburn. So don't forget high factor, waterproof suntan lotion.

and-a-half-acre lagoon that is fringed with palm trees and white sand beaches. If it wasn't for the high-season crowds, you could easily convince yourself you had been washed up on some tropical island paradise. With the exception of Blizzard Beach, Typhoon Lagoon goes in for the most extravagant landscaping and introduces some clever details that you will not find anywhere else. The walk up Mount Mayday, for instance, provides a terrific overview of the park as well as adding scenic touches like rope bridges and tropical flowers. Sun loungers, chairs, picnic tables and even a few hammocks are provided to add to the comfort and convenience of areas like Getaway Glen.

The park is overlooked by the 90-foot **Mount Mayday**, atop which is perched the luckless *Miss Tilly*, a shrimp boat that legend has it landed here during the typhoon that gave the park its name. Watch for the water fountains that shoot from *Miss Tilly*'s funnel at regular intervals, accompanied by the ship's hooter which signals the outbreak of another round of four-foot high waves in the lagoon itself (where you can hire innertubes to bob around on or just try body-surfing). Circling the lagoon is **Castaway Creek**, a three-foot deep lazy flowing river that offers the chance to float happily along on the rubber tyres that are provided for just this purpose (although around midday you may find yourself shoulder-to-shoulder with hundreds of people who all have the same idea).

The series of slides and rides are all clustered around Mount Mayday and vary from the breathtaking **Humunga Kowabunga**, which drops you 214 feet at up to 30mph down some of the steepest inclines in waterdom (make sure your swimming costume is SECURELY fastened before attempting this one!), to the children's area **Ketchakiddee Creek**, which offers a selection of slides and fun pools for all youngsters under four feet tall. In between, you have the three **Storm Slides**, another body slide-type which twists and turns through caves, tunnels and waterfalls, **Mayday Falls**, a 460-foot innertube ride down a series of twisting, turning drops, **Keelhaul Falls**, an alternative tube ride that takes slightly longer, and **Gangplank Falls**, a group or family ride whose tubes take up to four people down the 300 feet of mock rapids. The hugely imaginative **Shark Reef** offers the chance to snorkel around this upturned wreck and coral reef among 4,000 tropical fish and a number of very real, but quite harmless, nurse sharks. Like all the areas, this one is very carefully supervised, and those who aren't quite brave enough to dive in amongst the marine wildlife can still get a close up through the underwater port holes of the sunken ship (Shark Reef is also closed to swimmers during the coldest of the winter months). There are also height and health restrictions on Humunga Kowabunga (no bad backs, necks, or pregnant women), while the queues for this slide, plus the Storm Slides and Shark Reef can touch an arduous hour at times which can take a lot of the fun out of the experience (an hour's wait for a 20-second slide? Not for me, thanks). Getting out of the sun can lso be slightly problematic as the provision of shaded areas is not overwhelming, but a quick plunge into Castaway Creek usually solves any overheating problems. Typhoon Lagoon does have the most picturesque areas to just soak up the sun, though. The palm-fringed beaches of the Lagoon area are a great place to set up camp, either on the right (to be near the lockers) or on the left (near Ketchakiddee Creek if you have youngsters).

> BRIT TIP: If the main changing rooms are busy (as they will be throughout the morning during peak periods), go instead to one of the rest-rooms where changing facilities are also provided.

For snacks and meals **Lowtide Lou's** and **Let's Go Slurpin'** both offer snacks and drinks while **Typhoon Tilly's** and **Leaning Palms** both serve a mixture of burgers, sandwiches, salads and ice-cream. More than anywhere else, it is important to avoid main meal times here if you want to eat in relative comfort. You do, however, have the option of bringing your own picnic along here (unlike all the other theme parks) as there are several scenic areas laid out for you but no alcohol or glass containers are allowed). You CAN'T bring your own snorkels, rafts and inner-tubes into the park, but snorkles are provided at Shark Reef and you need to hire innertubes only for the Lagoon. If you have forgotten any vital item like a sunhat or bucket and spade for the kids, or even your swimsuit, they are all available along with the usual range of gifts and souvenirs) at **Singapore Sal's**.

To avoid the worst of the summer crowds (when the park's 7,200 capacity is frequently reached), Monday morning is about the best time to visit (steer clear of the weekends at all costs), while on other week days arrive either 30 minutes before opening time or in mid-afternoon when some people decide to call it a day to dodge the daily rainstorm. Early evening can also be quite pleasant as the park starts to light up.

Opening hours are 9am to dusk every day, with admission $22.50 for adults and $17.00 for kids three to nine (under threes free). It is free, of course, with a Five Day World Hopper Pass. **Attraction rating: AAAAA or TTTT** (depending on which slides you enjoy!).

River Country

At just a quarter of the size of Typhoon Lagoon, you might think this is a good, out-of-the-way spot that most people overlook. But you'd be wrong. It may be smaller, but the same number of folk seem to try to cram in here. As it is not unknown for the gates to close by late morning because capacity has been reached, it is a good idea to arrive early or after 4pm (when admission prices are also reduced).

However, just because it is the country cousin to Typhoon Lagoon and Blizzard Beach in terms of size doesn't mean River Country is any less well organized or lacking in charm. In fact, its theme as an old-fashioned swimming hole gives it a distinctly rustic, backwoods America flavour straight out of *Huckleberry Finn*.

The heart of the park is **Bay Cove**, a roped off section of Bay Lake which offers the chance to climb on ropes, tyre swings, a barrel bridge and boom swing and ride the cable, all finishing with an emphatic splash into the lake. **Whoop 'n Holler Hollow** contains the two main thrill opportunities, a pair of

6

similar bodyslide flumes that end

Wet 'n Wild

with a seven-foot drop into the heated swimming pool. **White Water Rapids** is a somewhat more sedate trip via innertube down a series of chutes and pools that gives you rather more chance to admire the scenery, while young children are also exceptionally well catered for with their own area, **Kiddie Cove**, which contains several small slides, pools and a separate stretch of beach. Just to do each of the main activities will take you about half the time that Typhoon Lagoon does, but there is a more relaxing, rural feel to River Country that encourages you to stick around for a while longer. And, if you get bored with splashing in the water, you can always take a boat ride or walk around on the Nature Trail, a 1,000-yard boardwalk through a pretty, well-shaded Cypress grove.

Pop's Place serves the usual array of fast food (and a Kid's Picnic Basket at $3.29) while the **Waterin' Hole** offers snacks and drinks. There is no gift shop here, however.

To find River Country, follow the directions for Discovery Island and bear left just before the boat jetty. Admission is $14.75 for adults and $11.50 for kids aged three–nine

while it also comes free with the five-day ticket. Opening hours are again 9am until dusk. **Attraction rating: AAA or TTT.**

Blizzard Beach

Ever imagined a ski-ing resort in the middle of Florida? You haven't. Well, Disney have, and this is the result. Blizzard Beach aims to put the rest of the parks in the shade for size as well as extravagant settings, with the whole park arranged as if it were in the Rocky Mountains rather than the sub-tropics. That means snow-effect scenery, Christmas trees and water slides cunningly converted to look like skiing pistes and toboggan runs. It delivers a real feast for water lovers and Disney admirers in general, and the basic premise of snow-surfin' USA is an unarguable five-star knockout. Feature items are **Mount Gushmore**, a 90-foot mountain down which all the main slides run (including the world's tallest free-fall speed slide, the frightening 120-foot **Summit Plummet**), **Tike's Peak**, a kiddie-sized version of the park with scaled-down slides and snow-beach, **Melt-Away Bay**, a one-acre pool fed by 'melting snow' waterfalls, and **Cross Country Creek**, a lazy-flowing river around the whole park which also carries floating guests through a bone-chilling 'ice cave'. Don't miss the standout rides – **Teamboat Springs**, a wild family inner-tube adventure, **Runoff Rapids**, a one-person tube plunge, and the **Snow Stormers**, a daring head-first 'toboggan' run. There is also a 'village' area including the **Beach Haus** shop and **Lottawatta Lodge** restaurant offering diners a view of Mount Gushmore and Melt-Away Bay beach. The names alone should prepare you for a positive riot of visual jokes and clever imagery, and the crowds are suitably MASSIVE. AAAAA.

Blizzard Beach is located just north of the All-Star Resorts off Buena Vista Drive, and charges are $25 per adult and $16 per child (three to nine) with opening times from 9am to early evening.

Wet 'n Wild

If Disney scores highest marks for its scenic content, then Wet 'n Wild goes full-tilt for thrills and spills of the highest quality. If you really want to test the material of your swimsuit to the limit, this is the place to do it!

Wet 'n Wild is repeatedly one of the best attended water parks in the whole country, and its location in the heart of International Drive makes it a major tourist draw. Consequently, you will once again encounter some serious crowds here, although the 12 slides and rides, Lazy River attraction, an elaborate kids' park (with mini versions of many of the slides), Surf Lagoon and restaurant and picnic areas all manage to absorb a lot of punters before the queues start to develop. Waits of more than half an hour at peak times are rare. Its popularity with locals means it is busiest at weekends, with July the month that attracts most crowds.

You are almost spoilt for choice of main rides, from the relatively gentle bodyslide of the **Flash Flood** and the highly popular group innertube rides of **The Surge** and **Bubba Tub**, through the more demanding rides of **Raging Rapids** to the high-thrill factor of the **Black Hole** (like the Magic Kingdom's Space Mountain, but in water!), **Blue Niagara** (also an enclosed body-slide) and **Mach 5** to the ultimate terror of **Der Stuka** and the new **Bomb Bay**. These latter are definitely not for the faint-hearted. 'I was convinced I was going to die!'

Wet 'n Wild

was the mild observation of one battle-hardened water park veteran. Basically they are two 76-foot-high bodyslides with a drop as near vertical as makes no difference. Der Stuka is the straightforward slide version, while the Bomb Bay adds the extra terror of being hoisted into place and then allowed to free-fall on to the top of the slide. And they call it fun?! Suffice it to say, your author has not put himself at risk on these particular contraptions, and has absolutely no intention of doing so! For some reason only 15–25 per cent of the park's visitors pluck up the courage to try it. Can't think why.

The neighbouring lake is also part of the fun (although not in winter when its temperature drops below that of merely chilly), adding the opportunities to try the cable-operated **Knee Ski** and ride the **Wild One** (large innertubes tied behind a speedboat). Alternatively, take a breather in the slow-flowing **Lazy River** or abandon the water altogether for one of several shaded picnic areas. Staying cool out of the water is rather harder, however, especially at peak times when the best spots are quickly snapped up. For food, **Bubba's Bar-B-Q** serves chicken, ribs, fries and drinks, the **Beach Club Snack Bar** features burgers, hot-dogs, chicken and sandwiches and there are another seven snack bars offering similar fast-food fare, including a pizza bar and a kiddies' counter (for the likes of peanut butter sandwiches, hot dogs and chips). For the energetic there is also beach volleyball and the chance to ride the **Robo Surfer** at selected times, a watery version of the mechanical bucking bronco. All-day lockers, shower facilities, tube and towel rentals are all well provided, but if you bring your own floating equipment is has to be checked by one of the many lifeguards on duty. Picnics can also be brought in, provided you don't include alcohol or glass containers.

Wet 'n Wild is located half a mile north of International Drive's junction with Sand Lake Road and is open year-round from 9am in peak periods (10am at other times) until variously 5, 6, 7, 9 or 11pm. The extended hours from late June to late August, known as Wet 'n Wild Summer Nights programme, offer particularly good value as admission is half price after 5pm and you still have six hours of watery fun ahead of you. Admission to Wet 'n Wild also now includes the neighbouring mini-golf park, Congo River. Admission prices are $21.95 for adults, $17.97 for kids three to nine and under threes free. Parking is an additional $3. **Attraction rating: AAA or TTTTT** (you have been warned!).

Water Mania

If Wet 'n Wild attracts the serious water-thrill seekers, Kissimmee's version Water Mania is more family-orientated and laid back, with the crowds highest at weekend when the locals flock in and lowest early in the

week. That's not to say that Water Mania doesn't have its share of scary slides (or that Wet 'n Wild doesn't cater for families), it's just that their emphasis is slightly different and those looking to avoid the worst of the crowds often end up here.

Where Water Mania also scores a minor victory over its rivals is in the provision of three acres of wooded picnic area that makes a welcome change from the concrete expanses and from the feverish splashing activities. You are again welcome to bring your own picnic (although no glass bottles or mugs).

Eight different slides, including a patented non-stop surfing challenge called **Wipe-Out**, the usual **Cruisin' Creek**, a 750,000-gallon **Wave Pool** (waves every 15 minutes, up to four feet high) and two separate kids' areas provide the main attractions, and there is again enough here to keep you occupied for at least half a day. Top of the list for those daring enough to throw themselves down things like Der Stuka is **The Screamer**, an aptly-named 72-foot-high free-fall speed slide, and **The Abyss**, 300 feet of enclosed-tube darkness. **The Anaconda** and **Banana Peel** both feature family-sized innertubes down long, twisting, turning slides, while the **Double Berzerker** offers two different ways to be whooshed along and spat out into a foaming pool. **The Rain Forest** is designed for two to 10 year olds, with a 5,000 square-foot pool ranging from three inches to two feet deep and featuring mini-slides, fountains, water guns, and a giant pirate ship. **The Squirt Pond** offers kids more chances to ride pint-sized slides and flumes. However, the stand-out feature, for both trying and watching, is the **Wipe-Out**, one of only two such attractions in the world. The challenge is to grab a body surfboard and try to ride the continuous wave, risking going over the edge into

nother pool if you stray too wide or
eing sent flying backwards if you
ose your balance. A real blast!

In addition to the cooling picnic
reas, there are also several snack
ars, a mini-golf course, volleyball
nd basketball courts, a games room
nd a large shop in case you have
orgotten your swimming costume.
Apparently, people do all the time!)

Water Mania is located on
Highway 192, just a mile east of the
4 intersection and is open variously
rom 9.30am (June to early
eptember), 10am (March to the
eginning of June and September
nd October) and 11am (in January,
'ebruary and November) until 5, 6
r 7pm (8pm at weekends in peak
eason). It is closed from Nov
7–Dec 25. Admission is $20.95 for
dults and $12.95 for kids three–12.
'arking is $3. **Attraction rating:
AA or TTTT.**

Off The Beaten Track

fter several days in the midst of the
ectic tourist whirl of mainstream
)rlando, you may find yourself in
eed of a day or two's rest from the
on-stop theme park activities, a
oliday from your holiday, if you
ke. If that is the case, this next
ection is for you.

Hopefully you will already have noted
he relatively tranquil offerings of
Cypress Gardens and Silver Springs, but
o get away from it all more completely,
nd to enhance your view of central
'lorida still further the following are
uaranteed to take you well off the
eaten tourist track.

Winter Park

'his elegant northern suburb of Orlando
s one of its best-kept tourist secrets as it
little more than 20 minutes' drive from
he hurly-burly of areas like International
)rive and yet a million miles from the
elentless commercialisation of the city. It
ffers several renowned museums and art
alleries, some top-quality shopping, 17
estaurants (including the top of the
inge **Park Plaza Gardens**), several

pleasant walking tours, a delightful 50-
minute boatride around several of the
area's lakes and, above all, a chance to
SLOW DOWN!

The Winter Park Scenic Boat Tour

The central area is **Park Avenue**, a
classy street of fine shops, boutiques, two
museums and a wonderfully shaded park.
At one end of the avenue is **Rollins
College**, a small but highly-respected
arts education centre which also houses
the **Cornell Fine Arts Museum** (open
daily, except Monday, admission free)
and **Annie Russell Theater**. The
museum features regular art exhibitions
and lectures, as well as having its own
collection. **The Morse Museum of
American Art** is a must for admirers of
American art pottery, American and
European glass, furniture and other
decorative arts of the late 19th and early
20th centuries, including one of the
world's foremost collections of works by
Louis Comfort Tiffany (open
9.30am–4pm Tue–Sat, and 1–4pm Sun,
admission $2.50 for adults, $1 for
children). The **Scenic Boat Tour** is
located at the east end of Morse Avenue,
and offers a charming, narrated tour of
the 'Venice of America', travelling 12
miles around the lakes and canals for a
fascinating glimpse of some of the most
beautiful private houses, boat houses and
lakeside gardens (properties in the area
start at $750,000 and top $3million in
several instances!). The tours run every
day from 10am to 4pm and cost $5.50
for adults ($4.40 for groups of 10 or
more) and $2.75 for children two to 11,
and it is one of the most relaxing hours
you will spend in Orlando.

The shops are also a cut or two above
anything you will encounter elsewhere,
and while you may find the prices equally
distinctive, just browsing is an enjoyable
experience with the charm of the area

6

highlighted by the friendliness of everyone hereabouts. From predictable fashions to totally unpredictable stores like **Lee Morgan**, a one-off gift shop and antiques and furniture store, and **The Rune Stone**, a one-off toy shop, the notable feature of all the shops is that they seem to have window-dressers who really know what they're doing for a change (not a strong point of many American shops) and make each one look tempting. Regular pavement craft fairs and art festivals also add splashes of colour to an already inviting scenario. In addition to the Park Plaza Gardens, which specialises in continental cuisine (see Chapter Seven on Eating Out), you can dine on French, Italian, Thai and Vietnamese offerings.

An additional high point of a visit to Winter Park is the **Kraft Azalea**

Stowaway Adventures

Garden on Alabama Drive (off Palmer Avenue at the north end of Park Avenue), 11 acres of shaded lakeside walk-ways, gardens and hundreds of magnificent azaleas. The main focal point, the mock Grecian temple, is a particularly beautiful setting for the many weddings that are held here.

Winter Gardens is located off exit 45 of I4, Fairbanks Avenue. Turn left on to Fairbanks and head east for two miles until it intersects with Park Avenue; public parking is well indicated.

Stowaway Adventures

To go even further into the unspoilt side of central Florida, try one of the half-day tours offered on the St John's River by this small, independent company who specialise in boat trips and nature walks.

From April to the end of September,

Stowaway features a six-hour day cruise from 9.30am that stops to visit **Hontoon Island** (home of the Timicuan Indians) for a guided walk and then at **Blue Springs State Park** for swimming and snorkelling in the crystal clear spring waters (snorkelling gear and refreshments all provided). From October to March the itinerary switches to a longer nature walk with the chance to view the West Indian manatees (those half hippo-half walrus creatures featured at Sea World) nurturing their young calves as they swim about the spring run. There is also a four-hour sunset cruise on the river, with music, hors-d'oeuvres and complimentary wine or beer. Groups are limited to 18 on the day cruises and 12 in the evening, so there is a good personal touch to all the activities.

For a close-up view of the scenic waterways, tropical plantlife and local wildlife, including many species of birds, deer, alligators and the occasional black bear, this is a first-class trip. Stowaway Adventures are operated by Captain John Stowe and can be found at Hidden Harbour Marina, in the town of Sanford (exit 52 off I4) to the north of Orlando on the St John's River and cruises cost $46 for adults ($33 on the evening trip) and $38 for children three to 12. For full details call 407 695 2722.

Air Boat Rides

Staying with the watery theme for the moment, Florida also offers the thrill of airboat rides on many of its lakes, rivers and marshes. An airboat is a totally different experience to any boat ride you will have taken as it is more like flying at ground level. It is as much a thrill as a scenic adventure, but it also has the advantage of exploring areas otherwise inaccessible to boats. Airboats simply skim over and through the marshes, cross short stretches of land in places, to give you an alternative, close-up and very personal view. Travelling at up to 45mph also means it can be loud (hence you will be provided with headphones) and sunglasses are also a good idea to keep stray flies out of your eyes. It is also NOT the trip for you if you are spooked by crickets, dragonflies and similar creepy crawlies that occasionally land inside the boat!

There are a number of different operators in central Florida, but my personal favourite is **Toho Airboat Excursions**, who operate from Lake Tohopekaliga south of Kissimmee. Take Poinciana Boulevard south 18 miles from Highway 192 into Southport Road and then the picturesque and tranquil Southport Park. Here their daily tours operate at regular intervals from 9.30am to 6pm, with the chance to see all manner of wildlife, from alligators and wild boar to herons, cranes, wild turkeys

Airboat rides

and a host of other water fowl. It's one of the smoothest boat rides you will ever take, while Toho Airboats also operates a night-time Alligator Hunt for which you need to book. This goes out at about 9pm and heads into the marsh for an hour, where you sit and wait for the gators to come and take a look. Their eyes glow red in the dark and it is a fascinating experience!

> BRIT TIP: Best time to do the daily ride is first thing on a weekday morning when the local wildlife is at its most plentiful

The day trip costs $15 per adult, half price for children seven and under, for the half-hour round trip (discount coupons are available which give you an extra $3 off), while the night-time Gator Hunt is $25 and $12.50. Contact Toho Airboat Excursions on 407 931 2225 for details of the next night trip, which is usually run on an invitation basis.

'Old Fashioned' Airboat Rides are another reliable operation out to the east on St John's River, some 45 minutes drive from I4 and 15 from the Kennedy

Space Center. They offer one-and-a-half-hour guided tours into more little-seen corners of Florida's waterways at $25 for adults and $15 for kids under 12. However, their daily tours, barbecues and special night-time alligator excursions must all be booked in advance by calling Airboat John on 407 568 4307.

Balloon Trips

Florida is one of the most popular areas for ballooning and, if you are up early enough in the morning, you will quite often see three or four balloons floating over the Orlando countryside.

The experience is a majestic one. If Orlando represents the holiday of a lifetime, then a balloon flight is the ride of a lifetime. Believe me, Disney has nothing to touch this one! The utterly smooth way in which you lift off into the early morn-

Spectacular views from hot-air balloons

ing sky is breathtaking in itself, but the peace and quiet of the ride, not to mention the stunning views from up to 2,000 feet above ground, are quite awesome. It is not a cheap experience, however, but it is equally appealing to couples and families, although small children can be a little scared by the unusual nature of it all. Needless to say, it is not recommended for anyone who suffers vertigo or a fear of heights! It is also a very personalised ride, as four people make for a full trip. Most baskets will take five, or occasionally even six, but you need to be on good terms with each other!

There are numerous outfits offering balloon flights in the Orlando area, and you should be advised that several have earned themselves a bad reputation for lacking full safety requirements or showing scant regard for the areas where they take off and land. Hence, if you are considering a balloon flight, it is important to ensure your trip is with a

6

reputable operation. **Central Florida Balloon Tours** fit that description admirably, under the control of Captain Richard Davenport, an experienced and very personable flier. For most of the year they operate early morning flights (giving you a 'phone call at around 5am before picking you up about an hour later) to take advantage of the calmest winds, while in the winter months they usually fly in late afternoon.

Occasionally, weather conditions prevent their flights, in which case they very thoughtfully refrain from the 5am phone call! The full experience includes seeing the crew set up and inflate the balloon (you can help if you wish), an hour's flight (marvelling at the sights, sounds and amazing amount of control your pilot has over the craft, right down to being able to come within inches of one of the many lakes you fly over), the landing and a traditional balloonist's champagne breakfast in some peaceful, remote spot. With the return journey to your hotel (by van!), the whole thing lasts around three hours and also includes your special memento flight certificate. Wear sensible shoes but otherwise dress as you would for being on the ground as there is little temperature difference and no wind chill factor from being at these altitudes (although ladies please note that dresses are not advisable for clambering in and out of the basket!). If anything, the balloon's propane burners make things slightly warmer rather than cooler once you are under way. Prices are $175 per person, and you can call Central Florida Balloon Tours to book a flight on 407 294 8085. And don't forget your camera and/or camcorder. It makes for magnificent photography and filming.

For a bigger scale experience you should try **Aerial Adventures of Orlando**, who operate Rosie O'Grady's Flying Circus with up to five balloons at a time. You have to meet at 5.45am at Apple Annie's in Church Street Station, from where you are taken to the launch site and then brought back again for the inclusive breakfast at Lili Marlene's Aviator's Restaurant. Extra touches include pre-flight coffee and orange juice, a polaroid photo of you and your pilot, a Church Street Station champagne glass and a free entry to the Station. Their breakfasts are of the cooked variety, but you do miss out on the wonderful experience of sipping champagne in the middle of nowhere in Florida's great outback. The full Aerial Adventures package is $165 per person, while they also offer an economy fare of $110 for flight only.

Cypress Island

This 200-acre nature attraction is another heaven-sent opportunity to get away from the crowds and enjoy more authentic Florida countryside, with the added feature of more than 400 local and imported animals like African pygmy goats, emus, mountain sheep, llamas and the cute Patagonian cavy all roaming around in splendid freedom.

Situated in south Kissimmee on Lake Tohopekaliga (Toho for short), it offers miles of nature trails, a four-mile ecological tour by golf cart, plus the extras of seaplane ($15 extra) and waverunner (a safer, sit-down type of jetski, $8 extra) rides. Their latest additions are the Wildlife Refuge and Rehabilitation Center, which rescues injured animals and uses them to educate visitors, and the Animal Nursery, which offers a close-up view of the Island's latest arrivals.

Its wonderfully relaxed, open-air style is also geared up for picnics, volleyball, softball and horseshoe-pitching, while other extras include airboat rides, a swampy buggy ride (on a 12-wheel, 2½-ton truck), horse rides and their night-time alligator photo safari. Cypress Island is reached by a 3-mile boat ride from their Country Store at the end of Scotty's Road, which is well signposted from Highway 192's junction with the Florida Turnpike. Just turn right into Shady Lane and it is about 2½ miles further south. Basic adult admission is $24 while kids (3–12) are $17, and the first boat leaves the Country Store at 9am every day, with the last boat returning an hour before dusk. For reservations or information about this unique local treasure, call 407 935 9202.

Warbird Air Museum

Vintage aeroplane and nostalgia buffs will want to make a note of this offbeat museum adjacent to Kissimmee Airport, which builds and restores old World War II fighters and bombers. Kids who enjoyed building Airfix kits will specially enjoy the one-hour tour of the facilities, which basically represent a couple of large hangars with aircraft in various stages of restoration and repair. It is one of the most amazing programmes of its kind you will find, with the exhibits ranging from fully-restored Grumman Avenger torpedo bombers to scraps of fuselages and engines that will gradually be incorporated into the latest rebuilding project. The tour guides also have a detailed working knowledge of everything they show you. You could be forgiven for thinking you have walked into a scrapyard on your way in, but the main hangars reveal the full scale of the operation, with the wholescale restoration of a B-17 Flying Fortress being their pride and joy. The site also includes a charming little gift shop that houses some more museum pieces, costumes and models from World War II. It is open seven days a week from 9am to 5.30pm (9–5pm on Sundays), and there is always some reconstruction work under way, while the exhibits themselves change regularly as new ones are brought in and others flown away. Charges are $6 for adults and $5 for over 60s and under 12s. The museum can be found just off Highway 192, half a mile down Hoagland Boulevard on the left.

Cruises

A quick glance at any of the tour brochures for Orlando will reveal a hugely tempting array of full-scale sea cruises that can be taken in addition to enjoying this theme park paradise. If the prices there are slightly prohibitive, consider one of the one-day cruise excursions that operate on St John's River or from one of the ports that are little more than an hour's drive from Orlando. Again, it's a very different option for your holiday and they offer a little taste of what their big brothers have in store (at much greater expense!).

The **Europa FunKruz** operates daily from St John's Pass Village, Madeira Beach, St Petersburg, and offers a lively range of sightseeing, meals and live entertainment, including a full casino for those of a gambling inclination. The 500-ton *Europa Sky* can take up to 400 passengers on a six-hour day or night cruise up the east coast. Its facilities include a lounge, sports bar and games room, a VIP dining area and a passenger suite, and you are assured of top-quality food from their on-board chefs. Rates are $39.95 per person or $49.95 for the slightly longer evening excursion, plus $12 port charges and taxes. It departs 10am–4pm (Monday to Friday), 11am–5pm (Saturday and Sunday). 6.30pm–midnight (Sunday to Wednesday) and 6.30pm–12.30am (Thursday to Saturday). For more details call 813 393 5110.

The **Rivership Romance** offers another chance to escape the tourist throng with a three- or four-hour cruise along the St John's River, taking in some of Florida's more natural scenery and wildlife. Live entertainment, full bar service and excellent cuisine is again the order of the day, but things are altogether more relaxed and, on the evening cruise, more romantic and intimate. The three-decked, 110-foot catamaran offers three different cruises, a three-hour lunch excursion (Wed, Sat and Sun, from 11am, $30), a four-hour lunch (Mon, Tue, Thur, and Fri from 11am, $40) or a four-hour evening dinner-dance (Fri and Sat, from 7.30pm, $41 and $46). The Rivership Romance can be found by taking I4 18 miles northeast of Orlando, turning off on exit 51 and going east through five sets of traffic lights into downtown Sanford. Turn left on to Palmetto Avenue and go three blocks to Monroe Harbour Marina. Call 407 321 5091 for more details and reservations.

Beach Escapes

When the temperatures start to soar (and even when they are only gently climbing), the lure of Florida's many white sand beaches becomes very strong, and there are some excellent choices little more than an hour's drive away. Be warned first, though, that Orlando natives all get the same idea at the weekend, so unless you head out EARLY (ie. before 9am and come back late, ie. after 8pm) you are likely to encounter some serious traffic. The choice is actually quite simple for a change. If you head EAST, you have **Cocoa Beach**, at about 40 miles the closest to Orlando (straight along the Beeline Expressway, then south on Highway A1A) and a great mix of wide sands, gently-sloping beaches and moderate but fun surfing waves. As it's the Atlantic, the sea can be pretty chilly from November to March (and a good degree or two less than the Gulf Coast even during the summer), but Cocoa Beach is rapidly developing into a major coastal resort, so the facilities are never less than excellent. While in Cocoa Beach, be sure to visit

Daytona Speedway

Ron Jon's Surf Shop, a mind-boggling pink and purple emporium of warehouse proportions open 24 hours a day, stocking every kind of beach paraphernalia imaginable, and the **Cocoa Beach Pier**, an 800-foot stretch of restaurants, bars and shops built out into the Atlantic and open until 2am every day. From here north to **Daytona Beach** you have almost 100 miles of beautiful beaches that have been developed to a lesser extent, while Daytona itself (home to some great annual motor-sport, see below) is one of the most famous beaches in the world. To reach Daytona Beach direct from Orlando, it is about 60 miles and 90 minutes' drive along the full length of I4 out of Orlando, pick up I95 north then Highway 92 east, which turns into International Speedway Boulevard and leads straight to the beaches.

To the WEST you have the **Gulf Coast**, which is a good 90 minutes' drive down I4 and through Tampa on I275 south to **St Petersburg Beach** (105

St Petersburg Beach

miles) or **Clearwater Beach** (110 miles) or two hours-plus down I4 and then I75 to **Bradenton** (130 miles), **Sarasota** (140 miles) and **Venice** (160 miles). The beaches are less 'hip', that is more relaxed and refined, and the sea a touch warmer and much calmer, so it is better for families with small children. You will find it easier to get away from the crowd here, too.

> BRIT TIP: You will be tempted to join in the locals' craze for driving right on to the sand at Daytona Beach, but watch out for tolls to do so, stick rigidly to the VERY slow speed limits and don't stray off the main tracks as you can easily get bogged down.

Sport

In addition to virtually every form of entertainment known to man, central Florida is also one of the world's biggest sporting playgrounds, with a huge range of opportunities to either watch or play your favourite sport.

Golf

Without doubt, the number one activity is **Golf**, with almost 200 courses within an hour's drive of Orlando. The weather, of course, makes it such a popular pastime, but some spectacular courses add to the attraction, and there are numerous holiday packages geared entirely towards keen golfers of all abilities. With an 18-hole round, including green fees, cart hire and taxes, from as little as $25 on some courses (and the average around $35), it is a very attractive proposition and a very different one from those used to British courses. If you go in for 36-hole days, it is possible in most cases to save up to $25 by replaying the same course. Sculptured landscapes, manicured fairways and abundant use of spectacular water features and white sand traps make for some memorable golfing. January to May is the busiest golf 'season', but many courses are busy year-round. Check also when you book about each club's dress code, as there are quite a few differences from course to course.

Inevitably, Walt Disney World has been quick to seize on the opportunity to attract the golf fanatic, with no less than five highly contrasting championship quality courses within its bounds, plus a nine-hole practice course, a full range of teaching and training programmes and fully-equipped pro shops. The five include **Magnolia**, a typical US PGA course that features the final round of the Walt Disney World/Oldsmobile Classic every year (as well as a bunker shaped into the form of a familiar pair of mouse-like ears!), and the massive **Palm**, a 7,000-yard course rated one of Disney's toughest and one of *Golf Digest*'s Top 25. Their reputation precedes them, however, so they are inevitably the busiest courses in Orlando, not to mention among the most expensive. Palm, Magnolia and **Lake Buena Vista** are all $75 a round, while **Osprey Ridge** and **Eagle Pines** are $85, although you can play for half-price after 3pm. Walt Disney World resort guests can book their tee-times up to a month in advance, while day visitors can book only seven days before. Call 407 824 2270 to arrange your tee-time.

Greneleafe Golf and Tennis Resort has three challenging courses that are

Golfing in Orlando

open to the non-resident public outside January to April. Located near Haines City, to the south west, tee-times are available three days in advance, prices from $45–$95, call 813 422 7511. The **Poinciana Golf and Racquet Resort** (on Cypress Parkway, to the south of Kissimmee) has an 18-hole course featuring a mind-boggling 69 bunkers and 17 water-hazard holes. Call up to seven days in advance for tee-times ($25–$40) on 407 933 5300. **MetroWest Country Club** (on South Hiawasee Road, Orlando) offers a fair, yet demanding test on a graceful 6,500-yard course featuring 100-foot elevations. Book seven days in advance, $50–$60, on 407 299 1099. The magnificent facilities of **Marriott's Orlando World Center** (on World Center Drive just before it runs into Walt Disney World's Epcot Drive) are home to a course of modest length but fiendish design, with 15 water holes and acres of sand in 90 bunkers! You can book seven days in advance (90 if you are staying at the resort hotel) on 407 239 4200, with fees from $60–$95.

Alternatively, if you would like some advice in choosing and booking the right course, contact **Tee Times USA**, Florida's only golf reservation network. They can arrange tee-times at most of Orlando's best courses — at NO surcharge — as well as offering a range of all-inclusive golf packages. They are staffed by local golfers with expert knowledge of where and when to play and offer discounts at quieter times of the year. Their guaranteed service takes a lot of the hassle out of organising your golf and can save a lot of time, whether it be for advance reservations, same-day tee-times, club rentals, golf schools or private lessons. Call 1–800 374 8633 in

6

Florida, or write for more details to Tee Times USA, PO Box 641, Flagler Beach, Florida 32136. There is also an independently published free magazine, *Tee Times*, available at most courses and the golf shops around town, that details nearly all of the courses available to tourists.

Tennis

Tennis is another huge activity, with many hotels having floodlit courts and always offering racquet and ball hire. The **Contemporary Resort** offers the best opportunities in Walt Disney World with six cushioned-surface courts open to non-residents (tel 407 824 3578 to book one), while the **Lake Cane Tennis Center** (on Turkey Lake Road) has 13 asphalt courts (tel 407 352 4913). The **Orange Lake Country Club** on Highway 192 has 16 hard courts in addition to three nine-hole golf courses (tel 407 239 0000) and in Altamonte Springs to the north is **Sanlando Park**, a 25-court complex (tel 407 869 5966). Charges vary from $2–$10 an hour (guess who's the most expensive!), while all the above-mentioned centres also offer lessons from $30 an hour.

Fishing

Fishing also attracts a lot of specialist holiday-makers, although not that many, it has to be said, from Britain. The abundance of lakes and rivers make for plentiful sport of the angling variety, with bass the prime catch, along with pike, perch and catfish. A seven-day licence will cost you $16.50 (available from all tackle shops, fishing camps, sports stores and Wal-Mart and K-Mart supermarkets), and there are dozens of boats for hire on the St John's River, Lake Toho in Kissimmee, Lake Kissimmee and both coasts for some serious sea fishing. Expect to pay $125–$150 for half a day and $175–$200 for a full day trip bass-fishing. For the most complete angling service in central Florida try **Cutting Loose Expeditions**, a highly-experienced, personalised operator who can organise fresh or sea-water expeditions and arrange hotel pick-up if necessary. The service is masterminded by A Neville Cutting, one of America's greatest fishing adventurers, and he maintains very high standards with his guides and other staff. Rates

start at $175, going up to $600 for a day's offshore fishing for the likes of marlin. Phone 407 629 4700 or write to Cutting Loose Expeditions, PO Box 447 Winter Park, Florida 32790–0047.

Water Sports

Florida is also, of course, mad keen on **Water sports** of all persuasions. Consequently, on any area of water bigger than your average pond don't be surprised to find the locals water-skiing, jet skiing, knee-boarding, canoeing, paddling, wind-surfing, boating or otherwise indulging in watery pursuits. Walt Disney World offers all manner of boats, from catamarans to pedaloes, on the main **Bay Lake**, as well as the smaller lakes of **Seven Seas Lagoon, Club Lake** and **Lake Buena Vista**. There are several operators on the lakes around Orlando and Kissimmee, too, but some of them leave much to be desired, safety-wise. **Splash 'n Ski** get the official Brit's Guide recommendation because o

Knee boarding is a favourite

their safety-conscious approach, the high qualifications of their instructors (they GUARANTEE to get you skiing) and the extra personal touch from their British-owned operation. Try jet-skis, waverunners, paddle-boats and top-quality skiing on one of the prettiest (and cleanest!) lakes in Florida. Splash 'n Ski can be found behind the Westgate Lakes Resort on Turkey Lake Road, and benefit also from using some of the Resort's facilities. Tel 407 345 0000 ext. 137 for more details. For a more gentle experience and a close-up of the local wildlife try **Katie's Wekiva River Landing**. Here you can try up to a full day's canoeing on some of the most scenic waters of central Florida (take I4 [North] east to exit 51 and Highway 46 west for almost five miles, and Wekiva

ark Drive is on your right). It's fairly
isurely, but does have its faster-flowing
ctions, and you can take time-outs for a
icnic or to go fishing. The entire
ortion of the Wekiva River here has
een designated a protected Scenic and
Vild area, while the neighbouring forest
ith its hiking trails is an official aquatic
reserve, which gives you an idea of the
rritory. Thick Cypress forest, clear,
oring-fed waters, abundant water and
ildlife, it's all here for nature-lovers.
atie's offers four different canoe trips,
om a leisurely two-hour, six-mile
addle to a 19-mile overnight camping
ip, all with a pick-up service at the end
r transport up-river to start with. Prices
nge from $15 to $26 (children three to
2 half-price), and the trips are suitable
r beginners and more experienced
noeists alike. Katie's also offers
mping, boating and fishing, for more
etails call 407 628 1482.

> BRIT TIP: Don't forget insect
> repellent in the summer
> months when the bugs are out
> in force, and bring a
> waterproof bag for your car
> keys and wallet.

Mini Golf

ot exactly a sport, but definitely for
urist consumption are the many and
uite extravagant opportunities for
ini-golf around Orlando. Not only are
ey quite picturesque, some of them
fer prizes for particularly tricky shots.
hey are a big hit with kids and good
n for all the family (if you have the legs
ft for 18 holes after a day at the theme
rk!). Several other attractions and
rks offer mini-golf as an extra, but for
e best try out the big self-contained
ntres, of which there are five main
es. **Pirate's Cove** has a twin-course
t-up on Florida Plaza Boulevard (off
ighway 192, just past Old Town) and
ternational Drive (just south of the
ercado Centre), with mountain caves,
aterfalls and rope-bridges to test your
ill and please the eye. **River
dventure Golf** (on Highway 192,
most opposite Medieval Times) offers a
ississippi River adventure with rolling
pids, waterfalls and an authentic water

Canoeing on Wekiva River

wheel. **Bonanza Miniature Golf and
Gifts** (next door to the Magic Mining
Co restaurant on the western side of
Highway 192) has another imaginative
— and very tricky — 36 holes set in a
gold-mine theme with the backdrop of
huge waterfalls. **Pirate's Island** (further
along Highway 192 to the east) is
another spectacular 36-hole spread,
while arguably the most impressive of
the lot is the **Congo River Golf and
Exploration Co**, which has courses on
Highway 192, International Drive and
Highway 436 in Altamonte Springs.
They could almost be Disney-inspired
they are so artificially scenic. The
Kissimmee location also has paddle boats
to try, while International Drive has the
option of go-karts, and all three have
games and video arcades. Charges are $6
or $7 per round, but look out for
coupons which all have a couple of
dollars off each one. They open from
9am to 10pm or 11pm daily. **Million
Dollar Mulligan** is also worthy of
mention here, although it is neither
mini-golf nor the real McCoy. Instead,
Million Dollar Mulligan, just off
Highway 192 on Florida Plaza Boulevard
(next to Old Town — look for the giant
golf ball), is a nine-hole, floodlit pitch-
and-putt course, plus driving and target
range, that looks spectacular at night
with its lake and fountains lit up. The
pitch-and-putt is $10 ($6.50 for kids), a
practice bucket for the range $3.50,
while there is also a natural grass putting
course ($4 and $2.50), all open from
9am–midnight.

Go-Karting

On a similar footing, there are a number
of **Go-kart** tracks around the main
tourist areas that will also seek to side-
track you for an hour or two. The

6

Fun 'n Wheels go-karting

biggest is **Fun 'n Wheels** (on International Drive at Sand Lake Road, and on West Vine Street, Kissimmee), which is open daily from 9am to either 7pm or 11pm (depending on the season). You buy tickets at $1.25 each (or 30 for $30) and then have the choice of four kart tracks, mini-golf, bumper boats and cars, waterslides, a Big Wheel, a kiddie play area, games arcade and snack bars. You really do need plenty of energy to tackle this (not surprisingly, it's a big hit with kids), and the almost non-stop roar of the karts can get a bit tedious. **Malibu Grand Prix** (on American Way) has scaled-down Formula One and IndyCar racing on professionally-supervised tracks, plus mini-golf, bumper cars, more than 200 arcade games and a batting cage if you want to try your hand at baseball. **Old Town** also has its own go-kart track, while **Zooma**, just a mile to the east, has a replica mini Daytona 500 Speedway to try out, as well as a Sky Coaster, which is a cross between bungee jumping, hang-gliding and para-sailing. **Kartworld** (at the top of International Drive and on Highway 192) has some of the largest tracks in the world, up to a mile long, as well as large games arcades. **Action Kartways Family Fun Park** (at the eastern end of Highway 192) has a fast track, pro track, family track and kiddie track, as well as bumper boats and a video arcade. For the complete experience, **The Great American Racing Place** (formerly known as Jungle Falls), also on Highway 192 almost opposite Capone's Dinner Show, has no less than five tracks, plus two mini-golf courses, bumper boats and games arcade.

Horse-riding

If **Horse-riding** takes your fancy (or your children's), you will certainly want

to know that Orlando is home to one of the foremost equestrian centres in America, if not the world! It is the **Grand Cypress Equestrian Center**, part of the 1,500-acre Grand Cypress Resort, and all its rides and facilities are open to non-residents. This stunningly well-equipped equine haven offers a dazzling array of opportunities for the horse enthusiast of all abilities. A full range of clinics, lessons and other instructional programmes are available, from half-hour kids' sessions to all-summer academies, plus a variety of trail rides, and the centre's facilities include floodlit covered arena, a dressage ring, a floodlit outdoor jumping ring, an exercise track, turnout paddocks, tack and gift shop, lounge, classroom, snack bar and locker rooms. Serious horse riders will note that this was the first American equestrian centre to be approved by the British Horse Society, and it operates the BHS test programme. Inevitably, this five-star facility does not come cheap, but, especially for children, it is a highly worthwhile experience. Private lessons are $45 per half hour or $75 per hour, while a week's package of eight half-hour lessons is $260. Young Junior Lessons (15-minute supervised rides for under-12s) are $25, while the Western Trail Ride (an hour's excursion for novice riders) is $30 per person and the Advanced Trail Ride $45. The centre is open from 8am to 5pm daily and can be found by taking exit 27 on I4 on to Route 535 north, turning left after half mile at the traffic lights and then following the road north for a mile (past the entrance to the Hyatt Regency Grand Cypress Hotel) until the equestrian centre is on your right. For more details and to book rides (which are most popular from late November through to March), call 407 239 1938. On a smaller scale and none the less charming is the **Poinciana Riding Stables** on Poinciana Boulevard, just a couple of miles south of Highway 192. This gets you more out into the wilds as it is further away from the main tourist areas, and you can spend anything from half an hour to a full day enjoying the different rides and lessons on offer. Their two main trail rides are the Nature Trail ($29.95), a 45-minute to an hour ride for beginners through 750 acres of untouched Florida countryside (no reservations required), and the private Trail Ride, a 90-minute trip for advanced riders with a private guide ($39.95, reservations required). There is also a picnic area with fishing pond, plus paddle boat rentals, playing fields and farm animals to pet. Catering is provided by Sonny's Real Pit Bar-B-Q, with chuck-wagon style beef, chicken, pork and ribs, accompanied by corn on the cob, baked potatoes, hot bread and gallons of iced tea. Sounds tempting? I'm there already and I've never ridden a horse in my life! There is no charge to just look around, and the stables are open from 9am to 5pm daily, call 407 847 4343 for details and reservations.

The Orlando Arena

Ice-skating

For **Ice-skating** there is the new **Rock on Ice** skating arena on Canada Avenue (off either Carrier or Sand Lake Roads), just behind International Drive, which is open from 9am to 11pm daily (1am at weekends in high season). This huge arena features disco-style lighting and sounds, its own resident DJ, a video arcade, snack bar and skate rental. Admission is $6 and skates will cost you an extra $1.50. Evening sessions vary from Monday's Youth Hockey to Wednesday's Girls Nite Out, The Famous Friday Nite Chill Out (with prizes to be won), a Saturday Moonlight Skate and Family Night on Sunday. Times vary so call 407 363 RINK for full details.

Bowling

If you are into 10-pin **Bowling**, the neighbouring **World Bowling Center** on Canada Avenue is a state-of-the-art venue for both league and open play, with fully automatic scoring and giant video screens. Finally, if anyone is into the sanity-questionable 'sport' of bungee-jumping, there are several opportunities

Tampa Bay Stadium

to experience this particular thrill, with the **Mystery Fun House** having a giant, pink crane to leap from, **AJ Hackett Bungy** at Old Town on Highway 192 offering a video of your jump from their 80-foot tower (5pm–midnight, $29 for adults, over–65s free!!!) and **Ricky's Rocket** also at Old Town, a bungee 'chair' which starts at ground level and catapults you into the sky at an alarming rate ($20 per person, 2pm–midnight), 0 to 60mph in two seconds, straight up! (then down, up, around, down again, up again, and so on…).

Spectator events

When if comes to **Spectator events**, Orlando is not quite so well furnished as other big American cities, but there is always something on offer for the

Florida Citrus Bowl

discerning sports fan who would like to sample the local version of the big football or cricket match. There are no top-flight American Football or baseball teams in Orlando, but there is an indoor version of gridiron, called Arena Football, plus two Minor League baseball teams. The big sport in town, though, is **Basketball** and the Orlando Magic, who, in Shaquille O'Neal, have one of the world's great up-and-coming sports stars. The basketball season runs from November to May (with exhibition games in October), and the only drawback is Shaq and the Magic are so popular the state-of-the-art, 16,000-seat Orlando Arena where they play (on Amelia Street, exit 41 off I4, turn left, then left again) is nearly always fully-booked for home games. The Arena box office (407 649 4200) can always tell you if there are any tickets left, although you need to call in person to buy them (from $10 up in the Gods to $45 courtside), or you can try calling Ticketmaster on 407 839 3900 for credit card bookings. The Orlando Predators, one of America's top **Arena Football** teams, are also popular at the same venue (from May to August, ticket prices from $10–$30) and you would need to call several days in advance to avoid missing one of their lively home games that feature some great entertainment as well as their fast, hard-hitting version of indoor American Football in the state-of-the-art Arena. For the Real Thing in gridiron terms, the nearest teams in the **National Football League** are the Tampa Bay Buccaneers, 85 miles to the west, the flashy Miami Dolphins, some 3½ hours drive to the south down the Florida Turnpike or the brand new Jacksonville Jaguars (the trendiest sportswear in the shops, too!) way up the east coast past Daytona, a 3-hour drive up I4 and I95. Again, Ticketmaster can give you ticket prices (they vary from $20 to $40) and availability. College American Football is also a big draw in America and Orlando's **Citrus Bowl Stadium**, which staged four World Cup games last year, is home to one of the biggest annual games, the New Year's Day Citrus Bowl, which pits two of the season's top college teams in an end-of-season playoff. However, tickets are again hard to come by as it is nearly always a sellout, so call the Stadium (which is in the downtown area, just off the North Orange Blossom trail, take exit 36 off I4, turn left then right) on 407 423 2476 at least a month in advance if you are interested. The University of Central Florida also draw big crowds here for their games (September to December), while the Stadium holds one-off events like big rock concerts, too.

Baseball

Baseball is still America's traditional sporting pastime and Orlando is home to the spring training headquarters of two Major League clubs, the Houston Astros and the Kansas City Royals. Spring training in March and April is the equivalent of our soccer pre-season friendlies but is taken rather more seriously because players are battling to make their team's squad for the coming season, hence their training sessions and warm-up matches are often as competitive as the real thing. Houston play their pre-season baseball at Kissimmee's Osceola County Stadium on Bill Beck Boulevard at the eastern end of Highway 192, while Kansas City are based at Baseball City, 25 miles to the south on I4 (exit 23, then Highway 27 on your left). From April to September Orlando is also home to two Minor League teams, the Orlando Cubs (who play at Tinker Field, next to the Citrus Bowl on Tampa Avenue) and the Kissimmee Astros (at Osceola County Stadium), who are also worth a look.

Rodeo

For another all-American pursuit straight out of the Old West, go and see the twice-yearly **Silver Spurs Rodeo** at Osceola County Stadium. This is the biggest event of its kind in the south-east United States and is held the first week in July and the last week in February every year, but it sells out fast so you need to call at least a month in advance for tickets on 407 847 5118 or 407 628 2280. The event features some classic bronco and bull riding and attracts top rodeo competitors from as far away as Canada, with some big-money prizes for the winners.

Daytona

Motor-Sport fans will definitely want to make a pilgrimage to the world famous Daytona Speedway, which draws 200,000 fans each year to the Daytona 500 in February and the Firecracker 400 on the 4th of July. Other auto and motorcycle races are held throughout the year; call 904 253 7223 for more details. Take I4 (North) east straight to Daytona, go north on I95 for 15 miles then take Highway 92, International Speedway Boulevard, east for one mile.

Shooting

Anyone who fancies themselves a dab hand with a gun can let loose a few salvos at one of the two target ranges which are open to tourists. **Shooting Sports Inc**, just off International Drive opposite Wet N Wild, is open from 9am to midnight with a 25-yard indoor range and some clever action shooting, while **Quick Shots**, at the top end of International Drive, just south of Belz Factory Outlet shopping centre, has 18 live ammunition ranges and nine paintball lanes with moving targets. You can fire modified AK47s, M16s and .44 Magnums all with no special permit required, and it's open from 10am to 11pm. For paintball fanatics there is a **Paintball World**, on Holiday Trail just behind Old Town, Kissimmee, which promises 60 acres of outdoor adventure for ages 10 and up, referees and all equipment provided! Call 407 396 4199 for the various times and dates of operation.

The Dogs

Finally, for those who can't resist a mild flutter, there are two Greyhound Tracks in the area that allow pari-mutuel wagering (that's Tote betting to us). The nearest is **Seminole Greyhound Park**, on Seminole Boulevard in the northern suburb of Casselberry (exit 47 off I4, and follow Maitland Boulevard three miles to the north east) which is open daily from May to September, evenings (except Sunday) at 7.30pm and matinees from 1pm on Monday, Wednesday and Saturday. Admission is $3, for more details call 407 699 4510. About an hour's drive to the east, **Melbourne Greyhound Park**, on North Wickham Road in the coastal town of Melbourne (take Highway 192 all the way east) operates year-round every night at 7.30pm except Sunday, with matinees at 1pm on Monday, Wednesday, Saturday and Sunday. Again, admission is $3, tel 407 259 9800.

Rosie O'Grady's Saloon at Church Street Station

Orlando By Night

When it comes to night-time entertainment, Orlando once again has a dazzling array of attractions, particularly in its two, purpose-built entertainment complexes at Church Street Station, in the heart of the downtown area, and Disney's Pleasure Island. Both of these will require a full evening of your attention, with Church Street Station being unmissable for its elaborate settings and Pleasure Island for its slightly greater range of entertainment. Children are welcome throughout Church Street Station, except for the big disco Phineas Phogg's where you must be 21 to get in, while at Pleasure Island you must be at least 18 or with your parents (and it is strictly over-20s ONLY at Mannequins and 8TRAX nightclubs).

Church Street Station

This converted old railway depot has quickly become the focal point of Orlando nightlife, with a number of bars, nightclubs, restaurants and other minor attractions springing up all around it. Its combination of shops, restaurants and bars has its highly sophisticated touches, but this is largely a lively, occasionally raucous, centre that caters for contrasting musical tastes from jazz, Country and Western to rock. It is open all day, but from 5pm there is an admission charge of $16 for adults and $10 for children to the nightclub part of

Church Street Station

the Station. If the attractions of New Orleans-style trad jazz and Can-Can girls, live Country and Western music with line dancing, or 60s and 70s rock classics played by the resident band do not appeal, visit Church Street during the day just to browse in the shops, look inside each of the venues and marvel at the magnificent interior architecture and furnishings. The Cheyenne Saloon, in particular, is visually stunning with its intricate oak railings and panelling. Be warned, however, Church Street Station is not a cheap place to eat or drink, even after you have paid your admission fee. A simple beer will set you back $4 (plus tip) and dinner for two at Lili Marlene's or Crackers is likely to be a $50–$60 touch. They also serve a couple of howitzer house cocktails, but again at $9 a time (including souvenir glass) it's a one-off rather than an oft-repeated experience! Here's a full rundown of the entertainment: **Rosie O'Grady's Good Time Emporium** (formerly the dilapidated Orlando Hotel) is the centrepiece of Church Street and a must-see venue for its Dixieland saloon setting, lively jazz music and trademark Can-Can girls who dance on the bar. Rosie's also serves Deli sandwiches and hot-dogs. The **Cheyenne Saloon** hosts the Country and Western scene, but if you're not a fan of the music don't let it put you off as the magnificent setting and atmosphere are definitely worth sampling, while the sight of the locals doing their line-dancing is equally fascinating (and there are Country dance lessons on Sunday afternoons from 2pm–6pm). The Cheyenne restaurant also offers barbecue chicken, ribs and beef. The **Orchid Gardens** belies its peaceful-sounding name by hosting the rock 'n roll scene in another superb

setting of ironwork and glass in a mock-Victorian style. Yes, I know that sounds bizarre, but it works a treat. **Phineas Phogg's Balloon Works** (8pm–1am, 2am Fri and Sat) is the youngest end of the spectrum, a loud, lively disco that doesn't really get going until at least 11pm (don't forget your photo ID to prove you are 21 or over). For all four o these nightclubs, you need to pay the one-off admission charge, but if you just want to go shopping in the Church Street Exchange (11am–11pm), sit for a drink in **Apple Annie's Courtyard** (11am–11pm) or visit one of the restaurants — **Lili Marlene's** (5.30pm–11.30pm) for excellent prime rib and seafood (and a kids' menu at $6.95), **Cracker's Oyster Bar** (11am–11.30pm) for Cajun specialities and some of the best seafood in town (and a kids' menu $6.95) or the **Wine Cellar** for a huge selection of (expensive European and New World wines with food available from Cracker's — you are free to wander around.

At the weekends there is also live entertainment in the cobbled street that connects the two buildings of Church Street Station, but expect the crowds to be at their highest then, too. For a romantic half-hour (or to keep all the family amused) take one of the horse-drawn carriage rides from outside Church Street Station around the whole of the downtown area and its lakes, which are all magnificently lit at night. Church Street does make up for its rather high prices with some weekly specials that are well worth knowing about. Tropical Tuesday at Apple Annie's (4pm–7pm) features $2.75 margaritas, draught beer at $1.50 and pitchers at $5.95; Wednesdays at Phinea Phogg's (6.30pm–7.30pm) is Nickel Bee Nite (that's five cents a time, and the place gets PACKED!); the Cheyenne Longneck Night on Thursdays (4.30pm–7.30pm) offers $1.50 BBQ sandwiches and cheap beer; the Backyar Barbeque is Fridays (11am–3pm) at the Cheyenne Saloon with an unlimited buffet for $6.95; and Sundays at Lili Marlene's is their special brunch buffet (10.30am–3pm) at $9.95 for adults and $6.95 for kids.

The surrounding areas on Church Street can be equally lively, with a (slightly cheaper) range of restaurants and bars, like **Pebbles, Mulvaney's Irish Pub, Tanqueray's Bar and Grill** (another Cheers-style venue), and the pure fun of **Sloppy Joe's** (look out for their 4–7pm happy hour and live entertainment), while for those who like a bit of spice with their evening entertainment there is **Terror on Church Street**. Basically, it is a walk-through variation on the Haunted House theme, but with live elements and some of the cleverest special effects you will find. If you ever wanted to have a real close-up view of your favourite horror films, this is the place to come. Visitors form up into small groups and then take the 20–25 minute walk (depending on just how scared you are!) through the 22,450 square feet of terror on two floors, encompassing 23 separate scenes. To give any more detail would spoil the shocks and surprises in store, but suffice it to say it is only the hardiest or most cynical of souls who can come through Terror on Church Street without a significant increase in blood pressure and adrenalin levels! Admission is $12 per person (children under 10 must be accompanied, but it is really much too scary for youngsters) and the attraction is open every night from 7pm–midnight on Sunday to Thursday and 7pm–1am on Friday and Saturday. Visit the Little Shop of Horror at the end of your trip to buy some particularly gruesome souvenirs for your friends! **TTTT**.

> BRIT TIP: If this appeals to you, go before 9pm as the queues start to build up quite horrendously from then.

Pleasure Island

Disney's venture into the entertainment complex market is predictably large-scale and elaborate. Here you have seven different clubs, plus restaurants, cafés and nearly two dozen gift and craft shops, like **The Music Legends Shop**, for rock memorabilia, **DTV**, an upscale Disney Fashion emporium, and **Avigators**, featuring Indiana Jones 'roughwear'. The theme is New Year's

Eve, where every night is a celebration with live, open-air entertainment and music, and midnight fireworks, i.e. it's party time! It is free entry to the shops and eating houses until 7pm, but then there is a $15.95 entry charge, with age restrictions (which they are very strict about, so if you are under 30 don't forget your passport as ID!). Pleasure Island is only a short walk from the shops and restaurants of Disney's Village Marketplace but is completely self-contained in its own right and now boasts the new attraction of an Orlando branch of the **Planet Hollywood** showbiz restaurant chain. As with the Hard Rock Café at Universal Studios, you don't need to pay for admission for access to Planet Hollywood, so if that's all you want to see, save your $15.95. However, you will be missing out on some memorable nightclubs and several more restaurants, including the popular young hang-out the **Fireworks Factory** that does great barbecue and cajun food (average price $18.90 for a two-course meal), and the neighbouring **Portobello Yacht Club**, which offers some authentic and very tasty northern Italian cuisine in smart, lively surroundings, with excellent, friendly service (average price $24.90 for a two-course meal). Seafood lovers will want to make a note of the Yacht Club as one of the most spiffing places to enjoy typical favourites like crab and other shellfish and more unusual delicacies like grouper and dolphin fish (no, that doesn't mean Flipper!). **The Hill Street Diner** features New York-style deli sandwiches, and **Dezertz** is a chocolate-lover's haven. Back on the nightclub scene, you have the choice of: the **XZFR Rock 'n' Roll Beach Club**, a live music venue featuring classic rock from the last 40 years; **The Neon Armadillo**, a right rootin', tootin' local hoedown showdown (yes, more Country and Western music); **The Pleasure Island Jazz Company**, for some excellent contemporary jazz and blues in a smoky, intimate setting, plus a tapas bar; **Mannequins Dance Palace** (21s and over only), a huge, extremely popular, boppy young disco scene, featuring a revolving dance floor; the **Comedy Warehouse** for up-and-coming young comedians and the occasional well-established name act;

6

8TRAX, a homage to 70s-style music, dance and styles, with bean-bag chairs, lava lamps and mirror balls (again, over 21s); and the unmissable **Adventurers Club**, a unique live entertainment bar and lounge decorated like some sort of multi-level 1930s safari/explorers club, where the place almost literally comes alive around you (watch the various animal heads, if you don't believe me!) and the stars of the show are as likely to be sitting next to you as on the stage.

Anchored at one end of the island (and therefore also not requiring the admission fee) is the **Empress Lilly Riverboat** which offers three more up-market restaurants and a live entertainment lounge. **The Steerman's Quarters** (5.30pm–10pm) specialises in juicy steaks, the **Fisherman's Deck** (midday–2pm and 5.30pm–10pm) offers more seafood temptations (good-quality food, but the Portobello Yacht Club is more fun) and the **Empress Room** is a full, five-star, cordon bleu choice with an ever-changing menu. **The Baton Rouge Lounge** features live musical and comedy entertainment, with no cover charge. At the other end of the island is the cinema complex **AMC Pleasure Island 10**, with 10 screens offering all the latest film entertainment. There is obviously a separate charge for the cinema.

'Big Splash Bash' at Sea World

Shows

Disney's other night-time extravaganzas are often overlooked by visitors unless they are staying at one of the main hotel resorts within the Vacation Kingdom. The most popular with those in the know (and it's free!) is the nightly **Electrical Water Pageant** on Bay Lake and the Seven Seas Lagoon in front of the Magic Kingdom. It lasts just 10 minutes so it is easy to miss, but it is

almost a waterborne version of the SpectroMagic parade in the Magic Kingdom itself, with thousands of twinkling lights on a floating cavalcade of boats and mock sea creatures. The best points to see it are outside the Magic Kingdom (in high season only), the Polynesian Resort and the shores of Fort Wilderness, but it can also be seen from the Contemporary Resort, the Grand Floridian and the new Wilderness Lodge. For a night of South Seas adventure and entertainment, try the **Polynesian Revue** (open to non-residents at the Polynesian Resort). It's a bit expensive at $32 for adults, $25 for juniors (12 to 20-year-olds) and $16 for under 12s (Sea World's version is slightly better value at $29 and $20), but the entertainment is quite thrilling (fire jugglers, hula-drum dancers and clever musicians) even if the food, in keeping with the majority of Orlando's dinner shows, is nothing out of the ordinary. For reservations (which are usually necessary), call 407 934 7639. The **Hoop-Dee-Doo Musical Revue** at Fort Wilderness is an ever-popular nightly dinner show that carries on where the Diamond Horseshoe Jamboree in the Magic Kingdom leaves off. Especially loved by young children, it features the joking, dancing, singing Pioneer Hall Players in a merry American hoedown-style show, with barbecued ribs, chicken and corn on the cob while you're watching. Okay, it's corny and a tad embarrassing to find yourself singing along with the hammy action, but you're on holiday, remember! The Revue plays three times a night at the Pioneer Hall, admission $33 for adults, $25 for 12–20s and $17 for under 12s, and reservations are ALWAYS necessary (tel 407 934 7639). A new family show is also available at Fort Wilderness through either your holiday company rep or Suncoast Tours (407 859 4211). The **Lion King Party In The Wilderness** is designed to appeal to overseas visitors and features dinner with various Disney characters, live music, kids' games and activities, comedy acts and fireworks. Prices are a bit steep at $55 for adults and $39 for under-12s, but that does include transport, a first-class (and plentiful) buffet meal, and the chance for your kids to meet their favourite Disney characters!

Having stumbled into the topic of themed dinner-shows, it would be appropriate here just to outline this particularly Orlando-based type of attraction for first-time visitors. As the name suggests, it is live entertainment coupled with dinner in a fantasy-type environment where even the waiters and waitresses dress in costume and act out roles. The staging is always of a large-scale, elaborate nature, the acting on the hammy side and the food hearty, plentiful but distinctly ordinary, usually accompanied by unlimited beer, house wine or soft drinks. There is always a strong family appeal and they nearly all seat you on large tables where you can get to know other folks, too, but, at an average of $30 for adults, they are not cheap (especially when you add on the taxes and tips). If you think of the price as $15 for the entertainment and $15 for the food, you get a better idea of what you're paying for, and if you go in with a willing suspension of disbelief and the attitude of being prepared to join in come-what-may, you WILL enjoy yourself!

Arabian Nights

BRIT TIP: NEVER pay full price for the dinner shows as there are always discounts to be had. Watch out for discount coupons among all the tourist brochures and magazines, while your holiday company may well offer discounted tickets as well.

There are currently eight different shows vying for your attention, and it is hard to recommend just one, so take your pick from the following:

Arabian Nights

This is the largest-scale production and one of the most popular with locals as well as tourists. It's a real treat for horse-lovers, but you don't need to be an equestrian expert to appreciate the spectacular stunts, horsemanship and marvellous costumes as more than 50 highly-trained horses perform a series of acts loosely based on the dreams of Princess Scheherezade in the huge, covered arena at the centre of this 1,200-seater Palace. The magnificent close-quarter drill of the Lipizzan stallions, the daring riding of acclaimed performers like Kim Barteau and Jason Straub, plus the comedy of 'Elvis' the talking horse, the 'Little and Large' act of a giant Frisian and Miniature American horse and the thrilling chariot race all add up to a memorable show that kids, in particular, adore. The food — green salad, oven-roasted prime rib with new potatoes, and a dessert (vegetarian meals on request) — is above average, but so is the price at $34.95 for adults and $19.95 for kids three–11. Arabian Nights, which is located just half a mile east of I4 on Highway 192 (it's on the left, just to the side of the Parkway shopping plaza, or just past Water Mania if you are coming from the eastern end of 192) runs every evening at 7.30pm in the winter and 8.30pm in summer, lasting about two hours, and tickets may be purchased at the gift shop between 10am and 5pm or by credit card if you phone 407 239 9223. There are also occasional matinees and additional performances, call the same number for details.

American Gladiators

New to Orlando in late 1995 is scheduled to be this new dinner-style

Arabian Nights

show which gives its audience front row seats for the nationally-popular TV show from which ITV's Gladiators programme was derived. Here, you will be able to sit and cheer the competitors through all the different events of the TV format, with contenders from all over America bidding to make a name for themselves. Each competition show is reckoned to run for about 90 minutes, during which you will be served a chicken dinner and the usual array of beverages, while there will also be an American Gladiators Live! shop and an extensive video arcade for the kids. Provisional prices are around $30 a ticket, but call 407 397 7100 for more details. The Gladiator Arena can be found on Highway 192, two miles east of its junction with I4.

Capone's

Song, dance, mystery, comedy and a personal invitation from Al himself to make sure you really enjoy yourself in this mock Speakeasy diner where the threat of a raid from 'the Feds' is ever-present. A big, all-you-can-eat Italian buffet, plus the addition of Sangria and Rum Runners to the free drinks list, make this as much an invitation to stuff yourself silly as to enjoy the rather hammy musical revue. It's all good, harmless, knockabout fun though, and, at $29.95 for adults and $14.75 for kids 12 and under, pretty good value. Capone's runs every night at 8pm and is located on Highway 192 just past its junction with Poinciana Boulevard heading east. Call 407 397 2378 for reservations.

Mark II Dinner Theater

This variation on the dinner-show theme offers a full-scale Broadway musical production after you have been able to chow down on another well-stocked buffet and salad bar, with home-made desserts and an (extra) full cocktail service and wine list. The quality productions change every six weeks or so, but include works like *Fiddler On The Roof*, *La Cage Aux Folles* and *Cabaret*. The interior is also tastefully designed with tables of two or four in tiered ramps surrounding the stage. An additional feature after Friday and Saturday evening performances is the Afterglow, a chance to meet the performers in the lobby, enjoy a few drinks and join in with a few well-known songs or even have a go in the spotlight yourself! You can call in even if you haven't been to the show. There are eight performances in the 320-seat theatre every week, but no shows Monday or Tuesday. Matinee performances (Wednesday, Thursday and Saturday, buffet opens from 11.30am, show starts at 1.15pm) are $29, Wednesday and Thursday evenings (buffet from 6pm, show at 8pm) and the Sunday twilight performance (buffet from 4.30pm, show at 6.30pm) are all $31, and Friday and Saturday evenings (buffet from 6pm, show at 8pm) are $33. Call 407 843 6275 for details of the current show and reservations, and the Theater can be found off exit 44 travelling (North) east on I4, turn left on to Par Avenue and one mile on the left.

Medieval Times

Eleventh-century Spain is the entertaining setting for this two-hour extravaganza of medieval pageantry, sorcery and robust horseback jousts that culminate in furious hand-to-hand combat by the six knights. It is worth arriving early to appreciate the clever mock-castle design and costumes of all the staff as you are ushered into the pre-show hall and then taken into the arena itself with banks of bench-type seats flanking the huge indoor battle-ground. You need to be in full audience participation mode as you cheer on your own knight and boo the evil and dastardly Green Knight, but kids get a huge kick out of it (not to mention a few adults) and they also love the fact that eating is all done without cutlery —

don't worry, there are handles on the soup bowls! The elaborate staging takes your mind off the fact the chicken dinner is only average, but there is plenty of it and the serfs and wenches who serve you make it a fun experience. Admission (inclusive of Medieval Life also) is $33.95 for adults and $22.95 for kids three to 12 and the doors open 90 minutes prior to each performance, the times of which vary according to the season, so call 407 396 1518 for details. The castle is located on Highway 192, five miles east of the junction with I4. If you have 45 minutes to spare, the adjoining **Medieval Life** exhibition makes an interesting diversion. This mock medieval village re-enacts the life and times of 900 years ago, with artisans demonstrating the crafts of pottery and tool-making, glass-blowing, spinning and weaving. There is also a Chamber of Horrors that might be a touch gruesome for small children. Admission to Medieval Life only is $9 for adults, $6 for children three to 12.

> BRIT TIP: Visit Medieval Life before the main show rather than after it as it tends to wind up pretty quickly after a performance.

Medieval Times

Medieval Times dinner show

King Henry's Feast

Continuing the theme of Middle Ages entertainment, this castle setting offers more deeds of derring-do, but the accent is more on the humorous than the epic. A hilarious court jester acts as MC for the evening with a rather underfed King Henry VIII making regular appearances in search of another wife (ladies beware!). The entertainment is provided by strolling players, singers and speciality acts like jugglers, fire-eaters and trapeze artists, and woe betide anyone who doesn't enter into the spirit of the evening! The chicken dinner is again pretty ordinary and the wine and beer mugs are among the smallest you'll find (it's a real challenge to drink a lot here!). King Henry's Feast is located in the heart of International Drive (you can't miss its huge castle-like structure next to Caruso's Palace) and tickets are $31.95 for adults and $19.95 for kids three to 11. Showtimes vary, so call 407 351 5151 for details.

Wild Bill's

Operated by the same people who run King Henry's, this show is more likely to appeal to us Brits as its Wild West theme is more what we associate with a holiday in America. It's located at the magnificently built Fort Liberty in the heart of Highway 192's tourist area and features two hours of western-style entertainment and hearty food all served by cavalry troopers in full gear. Rope tricks, knife throwing, Indian dancing, Can-Can girls and a Country and Western hoedown (with special audience 'victims'!) are the featured entertainment, while the meal comprises vegetable soup, fried chicken and barbecued ribs, corn on the cob, baked potato, biscuits, salad and apple pie. It's

6

Medieval Life – basket weaving

one of the most popular shows for foreign tourists and goes down well with kids too. Tickets are $31.95 for adults and $19.95 for three to 11s, and showtimes again vary so call 407 351 5151 for information and reservations. The Fort is also home to a 22-acre **Trading Post**, complete with authentic Western shops and photo spots, open from 10am to 10pm daily, while the **Brave Warrior Wax Museum** charts the history of the Wild West, with a dramatic soundtrack, at an extra charge of $4 for adults and $2 for children.

Sleuth's

Ever wanted to be part of your own real-life game of Cluedo? Well, now's your chance with central Florida's only full-time mystery dinner show. The two theatres are both little more than medium-sized restaurants, and the stages are pretty small, so be prepared for the action to happen all around you — and for some of the 'guests' to be part of the show! There are seven different murder-mysteries that commence with hors-d'oevres and pre-dinner drinks, and your servers are just as likely to be part of the cast, hence you must be ready to catch all the clues that come your way. The food is also above average, with honey-glazed chicken, baked potato and fresh vegetables or a vegetarian alternative and the house wine is fairly drinkable, but don't expect a major prize if you guess the murder solution correctly! Sleuth's can be found in Republic Square, just off Republic Drive, little more than a quarter of a mile south of its junction with International Drive (exit 30A off I4). Showtimes vary between 6 and 9pm daily, but tickets are all either $32.95 for adults or $22.95 for kids 3 to 11. Call 407 363 1985 for details.

Night Clubs

Orlando is also blessed with a huge variety of other nightlife, from common or garden discos to elaborate live music clubs and new features like Blazing Pianos, although the majority are situated in the downtown area, ie, away from the main tourist centres. The local paper, the *Orlando Sentinel*, has a regular Friday listing section called 'Calendar' which details every local nightspot worth knowing about as well as individual events and one-off concerts, and it is worth checking out as there is an amazing turnover in the success/failure rate of bars and discos. Don't be surprised if a nightclub suddenly undergoes a complete change of name and personality, as this is fairly common too. The basic distinctions tend to be **Live Music** clubs, **Mainstream Discos**, which can also have the occasional live band, **Alternative** or **Progressive Clubs** and then **Bars** which specialise in evening entertainment.

> BRIT TIP: The local music radio stations — of which there are many — regularly advertise the different nightly sessions at most clubs. The various inducements include free entry for ladies, live bands and 'all-you-can-drink' nights (which are unsurprisingly popular!). Don't think you have to confine your nightclub attentions to the weekend, either. There is usually something happening EVERY night, hence Sunday or Monday can be as busy as Saturday.

Live Music

The following should give you a representative taste of the most popular venues (for those 21 and over only in most cases), starting with the Live Music clubs.

Wolfman Jack's Rock 'n' Roll Palace, in Old Town, Kissimmee, takes you back to the dancing days of the 50s with live bands and occasional big-name acts like The Drifters (admission $8 for gents, $3 for ladies). **Blazing Pianos**, at the Mercado Centre on International Drive, formerly the Mardi Gras dinner show and currently the 'in' place for the young, trendy crowd, is a raucous cavern of a place featuring three duelling, fire-red pianos pounding out audience participation rock songs and regular contest spots (open 7pm–2am Sun–Thur, 6pm–2am Fri and Sat, cover charge is $5, and it's PACKED at weekends). The rock 'n' roll piano idea was pioneered, though, by the wonderfully-named **Howl At The Moon Saloon** on west Church Street and is equally popular there (Sun-Thur 6pm–2am, Fri and Sat 5pm–2am). Classic rock 'n' roll, show tunes, current hits, the Saloon's duelling pianists play them all, with full audience involvement and non-stop banter. There is no cover charge on Sunday, Monday and Tuesday, while on Wednesday and Thursday it is $2 after 7.30pm, on Friday it's $4 after 6pm and Saturday is $4 after 5.30pm, and the live piano action begins at 8pm every night.

More mainstream live music is the principle attraction of the relatively new and hugely popular **Jani Lane's Sunset Strip**, on the corner of Orange Avenue and Pine Street, a block up from Church Street. They borrow their decor theme from the Hard Rock Café, using a fascinating range of rock memorabilia, and also have pool tables and dart boards, but the focus is the stage and the massive dance floor which gets seriously crowded most nights. Open 8pm–3am every night except Monday, the main sessions are Wednesday to Saturday, with contemporary rock music provided by the house band and occasional guest groups. Wednesdays also feature a ladies male revue from 8–10.30pm (cover charge $5 plus free drinks!), with the guys allowed in from 11pm, Thursday has $1 draught beers until midnight and Friday and Saturday boasts 16-ounce beers for $2.50 (cover charge $5). Sunday is an 'unplugged' night, ie, acoustic music sessions, while Tuesday is 'London Calling', a DJ-hosted homage to the old wave punk and dance music of the 80s (18 to 21s free entry until 11pm). **Downtown Jazz and Blues** (on Orange Avenue between Washington Street and Central Boulevard) features nationally-acclaimed live jazz and blues performers from Tuesday to Sunday every week, with an 'alternative' choice on Mondays, a full and attractive dinner menu and happy hour from 4–7pm daily. The cover charge varies from $3–$5 and occasionally more according to who the headline act is, while the hours also vary. Monday's music session usually starts at 8pm, while Tuesday, Wednesday and Thursday kick off at 8.30pm (doors open from 4pm in each case), Friday is open from 11.30am with the live entertainment starting at 9.30pm and Saturday and Sunday both open at 7pm and start the music from 9.30pm. Jazz lovers will also want to check out **Pinkie Lee's** restaurant and jazz club (on west Amelia Street, just off the Orange Blossom Trail). Open 11.30am–1am (Tue to Fri), 6pm–2am (Sat) and 11am–3pm (Sun, for their Gospel Brunch, $13.95), it offers some terrific live sounds and an appetising dinner menu featuring a range of Southern dishes like corn-crusted catfish. Lunch buffets ($4.95 cold, $6.95 hot) run Tuesday-Friday and happy hour is 4pm–7pm — great value. Not exactly a music attraction but nonetheless a very 'live' one is **The Comedy Zone**, in the Holiday Inn on International Drive, which puts some top American comedians on stage twice a night at 8.30pm and 10.30pm as well as serving light snacks and drinks ($8 admission, $18.95 includes a full meal, and you must be at least 18 to get in).

Discos

For out-and-out, boppy, good-time discos, the huge **J.J. Whispers**, on Adanson Street (at the end of the Lee Road shopping plaza, just west of I4 exit 46, Lee Road, turn left), is one of the trendiest in town, with two state-of-the-art dance floors, a Games Room and a quiet VIP lounge (check for details on 407 629 4779), plus live entertainment nights with bands, all-you-can-drink sessions and all-male or all-female revues (we're talking Chippendale-type action for the girls and Teeny-Weeny Bikini contests for the guys; subtle it ain't! Cover charge varies from $5–$10, and it's open from 8pm to 2am nightly).

Olympic style ice skating at Busch Gardens, Tampa Bay

Borrowing from the success of J.J. Whispers and going for the same mass-market appeal is the new **Zuma Beach Club**, on North Orange Avenue, just up from Church Street. Formerly Dekko's, Zuma Beach has undergone a total revamp with a beach theme throughout, complete with palm trees, lifeguards and girls in bikinis. Its mainstream top 40 music approach is popular with the 25–30s something crowd and there is a different attraction most evenings: Monday is College Nite, with $2.50 16-ounce beers all night, Wednesday features a happy hour with free buffet from 4–10pm, Thursday is Ladies Nite, free drinks for the girls plus the Dream Team male revue from 8–10pm and free general admission after 10pm, Friday has another 4–10pm happy hour, Saturday is Zuma's Blow-Up beach party from 9pm–2am, with free admission for 21 and overs and Sunday is Hospitality Nite with $2 beers. Cover charge is $5 most nights. The **Baja Beach Club** (formerly the Cuda Bay Club, on West Palm Parkway, next to The Crab House restaurant and very visible from I4 junction 27) is another trendy, innovative nightclub featuring a very popular disco which plays music spanning four decades. It is open from 5pm–3am seven days a week, and the cover charge is $5 for out-of-state visitors (but free before 9pm) to enjoy a sophisticated range of facilities, including an outdoor deck and grill and even a beach volleyball court for the hopelessly energetic. The more eclectic **Big Bang**, on North Orange Avenue is one of the few places open until very late (9pm–4am Thur-Sat) and features a bar (wine and beer ONLY), dance area and the Winnebago Room, a novel lounge with a different, themed design every month ($3 cover charge).

Progressive

The alternative scene can boast three lively clubs that offer what the Americans term 'progressive' music but in real terms is more likely to be a techno-dance or even rave style, from Depeche Mode to the likes of Dee-Lite and other bands who will mean little to anyone over 25. **The Edge** is the biggest and most popular, a vast, warehouse-type place on the corner of Carr Lane and Livingston Street, six blocks north of Church Street. It is open from 9pm–5am (no drinks from 2am, though) Wednesday to Saturday, with admission charge $4 for 21 and over and $5 for 18–20s. The dark, cavernous interior boasts a straightforward high-energy disco, while outside a Tiki Bar offers the chance to sit and listen to some live, alternative bands. **Barbarella**, on Orange

Avenue on the corner of Washington Street, offers alternative and new wave music from 9pm–3am most nights although days vary — call 407 839 0457 for details). Again, it is more of a techno dance sound, although Mondays feature a 70s disco with a $5 cover charge and free bar (beer, wine and wine coolers only, no spirits) until 12.30am. The cover charge otherwise is $3, and their range of beers include Samuel Adams, Fosters and Bass. **The Club** is almost impossible to categorise as it ranges from mainstream disco to acid jazz lounge, with something different each night from Wednesday to Saturday. About half a mile north of Church Street on the corner of Orange Avenue and Concord Street, it is open from 9pm–3am with the cover charge ranging from $5–$8 according to the night. Free beers, live progressive bands, go-go dancers and no cover charge for ladies are additional attractions and the sounds run the full mixture of the progressive label.

Bars

Bars of all types simply abound in Orlando, as they do in every American city, but there are again several which offer a particular tourist appeal, especially to newcomers to the scene. Live entertainment, extrovert barmen, sports-themed bars and raw bars (offering seafood, often by the bucket!), the choice is, as ever, wide-ranging, but here are a few of the best. **Sports Dimension**, on 3001 Curry Ford Road, is the king of sports bars in Orlando, open from 11am to 2am daily and with SEVEN satellite dishes catching sport from all round the world and showing it on seven giant screens and 60 regular-sized TVs (no admission charge). **Fat Tuesday** (on Church Street next to the market) advertises the 'world's largest selection of frozen drinks' and we're not talking lemonade! Open seven days a week from 11am–2am it is a fun, lively bar for the younger crowd with live entertainment and no cover charge. **Chillers**, on Church Street is another young and trendy venue, basically a lively bar that serves, among other things, 20 varieties of frozen cocktails, plus bar snacks (5pm–1am, no admission charge). The neighbouring **Mulvaney's Irish Pub** is another good-time emporium

Medieval life exhibit at Medieval Times

with its flavour straight from the Emerald Isle (hence Guinness on tap!). Shepherd's pie and bangers and mash are the menu staples, while Irish folk singers add regular live entertainment and it is positively shoulder-to-shoulder at weekends. No cover charge, and hours from 11.30am–2am. Similarly, **Scruffy Murphy's Pub** offers an authentic Irish flavour three blocks north on Washington Street. Again, no cover charge and a real good-time atmosphere when it is busy (which is most nights). Finally, **Dad's Road Kill Cafe** is slightly more out of the way, difficult to describe and a great personal favourite. It's a very user-friendly bar and restaurant for lunch (great seafood, especially) and a lively, happening live music venue and bar in the evenings. The bar is littered with amusing items and curios, as well as games, dart boards and pool tables. To sample its particular brand of friendly charm, take exit 45 off I4, turn right on to Fairbanks then left into Orlando Avenue and it is in the small shopping plaza two miles up on your left. It is open from 11am–2am Tues–Sat, and there is no admission charge.

Right, if that doesn't give you enough to keep you occupied for the next fortnight, I'll be very surprised (it takes me all year just checking the information!). But it's all very well giving you all the lowdown on the attractions, you will also want to know a lot more about where, when and how to tackle that other holiday essential — FOOD! So, read on …

6

Eating Out

or watching the Americans at their national sport

If eating was an Olympic event, the Americans would take gold, silver and bronze every time. Forget baseball, basketball or American Football: eating is their national sport! To say they take meal times very seriously would be the understatement of the year.

I know I am doing a vast disservice to the majority of the inhabitants of their huge country, but it is hard to dispel the notion of the average American as a walking food intake, especially when so many of the local tourists you will encounter are so, well, not to put too fine a point on it, fat.

Variety

As a consequence, the variety, quantity and quality of restaurants, cafés, fast-food chains and hot-dog stalls is in keeping with this great tradition of eating as much as possible as often as possible. It is not out of the question to be able to eat around the clock, ie, 24 hours a day, and at first glance the full selection of food is rather overwhelming (hence this chapter). Cruising along either of the main drags of International Drive or Highway 192 will quickly reveal a dazzling array of different eating houses, the choice of which can be quite bewildering at first.

As a general rule, food is plentiful, relatively cheap, readily available and nearly always appetising and filling. You may not encounter many gourmet establishments (although Orlando DOES possess some outstanding high-quality restaurants), but you will get good value for money and you probably won't need to eat more than two proper meals a day, unless your appetite is of a similar Transatlantic nature. Put simply, portions tend to be large, food of a heavily steak, chicken or pizza-based variety, service of an efficient, friendly character, and it is ultimately hard to come by a really BAD meal.

Exceptional deals

In keeping with the climate, most restaurants tend towards the informal (T-shirts and shorts are usually acceptable) and cater readily for families. This also leads to two exceptional deals for budget-conscious tourists, especially those with a large tribe to keep happy. Many of the main hotels now offer 'Kids Eat Free' deals, provided they eat with their parents. The age restrictions can vary from under 10s to under 14s, but it obviously represents very good value for money if you are staying there. The second item of interest is the 'All You Can Eat' buffet, another common feature of many of the large chain restaurants in particular. These can be offered for breakfast, lunch and dinner for an all-in price (say $3.99 for breakfast or lunch or even only $5.29 for dinner), and when you consider they are catering for the American appetite it means you can have a pretty hearty meal for not too much and probably eat enough at, say, breakfast, to keep you going until dinner! A few establishments also offer 'Early Bird' specials, a dinner discount if you dine before 6pm. Also, don't be afraid to ask for a doggy-bag if you have a fair amount left over (and even if you haven't brought the dog!). It is common practice to take away the half of that pizza you couldn't finish, or those chicken legs or your leftover salad. The locals do it all the time and, again, it is very wallet friendly. Just ask for the leftovers 'to go'. (PS. It's not usually a bag, either!) Don't hesitate to tell your waiter/waitress if something isn't quite right with your meal. Americans will readily complain if they feel aggrieved, so restaurants are keen to make sure everything is to your satisfaction. And, please, don't forget to tip. The basic wage rate for waiters and waitresses is just $2.13 an hour, so they rely heavily on tips to supplement their wages. Unless service really is shoddy, in which case you should mention it, the usual rate for tips is 10 per cent of your bill at buffet-style restaurants and 15 per cent at full-service restaurants. However, it is usually worth checking to see if service has already been added to your bill. It is a common practice in many British restaurants nowadays, but not so common in America.

> **BRIT TIP:** A buffet breakfast at Ponderosa, Sizzler or any other of a dozen similar establishments will probably keep you going until tea-time and is a good way to start the day if you are tackling one of the Big Six theme parks.

Having implied that the majority of eating outlets tend to be of a

Elegant dining in Orlando

hearty rather than quality and variety-conscious kind it is still quite easy to encounter a monumental array of food types. Florida is renowned for its seafood, which also comes at a much more wallet-friendly price than the Mediterranean. Crab, lobster, shrimp (of a size which we would call king prawns), clams and oysters can all be sampled without fear of breaking the bank, as well as several dozen varieties of fish, many of which you won't have come across before. Cuban, Cajun/Creole and Mexican are other more local types of cooking which are well represented here (if you haven't eaten Mexican food, try fajitas — pronounced faheetas — they're delicious!), and you'll also be spoiled for choice of Oriental fare, from the more common Chinese and Indian to Japanese, Thai and even Vietnamese. The big shopping complexes and malls also offer a good choice of eateries in their food courts, and again they often represent particularly good value for money. Cracker cooking is original Floridian fare, and the more adventurous will want to try the local speciality — alligator meat. This can be stewed, barbecued, smoked, sautéed or braised. Fried gator tail 'nuggets' are an Orlando favourite, while barbecued gator ribs are the 'unofficial' food of Central Florida, according to the local press.

7

Delicious foods at End Zone food court at Disney's All-Star Resort

Ordering

Ordering your food can also be an adventure in itself. The choice for each item is often the cue for an inquisition of exam-type proportions from your waiter/waitress. You can never order just 'toast' — it has to be white, brown, wholegrain, rye, muffin or bagel; eggs and bacon come in a baffling variety of types; an order for tea or coffee usually provokes the response 'Regular or decaf? Iced, lemon or English?'; and salads have more dressings than the National Health Service. Whenever I've finished ordering I'm tempted to ask 'Have I passed?' after the barrage of questions. (NB: American bacon is always streaky and crisp-fried and sausages are chipolata-like and on the spicy side). Don't be worried about going in to a restaurant and asking to see their menu if it isn't prominently displayed. It is no big deal to Americans and the restaurant won't feel insulted if you decide to look elsewhere.

Drinking

Drinking is another matter altogether. Most British towns now have their share of American bars and diners and they give you a pretty good idea of what to expect, only there is a lot more of it here. The biggest complaint of Brits on holiday in the USA is of the beer. With the exception of a handful of English-style pubs (see below), American beer is always lager, either bottled or on draught, and ice-cold. It goes down great when it's really hot, but, as a general rule, it is weaker and fizzier than we're used to. Of course, there are exceptions and they are worth seeking out (try Old West, Molson Ice or Dos Equis for a fuller flavour), but if you are expecting a good, old-fashioned British pint, forget it. But I would suggest if you can't do without your pint of Tetley's, or whatever, for a couple of weeks, then you're probably going on the wrong kind of holiday here! Spirits (always called 'liquor' by Americans) come in a typically huge variety, but beware ordering just 'whisky' as you'll get bourbon instead. Specify if you want Scotch or Irish whiskey and demand it 'straight up' if you don't want it deluged under a mountain of ice! If you fancy a cocktail, there is a massive choice and most bars and restaurants have lengthy happy hours where prices are very consumer-friendly (hic!). Californian wines also work out much better value than imported European ones (and are usually of equally good quality). If you are sticking to soft drinks ('sodas') or coffee, most bars and restaurants will also give you free refills. You can also run a tab in most bars and pay when you leave to avoid having to shell out for each round.

> **BRIT TIP:** If there are several of you, ordering a pitcher of beer will work out cheaper than by the bottle or glass.

Another few words of warning. Florida licensing laws are stricter than ours and you need to be **21 or over** to enjoy an alcoholic beverage in a bar or lounge. Even if you are over 21 you will often be asked for proof of your age before you are served (or allowed in entertainment complexes like Pleasure Island) and this means your passport as it contains a picture of you (Americans use their driving licences as proof of ID because it also has to carry a photo of the owner). It's no good arguing or trying to reason with a reluctant barman. Local licensing laws are very strict and they simply cannot afford to take any chances. No photo ID, no beer! Anyone under 21 may NOT sit or stand near a bar either.

Right, that gives you the inside track on HOW to eat and drink like the locals, now you want to know WHERE to do it, so here's a handy guide to make sense of that veritable profusion of culinary variety. At the last count there were 3,515 restaurants in the metro Orlando area, with new ones being added and some biting the dust all the time, and, while it would be a very tall order to try to list every one, the following section will cover the main tourist areas and all the chain groups, as well as providing an insight into the more specialist, one-off establishments.

> BRIT TIP: Watch out for all the different free tourist magazines and brochures that can be found in the information centres, hotels and shopping areas. They all carry valuable money-off coupons for many of the restaurants and can save you lots of $s.

End Zone food court at the All Sports Resort

As a simple reference to the types of restaurants you will encounter, I have grouped them into four types, with the price scale gradually increasing through each one. They are: **Fast Food** outlets (McDonald's, etc); **Family Restaurants** (for example, Denny's, the American version of the Little Chef or Happy Eater); **American Diners** (the typical US-style establishment like the Hard Rock Café); and **Speciality Restaurants** (as a general rule, the one-off, more expensive places and 'foreign' food, like Chinese, Japanese and Italian).

Fast food

If you are a **McDonald's** fan you are coming to the right place as there are no less than 58 outlets in the greater Orlando area, varying from small drive-in types to the mega, 24-hour-a-day establishment on Sand Lake Road (near the junction with International Drive) that also has the biggest play area for kids of any McDonald's in the world and a number of differently themed eating areas! **Burger King** is also well represented, with 43 outlets, as is another familiar American franchise in Britain, **Wendy's**, which has 25 restaurants. If you're a burger freak and want to sample a variation on the theme, give **Checkers** (19 outlets) or **Hardees** (11) a try. **Kentucky Fried Chicken** (or KFC as it now likes to be known) has no less than 27 restaurants around the area, but you might like to try the local variations on the chicken theme at **Maryland Fried Chicken**, **Popeye's Famous Fried Chicken** or **Kenny Roger's Roasters**. If it's pizza you're after there is also a wide

7

choice, from the well-known **Pizza Hut** (with 53 restaurants) to the local varieties of **Flipper's Pizza** and **Domino's**, who all offer a local delivery service, even to your hotel room. A particularly American form of take-away is the Sub, or French-bread-type sandwich. This is what you will find at any one of the 25 local branches of **Subway**, or the 17 of **Sobik's** or 13 of **Miami Subs**. They're a rather more healthy option than yet another burger, and offer some mouth-watering varieties. Two other minor variations on the fast-food theme are **Arby's** (with eight outlets), which offers a particularly appetising roast beef sandwich and other beefy delicacies, and **Taco Bell** (27 outlets), which does for Mexican food what McDonald's does for the hamburger. If you've never had Mexican food before, this is not the place to start, but for anyone familiar with their tacos, nachos and tortillas, it's a quick and cheap spicy meal.

Two other restaurant chains worthy of mention at this point, although they are also of the diner type, are **Dairy Queen**, which offers a wider selection of buffet-style food (ice cream, yoghurt, hot dogs and hamburgers) for a quick snack, and **Dunkin' Donuts**, a glorified coffee shop that does a tremendous range of doughnuts (surprise, surprise) and other snack items. Practically all of these establishments will also have drive-through windows which are quite fun to try at least once on your Orlando visit. Simply drive around the side of the building where indicated and you will find their takeaway menu with a voice box that will take your order. Please, don't wait for the food to be miraculously produced from the voice box! Carry on around the building and your food will be served from a side window where the cashier will also take your money. You will probably find that your car has a slide-out tray from the central dashboard area that will take your coffee or soda cup and you can drive along with your meal and really pretend to be American!

Family restaurants

This is a section that may, at first appearance, seem very similar to the American Diner type, but there are two quite major differences. First, they are only restaurants. You won't find a bar here and some don't serve alcoholic drinks at all. And second, they make a big effort for family groups in terms of kids' menus and activities (in many cases the kids' menu doubles up as a colouring and puzzle book) and budget-conscious prices. They also all serve breakfasts, and you will find the best of the all-you-can-eat buffet deals here. Nearly all of them are chain groups in the same way as you find Little Chef and Happy Eaters all over Britain, but there are one or two individual restaurants worth knowing about.

Leading the way in terms of popularity with British tourists are the **Ponderosa Steakhouse** group and **Sizzler**. Whether it's breakfast, lunch or dinner, you will find great value and good, reliable food. In terms of style they are almost indistinguishable: you order and pay for your meal as you enter and are then seated, before being unleashed on some of the biggest buffet and salad bars you will have seen. Ponderosa have the rather flashier style, but you'd be hard pushed to tell whose food was who's. Expect to pay about $3.99 for their breakfast buffets and $4.99–$8.99 for lunch and dinner (there IS a difference in price depending on location, with the International Drive area tending to be a dollar or two dearer than elsewhere). Standard fare includes chicken wings, meatballs, chili, ribs, steaks and fresh seafood, while their immense salad bars in particular represent major value for money. Both are open from 7am until late evening and are handily located in all the main tourist spots.

A more homely touch can be found at the following selection of restaurant chains, with equally good if not better value for money. To my mind the best of the bunch are **Friendly's** restaurants for their exceptionally friendly service (naturally), well laid out and extremely appetising menus, hearty portions and positively mouthwatering desserts. They also do kids' fun menus that will keep the young 'uns amused and contented for the duration of the meal. Their big breakfast platter will set you back $3.99, chicken salad $4.99, a bacon cheeseburger with fries and coleslaw $5.29 and a Belgian waffle sundae $2.99, and they're open from 6am every morning with breakfast served until mid-day. **Bob Evans** restaurants (open 6am–10pm, or 6am–11.30pm Friday and Saturday) traditionally specialise in American downhome breakfasts, with all manner of pancakes, omelettes and egg platters guaranteed to fill you up without breaking the bank. They also do the inevitable burgers and hot sandwiches and a special dish of the day that might be shepherd's pie, roast turkey or hickory-smoked ribs. Their restaurant on Canadian Court, just off International Drive, is entered through a delightful General Store where you can buy country crafts and some of the homestyle foods on their menu. If it's a hearty breakfast you want at any time of day, then the **International House of Pancakes** (otherwise known as IHOP) or the **Waffle House** will both appeal to you. You will struggle to spend more than $4 or $5 on a full meal, whether it be one of their huge breakfast platters or a hot sandwich with fries. Waffle Houses are also open 24 hours a day, while IHOPs open at 6.30am right through to 1.30am. Another traditional American 24-hour family diner is **Denny's**, the nearest thing to our Little Chefs. Again, they make a traditional bacon 'n egg breakfast seem very ordinary with their wide selection, and they also do an excellent range of hot, toasted sandwiches and some imaginative dinner meals, like grilled catfish, as well as a Senior Selections menu, featuring smaller portions at reduced prices for the over-55s. Similarly, **Perkins Family Restaurant** is also open around the clock with a lookalike menu. For a really hearty breakfast try Perkins Eggs Benedict (two eggs and bacon on a toasted muffin with hash browns and fresh fruit, $5.59), while their bread-bowl salads at $5.89 are an equally satisfying meal.

Continuing the theme of American country cooking is the **Black Eyed Pea** group, where Mom's Meatloaf and fresh vegetables are the order of the day, along with huge salads and daily specials like chicken and dumplings and roast turkey. Their weekend breakfast buffet at $4.99 ($2.99 for kids) is also a highlight, as is

their kids' menu with puzzles. **Shoney's** is another buffet specialist, offering an impressive breakfast bar for an all-in $4.99 ($2.99 for kids) and a range of different dinner buffets at $8.99 a head that includes soup, salad and fruit bar. Their country buffet, boasting Cajun jambalaya and barbecue chicken, is a particular favourite, and Shoney's also do a neat little Just 4 Kids menu and fun book. Another 'homestyle' 24-hour establishment is the oddly-titled **Kettle**, otherwise known as America's Kitchen. Features include the Kettle Snippets menu, which is also a kids' activity book, some tasty snacks for the smaller appetite, a big breakfast choice and a hearty range of country dinners that all fall within the $5.89–$8.59 range. Finally, the last of the big family restaurant chains is **Morrison's Cafeteria**, a simple but efficient cafeteria-style establishment, not dissimilar to our motorway service stations but rather better value for money. Open 7.30am to 9pm, their kids' meals at just $1.99 are a snip, and their set meals at $4.29 offer a good choice of entrée, potato, vegetable and bread for the one price.

Two one-off restaurants that will appeal to the family as a whole are **Captain Nemo's**, on Highway 192 opposite Fort Liberty, and **Billy The Kid's Buffet**, a little further east on the same route. Captain Nemo's, open from 7am to 11pm (and serving breakfast until noon), offers a reasonable, balanced menu for all three meals of the day, but their speciality is seafood, with shrimp, oysters, lobster and daily specials like salmon, swordfish and grouper. Kids' meals are $2.95, including the inevitable fish fingers, but its real benefit is that if mum and dad would like to try the seafood while the children want yet another burger, Nemo's faithfully caters for both tastes as well as being a good, budget-price establishment, with the addition of early-bird specials (noon to 6pm) for just $6.95. Billy the Kid's Buffet is a more straightforward eat-all-you-can establishment with the extra benefit of a games room for kids and 99 cent children's meals (when eating with their parents). Breakfast buffet is $2.99, lunch $3.99 and dinner $6.99 (kids $3.49), and the youngsters are sure to love the Wild West atmosphere.

7

Arabian Nights

For a real fun family treat, (and the biggest crossover into the Diner-type restaurant) take the clan to one of the three **Jungle Jim's** in the Orlando area (at Crossroads of Lake Buena Vista, West Church Street and International Drive on Goodings Plaza). From the parrots that welcome you to the restaurant, you know you are in for an unusual dining experience, and sure enough you will eat in a truly entertaining jungle setting, with the menu promising 'An epic dining adventure of lost legends, forbidden pleasures and ancient rituals'. There are 63 (count them, 63!) choices of burger, including the World Famous Headhunter, a one-pound burger, with ham, bacon and cheese and a full pound of fries — polish off the lot and your next one is free! The alternatives are ribs, steak or chicken, but it would be a shame not to try at least one of the 63 varieties. The kids' menu is suitably varied, and there is a huge range of cocktails served by Dr S'Tiph Shotta Likker (ouch!). The International Drive location is open from 11am–2am every day, while the other two are open 11am–1.30am Sun–Thur, 11am–2am Fri–Sat.

British

To complete this section, it would probably be appropriate to mention the handful of British pubs and diners which seek to attract the UK visitor. All offer a fairly predictable array of pub grub along the lines of pies, pasties and fish and chips and a few imported British beers (Guinness has become very popular since the Irish were here for the World Cup in 1994!). You'll find the odd Brit or two working behind the bars, and you can happily take the kids into all of them, providing they don't sit at the bar. First and foremost among them is the **Cricketers Arms** in the Mercado Mediterranean Village on International Drive. This has become a favourite haunt for many British visitors due to the large selection of beers, appetising food (Ploughman's $6.25, cottage pie $6.50, bangers 'n mash $6.55), live evening entertainment and (soccer fans take note) live Premiership matches on their giant TV screen on a Saturday morning (from 10am — remember the time difference!) It gets very busy in the evenings, their live music is usually pretty good, and many of the staff are Chelsea fans, but we won't hold that against them! **Sweeney Todd's** in Church Street Market is similarly authentic, with a good range of beers (try Sweeney's Red, their home brew!), sound food (steak and kidney pie $7.75) and happy hour from 4.30pm to 7.30pm. Again, it gets very lively in the evenings, and positively shoulder-to-shoulder on Saturday nights. **Harry Ramsbottom's** can be found at Fort Liberty on Highway 192, with a pub/diner next to a proper fish 'n chippie. Sink a pint of Bass and have cod and chips for $4.95. Also along Highway 192 are the smaller and more derivative pubs of the **Merry Fiddlers** and the **Rovers Return** for *Coronation Street* freaks only.

The next section is the one where it would be easiest to go OTT. Not surprisingly, there are so many American-style restaurants of one kind or another it would be a full-time job just to keep track of them all. Therefore, I will limit this particular survey to the main tourist areas of International Drive and Highway 192, plus a couple off the beaten track that are well worth finding. The 'average price' listing is for a typical starter (Americans always refer to them as appetizers) and a main course (or entrée), plus a beer. In almost all cases you can call in just for a drink if you want.

American diners

Steak and Ale is a popular choice and can be found at seven locations around Orlando (11.30am–10pm Mon–Thur, 11.30am–11pm Fri, 12noon–11.30pm Sat, 12noon–10pm Sun; ave price $18.65). They do some great steaks and ribs, plus tempting seafood and chicken dishes, with early-bird specials of a three-course set meal for under $10 from 4–7pm (4–6pm November–March), and two-for-one drink specials at the same time. **TGI Friday's** will already be well-known from their outlets springing up all over Britain and their fun style of lively mealtimes is served up in exactly the same way in their six Orlando restaurants. (11am–1am; ave price $16.90). They do a great range of burgers, plus Mexican dishes, pizza, pasta, steak, ribs and seafood. The nationwide chain **Bennigan's** has six outlets in Orlando and is a particular personal favourite for their friendly, efficient service, smart decor and tempting menu, especially at lunchtime (11am–2am; ave price $14.40). They make the ordinary seem appetising and have a bar atmosphere straight out of the TV programme *Cheers*! Their Irish flavour really comes into its own on St Patrick's Day (17 March), and they have a happy hour (!) every day from 2–7pm and 11pm–midnight. Another enjoyable dining experience can be found at the two branches of **Darryl's** (one on International Drive, the other at Fort Liberty on Highway 192). Their weird and wonderful decor is totally original; they also have a great bar area and a nicely varied menu with some interesting choices, like Cajun-fried shrimp (11am–1am; ave price $17.50). Thick steaks, delicious burgers and Southern-

> BRIT TIP: Don't miss Darryl's twice-baked 'smashed' potatoes, mixed with bacon and melted cheese!

style dishes are their main fare, but they also offer some tasty soups and quiches.

Hooters makes no bones about its style. 'Delightfully tacky yet unrefined' declares the menu proudly, and sure enough here is a relatively simple, lively establishment, especially popular with the younger crowd for its beach-party atmosphere (11am–midnight Mon–Thur, 11am–1am Fri–Sat, noon–11pm Sun; ave price $12.50). Their five restaurants have a truly entertaining menu featuring great value seafood, salads, burgers and Hooters Nearly World Famous Chicken Wings that come in five strengths: mild, medium, hot, 3 Mile Island or Wild Wing. You have been warned!

Longhorn Steaks (six locations) is another lively, friendly set-up that serves generous slices of steak, chicken, burgers, salmon and salads without breaking the bank, as well as having a pretty decent kids' menu (11.30am–11pm; ave price $14.95).

By contrast, **Pebbles** (four restaurants) goes for the casual but sophisticated style, with a genuinely imaginative menu that will appeal to the amateur gourmet and won't cost you a fortune (11am–midnight; ave price $20.85). You can eat burgers or roast duck, salad or steak and be sure of an individual touch with every meal. Their pastas are particularly appetising and they also do a kids' menu from only $1.95. **Uno Chicago Pizzeria** is the place to go if Pizza Hut has become *passé*. Their four outlets offer great deep-dish pizzas with the addition of pastas, chicken dishes, steaks and salads (11am–midnight; ave price $13.90). The **Olive Garden** restaurants (11 of them) are one of America's big success stories in recent years as they have brought Italian food into the budget, mass-market range (11am–10pm Sun–Thur, 11am–11pm Fri–Sat; ave price $16.25). Their light, airy restaurants make for a relaxed meal and, while they don't offer a huge choice, what they do they tend to do pretty well and in generous portions. Pastas are their speciality, but they also offer chicken, veal, steak and seafood and some great salads, and there are unlimited refills of garden salad, garlic breadsticks and non-alcoholic drinks that add to their good value. What the Olive Garden does for Italian cuisine, **Chilis** does for Mexican. Actually, its an Americanised version of Mexican cooking with the emphasis more on steak and ribs and less on tortillas and hot spices (11am–1am

7

Mon–Sat, 11am–11pm Sun; ave price $11.20). Service is frighteningly efficient, and, if you are looking for a quick lunch or dinner, you'll be hard-pushed to find a quicker turnaround. Atmosphere is lively and bustly and they do a good kids' menu that is also a colouring/puzzle book. The one-off **Hollywood Diner** (on Highway 192, opposite Jungleland) is another fun place to take the family. You enter through a giant jukebox and are suddenly transported back to the 50s with the decor and music. Buffet specials and kids' deals abound (breakfast at just $2.99, and dinner at $6.99) to make it excellent value for money and there is a huge choice of ribs, chicken, burgers, fried shrimp, roast turkey, steaks and salads (7.30am to 11pm; ave price $10.35).

The Mill Bakery is another unusual selection, on south Kirkman Road, which offers some great home-brewed beers in addition to a thoughtful menu, featuring generous hot sandwiches, pizza, pasta, steaks and chicken, as well as 'Lite Bites' for the small appetite (6.30am–2am; ave price $14.90). Stop by the bar at happy hour (4pm–8pm, $1 beer and two-for-one drinks) or just sample their home-baked breads, muffins and desserts. Similarly, **Jack's Place** (in the Clarion Plaza Hotel on International Drive) refuses to be easily categorised. Here in this lively eaterie you dine surrounded by 'the stars' — dozens of signed celebrity caricatures by the famous New York artist Jack Rosen. The menu is pretty good, too — grilled yellow fin tuna, rosemary roasted pork and slow-roasted prime rib, as well as some more delicious pasta and steak dishes (6pm–10pm; ave price $21.90).

Ribs

When it comes to steaks, ribs and all manner of barbecue food, Orlando has a magnificent array of one-off restaurants that all proudly proclaim some kind of 'world famous' variety. In many instances they are right, and here's a good selection of the best on offer. **Austin's** (on International Drive, just south of the Mercado centre) is one of the new kids on the block, but does everything in good cowboy style, with an inviting gas-lit saloon-style bar and live Country and Western music (11am–midnight; ave

price $20.00). Ribs are their stock-in-trade, and portions are huge, but they also do very acceptable pasta, chicken and seafood as well as some massive steaks. Serious steak lovers will have to pay a visit to **Ruth's Chris Steak House** (999 Douglas Avenue in the suburb of Altamonte Springs just to the north of the city) where prime beef in a mouth-watering variety of choices is the order of the day. It isn't cheap or even budget-priced, but you'll be hard-pushed to get a better steak anywhere (5pm–11pm Mon–Sat, 5pm–10pm Sun; ave price $32.50). 'Only the best,' proclaims the restaurant's slogan. 'Come judge for yourself, but come hungry.' Nuff said. Similarly, the **Butcher Shop** (in the Mercado Centre on International Drive) offers steaks, steaks and more steaks. Hugely impressive is the cold counter where you can select your own piece of meat, and the hickory charcoal open grill where you can actually cook your steak to the desired degree (of course, there is also a chef to do it for you or offer advice). It's a novel approach and is

> BRIT TIP: Don't miss the Butcher Shop's skillet-fried mushrooms in garlic and butter sauce!

worth checking out if you fancy yourself as a bit of a Cordon Bleu in the kitchen (5pm–midnight; ave price $24.90).

While in the Mercado centre, you may decide to try **Damon's**, which pronounces itself The Place For Ribs. While they also do salads, chicken, seafood and burgers, their rib platters are simply humongous. (11am–10pm; ave price $19.40.) Try their onion loaf as a starter as it is rightly 'famous', while their lunch selections are particularly good value and, they promise, served within 15 minutes with their 'express' label. **Cattleman's Steak House** (on Vineland Road, Kissimmee, near the junction with Highway 192) goes for the cowboy approach once again, with a neat saloon bar (happy hour 4–7pm), earlybird specials at just $8.95 from 4–6pm and the Little Rustlers' Roundup menu for the kids. Steaks are again the order of the day, but you can also order chicken and seafood, while their

Heavenly Duck is worth trying for something different (4pm–11pm, saloon open until 2am; ave price $21.40).
Cecil's Texas Style BBQ (on South Orange Avenue, junction 34 off I4) offers hard-to-beat value and typically large portions of deliciously cooked beef brisket, ham, Polish sausage, turkey, pork, chicken or ribs. It's more of a family-style restaurant and offers daily specials from as little as $4.75 in unpretentious surroundings (11am–9pm; ave price $10.20). The up-market version of this type of establishment is **Wild Jack's** (on International Drive, just north of Sandlake Road) where you are greeted by the most magnificent wood-smoked barbecue aroma as you walk in the door. The huge, western-themed interior features a big, open pit-barbecue where you can watch your food being cooked (11.30am–11pm; ave price

> BRIT TIP: Don't miss Wild Jack's jalapeno mashed potatoes, their dynamite chicken wings, cowboy baked beans and the Jack Daniels chocolate cake for dessert!

$17.65). Steaks, ribs, chicken and turkey represent your main choices and they are all served up with bags of panache and a big helping of Wild West style. There is happy hour from 4pm–7pm, kids eat free with a full-paying adult and you can even buy yourself a Wild Jack's souvenir boot-shaped beer mug for $5.25!

The Magic Mining Co (at the western end of Highway 192's main tourist drag) is another fun-themed restaurant where you can imagine you are inside a gold mine while you eat. The menu is the usual array of steaks, ribs, chicken and seafood, and an extra feature is the adjoining gold mine mini-golf course (5pm–10.30pm; ave price $20.40).

Mexican

Back at the Mercado Centre on International Drive you'll find the excellent Mexican food of **Jose O'Day's**, a neat, relaxed restaurant that won't blow your taste buds if you're new to this type

of food. In fact, it's an excellent introduction to Tex-Mex cooking with a fine array of fajitas, enchiladas and beef and chicken dishes, while their salads are big enough for two (11.30am–midnight; ave price $18.40). Similarly, **Fajita Grill** (on State Road 535, just north of Highway 192) offers a tempting slice of Mexican along with the biggest Margaritas you have seen! Sizzling fajitas, enchiladas and chimichangas are served in huge amounts, along with steak, ribs and seafood (4pm–11pm; ave price $12.90). Of the same stable as Fajita Grill is **Lazy Bones Ribs** (on Highway 192, just past the junction with State Road 535 going east), an authentic barbecue diner that also has a kid's playroom. Baby back pork ribs, prime beef ribs, steaks, chicken and seafood are all succulent choices, plus there are Gator ribs for the really brave (4pm–11.30pm, with the Riverboat Bar and Lounge open until 2am; ave price $16.95). Another new, one-off restaurant that has a lot of Brit appeal is **Café Tu Tu Tango** on International Drive, next to Austin's. The accent is artist-colony Spanish (whatever that means), with a really original menu, live entertainment and art-work all over the walls that changes daily. Vegetarians will find themselves well catered for here, while you can also try some particularly succulent pizzas, seafood, salads and paella. Mexican and Chinese dishes also make an appearance, and there is a kids' menu with all dishes at $4.95 (11.30am–midnight; ave price $18.40). The overall style is based more on a Tapas bar, so you order a number of different dishes rather than a starter and main course. Ultimately, it is as much an artistic experience as a meal, and the fun atmosphere perfectly complements the rich array of dishes.

Steakhouses

Del Frisco's Prime Steak House (on Lee Road, to the north of the city centre) gets the *Orlando Sentinel's* nod as THE best of the area's steak restaurants. It's also the most expensive, but the magnificent decor and steaks that positively melt in the mouth underline why it picks up all sorts of awards every year. Beware, however, all your side dishes are EXTRA and the wine list is also in the astronomical price range

7

Paddling across Lake Eola

(5pm–10pm Mon–Thur, 5–11pm Fri–Sat; ave price $35-plus!) **Charley's Steak Houses** (of which there are three, the biggest on International drive just north of the Mercado centre) continue the theme of excellent steaks, cooked over a specially-built pit woodfire. It's not cheap, but the decor and bar area are splendidly furnished, and if you don't fancy steak, which you can watch being grilled on their large, hardwood grill, there are seafood choices as well (5pm–11pm; ave price $30.00). **Barney's Steak and Seafood** (on East Colonial Drive to the east of the city centre) won't hit your wallet quite so hard and boasts an award-winning salad bar and live entertainment. Prime rib, steaks and fresh seafood, including lobster tails, are the order of the day, and there is also a kids' menu (11.30am–11pm Mon–Fri, 4pm–9pm Sat–Sun; ave price $23.45). **Black Angus** and **Western Steer** complete the line-up of steakhouses along more budget lines as they also serve breakfasts and aim for the family market. Black Angus (down at the east end of Highway 192) offers an all-you-can eat breakfast buffet ($4.59, $2.99 for kids) as well as a typical range of steaks, and also has a nightly Karaoke session (9pm–1.30am) in the lounge bar (hours 7am–11.30pm; ave price $15.70). Western Steer (on Palm Parkway, just north of Lake Buena Vista, and International Drive, opposite Wet 'N Wild) offers a $3.99 breakfast buffet (kids $2.99) as well as a $7.99 dinner buffet (kids $3.99). Steaks are still the main fare, and with a large tribe to feed it's great value (7am–11.30pm; ave price $14.40).

Seafood

After that exhausting trek through the steakhouses of Orlando, you won't be surprised to learn the choice of seafood restaurants is equally large. **The Crab House** (locations on Goodings Plaza on International Drive and Palm Parkway) should be self-explanatory. Garlic crabs, steamed crabs, snow crabs, Alaskan king crabs, etc. Yes, this is THE place for crab. You can always try their prime rib, pasta or other seafood, but it would be a shame to ignore the house speciality when it's done this well (11.30am–11pm Mon–Sat, noon–11pm Sun; ave price $21.20). **Red Lobster** (11 restaurants) is from the same company that has made a success of the Olive Garden chain. This is seafood for the family market, with a varied menu, lively atmosphere and one of the best kids' menus/activity books you'll find. They offer lunches for only $4.99, and while lobster is their speciality, their steaks, chicken, salads and other seafood are equally appetising and they do a great variety of combination platters (11am–10pm Sun–Thur, 11am–11pm Fri and Sat; ave price $19.70). **Charlie's Lobster Hous** (on International Drive at the Mercado Centre and Aloma Avenue, Winter Park has a similar menu, although their International Drive restaurant is slightly more expensive. The bar areas are immaculately finished and service has that extra bit of charm (4–10pm Sun–Thur, 4–11pm Fri and Sat; ave price $27.40). Completing the chain restaurants here are the three outlets of the **Boston Lobster Feast**, with elaborate nautical decor and an unlimited lobster and seafood buffet (hence the Feast, you see). They have early-bird specials at $19.95 from 4.30–6.00pm Mon–Fri, 2.00–4.30pm Sat–Sun (and that represents excellent value), while their 40-item Lobster Feasts start at $24.95 and are guaranteed to stretch the stomach more than a little

(4.30pm–10pm Mon–Fri, 2–11pm Sat and Sun; ave price $27.20).

Of the one-off restaurants, **The Ocean Grill** (on International Drive, just north of the Sand Lake Road junction) represents great seafood at moderate prices. Daily specials jostle with the likes of fried clams, Southwestern swordfish, fried catfish, shrimp creole and seafood lasagna. Their plain old fish 'n chips ($8.95) would put most British chippies to shame, and for the really hearty appetite they do a magnificent surf 'n turf (lobster or shrimp and steak), although admittedly at a hearty price ($23.95). They also do pasta, stir-fry, steaks, ribs and chicken, but these dishes are done better elsewhere (4pm–11pm; ave price $18.85).

Townsend's Fishouse and Tavern (on West Michigan Street, just off the Orange Blossom Trail) is a delightful bar-restaurant in the best American tradition. The interior decor is positively crammed with little oddities and the service is very friendly. As well as lobster, crab and their daily fresh fish specials, they also do very acceptable steaks and pasta, and there is live entertainment Wednesday to Saturday (11.30am–11pm; ave price $23.75). The **Atlantic Bay Seafood Grill** (on Highway 192, just east of I4) surprisingly offers a breakfast buffet on top of its full range of well-priced seafood dishes, early-bird specials from 4.30–6.30pm, and steaks, ribs and pasta. It's not gourmet fare but it is hearty and good value, especially their all-you-can-eat seafood bar (7am–2pm, 4.30pm–11pm; ave price $19.40). Finally, the two restaurants of **Straub's** (on East Altamonte Drive, just east of the Altamonte Mall, and East Colonial Drive) are rated among the best seafood diners in central Florida, with great service and good value for money, including early bird specials 4.30–6.00pm. Their surf 'n turf grill combination is simply the best you'll find, while their seafood is always unfailingly fresh and pasta lovers will also enjoy several marvellous dishes like pesto linguini with sautéed shrimp, mushrooms and sun-dried tomatoes (4.30pm–10pm Sun–Thur, 4.30–11pm Fri and Sat; ave price $22.40).

Canoe down the river to get away from it all

For a selection of all the above — and more — visit **Marriott's Orlando World Center** on World Center Drive. Here you will find no less than FIVE distinctive restaurants that beautifully encapsulate Orlando's dining choice. **Allie's American Grill** (6.30am–2pm and 5pm–10pm; ave price $18.90) is a versatile diner, **Champions Sports Bar** (4pm–2am Mon–Fri, mid-day–2am Sat and Sun; ave price $13.20) boasts 18 televisions, **JW's Steakhouse** (11.30am–10pm Mon–Fri, 7am–10pm

> BRIT TIP: Straub's main courses include homemade bread, coleslaw and either rice, potatoes or veg, so it may be wise to give the starters a miss!

Sat and Sun; ave price $29.25) offers indoor or outdoor dining overlooking the magnificent golf course, **Tuscany's** (6pm–10pm; ave price $28) is an elegant Italian option and the **Mikado** (6pm–10pm; ave price $26.45) goes for Japanese style and flavouring.

7

It could be said I've saved the best for last in this American Diners section as there are five other restaurants that sort of fit into this category but are really delightful, one-off restaurants in their own right. All five will provide a genuinely exciting dining experience in novel settings that will linger long in the memory, and without costing you a fortune.

Hard Rock Café: Okay, if you've been to the one in London (or elsewhere around the world) you'll know what to expect, but even so Orlando's Hard Rock Café (adjacent to Universal Studios, and with a separate entrance and free car park) is still a wonderfully fun place for a loud, lively meal. Their burgers are hard to beat (especially their trademark 'Pig Sandwich'), while they also do ribs, steaks and sandwiches, and pop music fans will be able to study the dozens of pop mementos and memorabilia that line the walls. Their Hard Rock merchandise is also a lot cheaper here than in London (10.30am–2am; ave price $15.70).

Planet Hollywood: The largest restaurant in the rapidly-expanding worldwide chain of this glitzy, showbiz-style venture can be found next door to Disney's Pleasure Island and is just a pure fun entertainment venue. The food is fairly predictable diner fare, although everything is served up with pizzazz, but the cavernous interior lends itself to a real party atmosphere, complete with numerous film clips and a stunning array of movie memorabilia. Some memorable house cocktails, too, but visit either mid-morning or mid-afternoon to avoid some serious queues! (11am–2am; ave price $18.95).

B-line Diner: Inside the Peabody Hotel on International Drive lurks an amazing Art Deco homage to the traditional 50s-style diner, faithful to every detail, including the outfits of the staff. You sit at a magnificent long counter or in one of several booths, with a good view of the chef at work, and with a rolling menu that changes four times a day (which isn't bad when it is open around the clock!). The food is way above usual diner standard, but the prices aren't so you can munch away on catfish in a papaya–tartare sauce or pork chop with apple–sage chutney, as well as the traditional favourites of burgers, steaks and ribs, happy in the knowledge you won't break the bank. Their desserts are displayed in a huge glass counter and I defy you to ignore them! (Open 24 hours; ave price $14.90).

The Bubble Room: How do you describe a restaurant that looks like something out of a mad collector's nightmare crossed with an explosion in a paint factory. Simple, you don't. Instead I'll just say that the Bubble Room (on South Orlando Avenue, Highway 17–92, take junction 47 of I4, in the northern suburb of Maitland) has to be seen to be believed. It is packed with memorabilia from the 1930s, 40s and 50s in a number of themed rooms. The menu is equally eclectic with choices like Flaming Socra Cheese (flambéed Greek saganaki cheese!), Duck Ellington (roast duck in a tropical banana sauce) and The Liebert Lombardo (Mediterranean paella), and their dessert counter features some of the most delicious and humongously large gateaux in the universe (for which they are justly famous). Specialities (without their menu's strange titles) are the prime ribs, thick pork chops and file of grouper. Service is provided by Bubble Scouts and, while the prices are rather high for diner food, the

experience is not to be missed
(11.30am–10pm Sun–Thur,
11.30am–11pm Fri and Sat; ave
price $27.40).

4th Fighter Group: War buffs
and kids will love eating at this large
World War II American Air Force-
themed restaurant on Rickenbacker
Drive, off East Colonial Drive, just
past the Orlando Fashion Square
Mall. Its entrance is guarded by a
Sherman tank and other WWII
memorabilia lurk in odd corners.
The restaurant has a number of
different rooms, including one that
has headphones on the tables so you
can listen in to the control tower of
the adjacent Executive Airport,
which makes a very pretty backdrop
at night. Reservations are nearly
always required (407 898 4251),
especially for their Sunday brunch,
which features unlimited Bloody
Marys and champagne with a
magnificent range of fresh salads,
pastries, potatoes, bacon, eggs,
waffles, fresh seafood, etc, all for a
bargain $15.95. Main menu choices
include chicken, veal, shrimp, steaks
and chops, and there are daily
specials. There is a large bar and
patio area and dining outside is also
a treat (5pm–10pm Sun–Thur,
5–11pm Fri and Sat, plus Sunday
brunch 9am–2.30pm; ave price
$25.45).

Speciality restaurants

This final section requires least
preamble as the type of fare is fairly
obvious. As I have already mentioned,
the food on offer varies enormously
from American to Japanese, through
all kinds of Asian, to the Middle East,
through Europe and back again.
Here are the main varieties.

Chinese

Chinese food is well-established in
America and well represented in
Orlando. The **China Coast** series of
restaurants are part of the same chain as

the Olive Garden and Red Lobster
outlets and they are equally successful at
cornering the mass market appeal. There
are three China Coasts around Orlando,
the most conspicuous being on
International Drive. Delicious
appetizers, imaginative chicken dishes
and regional specialities are all very well
prepared and served in fine pagoda-style
splendour. Their lunch buffet is also a
winner with the budget-conscious
(11.30am–11pm; ave price $13.70).
Ming Court on International Drive, just
south of King Henry's Feast, is the Rolls
Royce of local Chinese restaurants. With
the magnificent setting and live
entertainment you could easily convince
yourself you had been transported to
China itself. The menu is extensive and
many dishes can be had as a side order
rather than a full main course to give you
the chance to try more (11am–2.30pm
and 4.30pm–midnight; ave price $22.90).
Golden Phoenix in Bay Hill Plaza on
Turkey Lake Road also manages to bring
an authentic touch to its location with a
menu that has one or two out-of-the-
ordinary items (11am–10pm; ave price
$19.60) while **Bill Wong's famous
super buffet** (yes, they really do call it
that) on International Drive offers a
cross between Chinese and diner-type
fare. Their all-you-can-eat buffet
features jumbo shrimp (and they mean
Jumbo!), as well as crabs, prime rib, fresh
fruit and salad (11am–10pm; ave price
$16.90). Similarly, the **Sizzling Wok**, on
Sand Lake Road, just across from the
Florida Mall, offers an opportunity to
get stuck in to a massive Chinese buffet
at a very reasonable price (11am–10pm
Sun–Thur, 11am–10.30pm Fri and Sat;
ave price $15.25). Out on Highway 192
you'll find two fairly predictable but
budget-conscious restaurants. **China
Kitchen**, opposite the Manufacturer's
Outlet Mall, goes for the buffet approach
once again, with a lunch at just $4.95 and
dinner $7.75. The food is unremarkable
but difficult to beat for the price
(noon–10pm; ave price $11.75). **Peking
Gardens** goes slightly more up-market
with a tempting range of Szechuan,
Hunan and Cantonese cuisine
(noon–11pm Sun–Thur, noon–midnight
Fri and Sat; ave price $13.60). **Trey
Yuen** and **Hunan Chinese Cuisine**
complete the tourist area Chinese

7

Bass fishing in Orlando

offerings, and are fairly typical of Chinese restaurants in Britain. Both are located on the northern stretch of International Drive, with Trey Yuen specialising in the appetising small bite Dim Sum selections and offering a local delivery service (11am–midnight; ave price $12.90) and Hunan sticking to a more limited range of specialities but again at a sound price (11am–midnight; ave price $12.75).

Japanese

The more adventurous among you (and those already familiar with their cuisine) will want to try one of the fine Japanese restaurants with which Orlando is blessed. **Shogun Steakhouse**, on International Drive under the International Inn, is ideal for those who can't quite go the whole hog and get stuck into Sushi (raw fish). If you decide to chicken out, you can still order a no-nonsense steak or chicken, but their full Japanese menu is well explained and vividly demonstrated by their chefs in front of you at long, bench-like tables (6pm–10pm Mon–Thur, 6pm–10.30pm Fri–Sun; ave price $17.90). **Kobe** also brings a touch of Americana to its dining content so you need not feel Sushi is the only option (actually, to sum up Japanese cuisine as just raw fish is a massive insult

— their range of seafood, steak and chicken dishes are as tempting as any Chinese restaurant, only different!). With five locations around the area, Kobe go for the mass market appeal but still achieve individual style with the chef preparing your food at your table in a style that is as much showmanship as culinary expertise (11.30am–11pm; ave price $14.85). **Ran-Getsu**, on International Drive opposite the Mercado centre, does for Japanese cuisine what the Ming Court does for Chinese, ie, it's stylish, authentic and as much an experience as a meal, and it is still reasonably priced. The setting is simple and efficient, and you can choose to sit at conventional tables or their long, S-shaped sushi bar (5pm–midnight; ave price $18.40). **Benihana** completes a formidable quartet of outlets, situated in the Hilton Hotel at Walt Disney World Village, Lake Buena Vista. Again, it's a memorable experience, with everything cooked right in front of you by their expert chefs, and their steaks are among the most tender you will ever touch (5pm–10.30pm; ave price $18.30).

Indian

If you have come all this way and still fancy a curry, believe it or not you will be able to get one as good as any you have tried back home. There are already more than a dozen Indian restaurants around the Orlando area and they all maintain a pretty fair standard, from the up-market **Far Pavilion**, at the intersection of International Drive and Kirkman Road, to the budget-price **New Punjab** at the upper end of International Drive and on West Vine Street, Kissimmee, with its excellent lunch and dinner specials. For a medium range restaurant, **Passage To India** (also on International Drive) gets the locals' vote as best Indian restaurant and is a cut above the average, too, with unusual dishes like Chicken Kadhai, the exotic Chicken Hyderabadi and vegetarian Sabzi Dal Bahar (11.30am–midnight; ave price $19.65). It is a particular personal favourite for its attentive service and relaxed atmosphere, and you will probably find yourself dining with a few fellow Brits, too. Rock band The Cure and cricketer Imran Khan have also eaten here and left the photos to prove

! The **Akbar Palace**, on Highway 192 ust past Fort Liberty as you head east, lso does breakfast and a budget-priced unch buffet at $6.95, while the **Indian Palace** on Palm Parkway offers a set unch at $5.95, and, yes, you can get ake-aways as well!

Thai and more

'or other types of Oriental cooking, the **iam Orchid** (on Republic Drive, just round the corner from Wet 'n Wild) ffers exceptional Thai food in a icturesque setting overlooking Sandy ake (11am–2pm Mon–Fri only and .30pm–11pm all week; ave price 14.95). If you'd like to try another ariation, **Little Saigon** (on East Colonial Drive) will introduce you to /ietnamese cuisine and a whole new rray of soups, barbecue dishes, fried rice ariations and other interesting treats hat take up where Chinese food leaves ff (10am–9pm; ave price $10.95). **Santa e** (on Semoran Boulevard) takes you to outh America with a buffet-style, ever-hanging menu that makes a nice change f you're tired of Mexican food 11.30am–2.30pm and 5–8.30pm Mon–Fri only; ave price $9.20 — no redit cards!). Cuban food is a Floridian peciality and you will find one of the est examples at **Numero Uno** (on outh Orange Avenue, near its junction vith Michigan Street). Roast pork is a articular treat, as is their chicken with ellow rice, while desserts are also an dventure (11am–3pm and 5–10pm Mon–Fri, 1pm–10pm Sat; ave price 19.50).

Italian

No survey of Orlando's restaurants vould be complete without mention of ts fine tradition of Italian cooking. *acino's* (at the Crossroads shopping entre at Lake Buena Vista and in two ocations on Highway 192, their first estaurant opposite Old Town, and their atest to the west almost opposite plendid China) goes for the family narket and scores a big hit with value-or-money, friendly atmosphere and icilian style, with clever animated uppet operettas, a fountain that ccasionally spouts flame and a relaxing pen air feel that is enhanced by the lever use of the differently arranged

Wet 'n Wild on International Drive

seating areas (11am–midnight; ave price $20.25, with kids meals at $3.95). **Bergamo's**, in the Mercado centre, is actually German-owned but nonetheless authentic for all that. Don't be surprised if your waiter suddenly bursts into song — it's all part of the unique charm of this extremely tempting and ultimately highly entertaining restaurant (5pm–11pm; ave price $28.20). **Carmente's** (two locations, on International Drive just north of Sand Lake Road, and the South Orange Blossom Trail, again just north of its Sand Lake Road junction) won't hurt your wallet quite so much and does a great pizza among a typical selection of Italian fare. They also offer breakfast and lunch specials (7.30am–11pm; ave price $12.95). Similarly, **Rosario's** (on Highway 192, next to Capone's Dinner Show) does surprisingly good food for their relatively low prices, especially the soups and pastas (5pm–11pm; ave price $15.65). **Donato's** keeps up the budget appeal and adds the attractions of an Italian market, pizzeria and deli that make dining there a very appetising experience. No frills but very good food, and its location just south of the Belz Factory Outlet at the top of International Drive makes it a handy retreat after a shopping frenzy (11.30am–11.30pm; ave price $12.60). **Bertucci's** (International Drive, north of Sand Lake Road) is also more of a pizzeria, with its charming, open style built around its feature brick oven. The pizzas are very good, and a small one is big enough for two with a salad and garlic bread, but they also do a good range of pastas and calzones, and a very sensible kids' menu (11am–midnight; ave price $14.70). The

7

five-star version of Italian cuisine here belongs to two contrasting restaurants, **Christini's** on Dr Phillips Boulevard, and **La Sila** on Kirkman Road. Strolling musicians, elegant surroundings and a 40-year history of award-winning cuisine characterise Christini's, where their homemade pasta and filet mignon are as good as anything you will find in Italy (5pm–11pm; ave price $28.50). La Sila, just north of Universal Studios in Turkey Lake Village, promotes a candlelit atmosphere with live music in the cocktail lounge, formal, dinner-jacketed staff and a northern Italian cuisine that features delicious veal, snapper and pasta delicacies. Their pasta, bread and desserts are all homemade and it is all presented in an old-world style that is a million miles away from the tourist hurly-burly of the theme parks (6pm–11pm, 6–2am in the bar; ave price $29.35).

Splashing out

Finally, if you fancy really splashing out, there are three restaurants that deserve your attention for pure, unarguable culinary excellence. Prices are high and they all take a bit of finding, but for a memorable meal of the highest class, this is where you should go.

Park Plaza Gardens: part of the Park Plaza Hotel on Park Avenue, Winter Park, this beautiful courtyard restaurant gives you the feel of outdoor dining with the air-conditioned comfort of being indoors. Attentive service is coupled with an elegant, versatile menu that offers the choice of a relatively inexpensive lunch or a three-course adventure featuring escargot, pasta with salmon, medallions of beef or one of several tempting fish dishes. Cuisine is distinctly nouvelle rather than American, but nonetheless satisfying for all that. Its setting becomes even more intimate and charming in the

BRIT TIP: If you have something to celebrate, or are considering a romantic engagement, book a table for two in the evening, tel 407 645 2475.

evening with lights scattered among the foliage. Enjoy happy hour in the lounge 5pm–7pm (with complimentary buffet Thursday and Friday), while their popular three-course Sunday brunch features unlimited champagne and live jazz (11.30–3pm Mon–Sat and 11am–3pm for Sunday brunch, 6–10pm Mon–Thur, 6–11pm Fri and Sat, 6–9pm Sun; ave price $30.45).

Maison & Jardin: French cuisine is again the accent of this award-winner on South Wymore Road, Altamore Springs (tel 407 862 4410 for reservations). Set among five acres of beautiful gardens, the restaurant has all the character of an antique villa, with the choice of three different dining rooms. The Gazebo Room offers the most picturesque view, over the formal gardens. The wine choice alone is staggering – more than 800 selections in a massive and carefully stocked cellar — but the food is similarly impressive. A caviar crêpe flambéed at your table, lobster and crab ravioli, roast stuffed quail or grilled medallions of elk in a brandy cream sauce, everything has majestic touch (6pm–10pm, 11am–2pm for Sunday brunch; ave price $33.00).

Chalet Suzanne: Set among acres of orange groves overlooking a pretty lake is an unlikely Swiss 'village' that has been family-owned and run since 1931. To find it, take a 40-minute drive on I4 (South) west and Highway 27 south, 10 miles past the turnoff for Cypress Gardens to just north of Lake Wales and you'll find Chalet Suzanne Boulevard (tel 813 676 6011). Again, an extensive wine list leads you into a menu of continental delights, featuring seafood delicacies like shrimp curry and lobster Newburg, mouthwatering steaks and their speciality chicken Suzanne. There is a set price for their amazing seven-course meal, starting at $40, depending on your choice of main course. Men are required to wear jackets for dinner and the restaurant is also open for breakfast and lunch (8am–9.30pm).

Now on to another of my favourite topics. As already mentioned, and in keeping with the area's great diversity of attractions, the other main way in which Orlando will seek to separate you from your hard-earned money is in shopping. The choice is suitably wide-ranging …

8 Shopping

or how to send your credit card into meltdown

The vast area that constitutes metropolitan Orlando is a positive shopper's paradise, with a dazzling array of specialist outlets, malls and complexes, flea markets and discount retailers. It is also one of the most vigorous growth markets, with new centres springing up seemingly all the time, from the smartest of malls to the cheapest and tackiest of tourist gift shop plazas (and you can hardly go a few yards in the main tourist areas without a shop insisting it has the best tourist bargains of one sort or another).

You will be bombarded by shopping opportunities every way you turn, and the only hard part is avoiding the temptation to fill an extra suitcase or two with the sort of goods that would cost twice as much back home. As a general rule you can expect to pay in dollars what you would pay in pounds for items like clothes, books, records and CDs, while there are real bargains to be had in jeans, trainers, shoes, sports gear and T-shirts.

But beware! Your duty free allowance in the catch-all duty category of 'gifts' is still only £136 per person, and it is perfectly possible to exceed that sum by some distance. Paying the duty and VAT is still often cheaper than buying the same items at home, however, so it is worth splashing out, but remember to keep all your receipts and go back through the red 'goods to declare' channel on your return. You will pay duty of between 4 per cent and 19 per cent on the total purchase price (ie. inclusive of Florida sales tax, see below) once you have exceeded your £136 allowance, and then VAT at 17.5 per cent on top of that. Unfortunately, you can no longer pool your allowances to cover one item that exceeds a single allowance. Hence, if you buy a camera, say, that costs £200, you have to pay the duty on the full £200, taking the total to £213.20, and then the VAT on that figure. However, if you have a number of items that together exceed your £136 allowance, you pay the duty and VAT only on the excess. To give you some examples of duty rates (which fill three volumes and are up-dated regularly), computers are currently charged at 4.4 per cent, golf clubs 5.3 per cent, cameras at 6.6 per cent and

8

BRIT TIP: If you are tempted to use 'doctored' receipts to make them show a lesser value — don't! Your goods will be confiscated and there are heavy fines. Also, you can't escape the duty by saying the items have been used (in the case of golf clubs, for example) or that they are gifts for someone else.

mountain bikes at a whopping 16.6

KEY TO ORLANDO - SHOPPING CENTRES

A = CHURCH STREET EXCHANGE
    AND CHURCH STREET MARKET
B = OLD TOWN
C = NEIGHBOURHOOD SHOPS
D = LAKEFRONT PARK
E = FORT LIBERTY TRADING POST
F = THE PARKWAY SHOPS
G = DISNEY'S VILLAGE MARKETPLACE
H = MERCADO MEDITERRANEAN VILLAGE
I = GOODINGS INTERNATIONAL PLAZA
J = CROSSROADS OF LAKE BUENA VISTA
K = BELZ FACTORY OUTLET
L = QUALITY OUTLET CENTER
M = KISSIMMEE MANUFACTURER'S OUTLET MALL

N = FLEA WORLD
O = OSCEOLA FLEA AND FARMER'S MARKET
P = FLORIDA MALL
Q = ALTAMONTE MALL
R = OSCEOLA SQUARE MALL
S = COLONIAL PLAZA MALL
T = ORLANDO FASHION SQUARE MALL
U = COLONIAL PROMENADE
V = HERNDON PLAZA
W = THE MARKETPLACE
X = WINTER PARK MALL
Y = PARK AVENUE
Z = INTERNATIONAL DESIGNER OUTLET

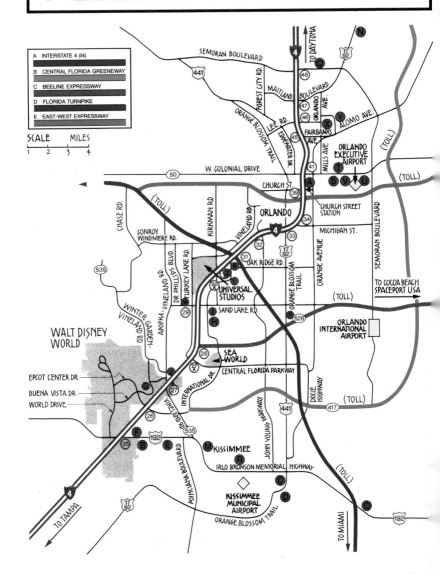

per cent, all plus VAT. If you have any queries about your allowances or the duty on specific items, consult the Customs and Excise office located in the departure lounge before you leave your home airport.

Your ordinary duty free allowances from America include 200 cigarettes and a litre of spirits or two litres of sparkling wine and two litres of still wine. Alligator products, which constitute an endangered species, require a special import licence, and you should consult the Department of the Environment first.

> BRIT TIP: As with the theme parks and restaurants, there are special coupons and discounts in the various tourist hand-outs for some of the shops. A few are worth keeping but the majority are pretty tacky.

Be aware, also, of the hidden 'extras' of shopping costs. Unlike our VAT, the local version in Orlando, the Florida State sales tax, is NOT added to the displayed purchase price, so you should add 6 per cent to arrive at the 'real' price. This frequently catches visitors out as they are convinced the wrong price has been rung up or that some clever con is being worked! The sales tax is added to everything you buy in Orlando, from your theme park tickets to a beer at the hotel and all meals (but not supermarket groceries, which are classed as 'essentials').

Here is a rundown of the main shopping attractions and the sort of fun and bargains that can be had, divided into four categories. Firstly, the purpose-built speciality shopping complexes, specifically out to catch the tourist. Second, Orlando's speciality flea markets and discount

outlets, third the large, typically American shopping malls and finally a few specific shops with the bargain-hunter in mind.

Shopping complexes

Top of the first category must come **Church Street Exchange** and **Church Street Market**, two separate but similarly intentioned restorations full of one-off gift-shops in downtown Orlando. The Exchange is part of the Church Street Station entertainment complex, but there is no admission charge to go shopping here. It is a grand, eye-catching old railroad station conversion now housing three levels of gift shops, cafés and

Park Avenue is Winter Park's main thoroughfare

restaurants, split into two sides, with live entertainment and sideshows in the evenings and at weekends. Open from 11am to 11pm every day, it also features Commander Ragtime's Midway of Fun, Food and Games, a floor of antique, carnival-style games and a usually uncrowded food court. Stores vary from the exclusive and expensive to typical tourist fare, but all with a distinctly stylish, Victorian flavour. Look out for the Bumby Emporium, Church Street Station's elaborate gift-shop, and the Buffalo Trading Company, for all things Western. Although the two tend to merge into each other, the two-storey Market is separately owned and run, built around a large brick courtyard, and consists of another two dozen specialist stores (check out Laser Magic for some clever

8

holograms and Brookstone for all manner of useful and useless gadgets), craft stalls and street performers, plus restaurants like the young and trendy Hooters, the English pub Sweeney Todd's and the excellent budget Italian eaterie the Olive Garden. The Market is open until 10pm (6pm on Sundays) and for both take exit 38 off I4. Parking is available and well signposted all around Church Street in either multi-storey or ground-level facilities.

Kissimmee's version of the purpose-built themed shopping centre is **Old Town**, a similarly picturesque, antique-style offering in the heart of Highway 192. More than 70 shops — including some novel T-shirt outlets — can be found along brick-built roads, with the additional features of a 1927 Ferris Wheel and 1909 Carousel, a two-storey Haunted House, go-kart track and free entertainment each evening on the Old Town Stage. Open from 10am to 11pm, Old Town will easily consume three to four hours of your time. Parking is free and it is easily located two miles east of I4, just look for the huge Ferris Wheel.

Other Kissimmee tourist-orientated shopping centres include the **Neighbourhood Shops**, which can be found two blocks south of Highway 192 on Route 17–92. These are a number of restored turn-of-the-century homes featuring gift shops, a children's boutique, country store and Chef's Pantry restaurant. Similarly old-fashioned in nearby Broadway, downtown Kissimmee, are the charming shops and restaurants of **Lakefront Park**. Further west on 192 are the **Fort Liberty Trading Post Shops**, an adjunct to Wild Bill's Wild West dinner show, featuring 20 craft shops and three restaurants, open seven days a week until 10pm. Just past Water Mania is the smaller

parade, **The Parkway Shops**, more speciality gift stores, restaurants and an ice cream club for those addicted to the cold stuff! The Neighbour-hood Shops are open 10am to 5pm (10am–3pm on Saturdays), Lakefront Park from 9am–5.30pm (Monday–Saturday only) while the Parkway will entertain you from 9am to 11pm seven days a week.

Not to be outdone, **Disney's Village Marketplace** in Lake Buena Vista provides a peaceful, leisurely atmosphere sprinkled with 17 rustic, shingle-sided shops specialising in fashions, jewellery and the inevitable mountain of Disney merchandise, including the largest store of its kind in the world, Mickey's Character Shop. There is also seasonal live entertainment, plus award-winning restaurants, all prettily located along the edge of the Buena Vista Lagoon where kids of 12 and older can go boating in various kinds of watercraft. The Marketplace is open from 9.30am to 10pm every day and parking is free. It is best located off exit 27 on I4, then north on Apopka-Vineland Road and first left into Hotel Plaza Boulevard.

Similarly cleverly built to attract the eye of passing tourists is the **Mercado Mediterranean Village** in the heart of the southern International Drive tourist drag, with more than 60 speciality shops, some superb restaurants (including Bergamo's, Charlie's Lobster House Jose O'Days and The Butcher Shop), the new Blazing Pianos nightclub, live evening entertainment and an impressive international food court (especially for the budget-conscious). The wonderful Spanish architecture encourages browsing along the 'streets', lined with one-off shops like the amusing book store Novel Ideas, One For The Road, which sells gifts and clothes for the car enthusiast, and the environmentallyonscious Earth Matters. The Mercado is open from 10am to 0pm (longer at the bars and restaurants), and will happily amuse ou and your wallet for several ours. Parking is free and it is also ome to the official Orlando Visitor nformation Center, which is full of andy brochures on the attractions, vith many discount coupons to be ad, too.

Back on International Drive, just p-road of the Mercado Village, is **Goodings International Plaza**, nother speciality tourist shopping entre featuring discount stores like Denim World, a gourmet grocery, 4-hour supermarket and several estaurants, open from 10am to nidnight every day. Likewise, **Crossroads of Lake Buena Vista**, he rather cheaper neighbour of Disney's Village Marketplace, offers similar collection of 25 busy shops nd some fun restaurants like Jungle im's, Pebbles and Red Lobster, plus ne elaborate Pirate's Cove dventure golf, and is open all week ong from 10am to 10pm.

> BRIT TIP: A word of warning on videos. If you are tempted to buy those souvenir videos — beware! American video tapes are **NOT** compatible with European VCRs, so you will be wasting your money unless the video is specifically marked **PAL**, which signifies European use.

Discount Outlets

Belz Factory Outlet is by far the nost impressive of the second ategory of shops, the flea market or iscount outlet and is a positive Mecca for all serious shoppers. ctually, it almost defies description as it is too widespread to be a full shopping mall, too elaborate to be a flea market and too down-to-earth to be a straightforward tourist trap (the locals do a lot of shopping here, too). Belz can be found on West Oak Ridge Road at the top of International Drive and consists of more than 160 shops arranged in two indoor plazas (both with lively food courts and one with a vintage Carousel to amuse the kids), plus four separate annexes that all require a separate journey by car (unless you want to wear out a lot of shoe leather!). Avoid Belz at weekends, if you want to beat the crowds. The aim is to sell name brands at factory-direct prices and, while you may have to wade through a fair amount of stuff you wouldn't want if they were giving it away, you will find shoes, clothes, books, jewellery, electronics, sporting goods, crockery and much more at bargain rates. Check out the Calvin Klein outlet (Annex 2), Reebok footwear (Annex 4), the Van Heusen factory store (Mall 1), Christian Dior lingerie at Carole Hochman designs (also Mall 1) and Guess Jeans (Mall 2). Serious shoppers will want to spend several hours here, and Belz is conveniently open from 10am to 9pm Monday to Saturday and 10am to 6pm on Sundays. **Quality Outlet Center** (9.30am to 9pm Mon–Sat, 11am–6pm Sun) further down on International Drive offers much of the same, although not quite in the same quantity. For a slightly classier version, the new **International Designer Outlet** plaza just south of Belz on I-Drive has a more up-market range of shops, including Eagle Outfitters, Rocky Mountain Chocolate Factory and Westpoint Pepperell for fine linens (10am–9pm Mon–Sat, 10am–6pm Sun). Kissimmee's version of the discount outlet is the **Kissimmee Manufacturer's Outlet Mall** on Old Vineland Road (just off the

8

Mercado Mediterranean Shopping Village

central drag of Highway 192). Again featuring name brands like Nike, Totes and Fieldcrest-Cannon, it is open 10am to 9pm Monday to Saturday and 11am to 5pm on Sunday.

Flea World boasts America's largest covered market, with 1,700 stalls spread out over 104 acres, including three massive, themed buildings, plus a seven-acre amusement park. It is open Friday, Saturday and Sunday only from 8am to 5pm and can be found a 20-minute drive away on Highway 17–92 (best picked up from exit 47 of I4) between Orlando and Sanford (to the north). The stalls include all manner of market goods, from fresh produce to antiques and jewellery and a whole range of arts and crafts, while there is a full-scale food court and a 300-seat pizza and burger eatery, the Carousel Restaurant.

On a slightly smaller scale is the **Osceola Flea and Farmers Market** at the eastern extremity of the tourist area of Highway 192 in Kissimmee, open Saturday and Sunday (8am to 5pm) from May 1 to September 30, and Friday, Saturday and Sunday (same hours) from October 1 to April 30.

Malls

The inevitable indoor malls are all big, efficient and much of a muchness, offering rather run-of-the-mill shopping compared to the tourist-orientated centres. However there are two exceptions to this rule and both are worth seeking out for a couple of hours. The **Florida Mall** has a much more stylish appearance than most of its counterparts, featuring some 200 shops in three themed areas, with several large department stores and an excellent food court offering a choice of 18 speciality restaurants, plus the lively bar-restaurant, Ruby Tuesday. It is located on the South Orange Blossom Trail, on the corner of Sand Lake Road, and is open 10am to 9pm Mondays to Saturday, 11am to 6pm on Sunday.

The huge two-storey **Altamonte Mall**, on Altamonte Avenue in the suburb of Altamonte Springs (take exit 48 on I4 and head east for half mile on Route 436), is also well above average. It is one of the largest in America, featuring 175 speciality shops, four major department stores, a choice of 16 eating outlets in Treats food court, plus another 3 restaurants, including Ruby Tuesday, and an elegant overall design with marble floors that makes visiting a pleasure. You can also get away from the usual tourist hordes here to do some serious shopping from 10am to 9pm Monday to Saturday and from noon to 6pm on Sunday (weekdays are best, though). Out of town visitors can also benefit from the mall's Privilege shopping programme, which offers discounts in many of the stores. Simply show your hotel room key or your driving licence or passport at the Customer Service Center in the middle of the lower level to pick up your Privilege card.

The large and spacious **Osceola Square Mall** (where Highway 192 mysteriously becomes Vine Street along its central stretch) is the only enclosed mall in Kissimmee, with 3 shops and a 12-screen cinema complex (open 10am–9pm Mon–Sat, 9am–5pm on Sun), while also worth a look if you are in the vicinity are the series of malls and shopping plazas along East Colonial Drive (Exit 41 off I4), including **Colonial Plaza Mall, Orlando Fashion Square Mall, Colonial Promenade, Herndon Plaza** and **Herndon Village Shoppes**, all of which offer more leisurely browsing, especially during the week. **The Marketplace** on Dr Phillips Boulevard (just west of I4 exit 29) is another friendly neighbourhood shopping centre, with Victorian styling, cobblestones and a clock-tower, as well as the striking Eco Art shop, a 24-hour grocery and the excellent Italian restaurant Christini's. **Winter Park Mall** on North Orlando Avenue is looking a bit tired and functional these days, and more interesting shopping can be found among the more exclusive, old-fashioned stores of Park Avenue in Winter Park itself (see Off The Beaten Track, Chapter Six).

Apart from the big chemist chain stores, Eckerd and Walgreens, already mentioned, there are a few more typical large-group stores. The main supermarkets you will find are Publix and Goodings, which are comparable with Asda, Safeway or (in the case of Goodings) Marks and Spencer, while for clothes, DIY, home furnishings, souvenirs, toys, electrical goods and other household items the big discount stores are K-Mart, Wal-Mart or Target (like a big version of Tesco's, but without the food department, if that makes sense!). If there is anything you have forgotten to bring, the chances are you can get it at K-Mart or one of the other two. For photographic supplies and film processing you should try one of the many branches of Eckerd Express Photo. Kids will also want to know Orlando is home to the biggest Toys Я Us shop in the world! It can be found on Florida Mall Avenue, just off Sand Lake Road and the Orange Blossom Trail.

Specialist shops

Finally, a few worth making a note of for specific items are the various outlets of **Denim World** (no explanation necessary), **The Sports Authority** and **Craig Sports**, the former on Sand Lake Road and the latter in Goodings Plaza on International Drive, which both offer all manner of sporting goods and apparel, while serious sportsmen and women will also want to visit either of the two outlets of **International Discount Golf and Tennis** on International Drive and the South Orange Blossom Trail, the magnificent range of the four **Edwin Watts Golf** shops, including their national clearance centre on International Drive, or any of the five **Special Tee Golf** shops. On golf clubs in particular you can pick up some great deals and save pounds on the same equipment back home. **Skips Western Outfitters** (on International Drive, just south of the junction with Sand Lake Road) and **The Great Western Boot Co** (in the Quality Outlet Centre on International Drive and opposite the Altamonte Mall) both offer the chance to get yourself fully kitted out in the latest cowboy fashions, while for an alternative statement in local fashion visit the **Orlando Magic Fanattic** (on the corner of Colonial Drive at its junction with I4) for an amazing range of clothing and souvenirs all bearing the colours or logo of the city's basketball heroes (including their mascot, 'Stuff' the Magic Dragon. I kid thee not!). Last, but by no means least, **Orlando Duty Free**, on Palm Parkway, offers tax-free shopping for perfume, tobacco, clocks, watches and other gift items.

Now you should be completely familiar with all the delights in store, let's move on to some practical advice on safety …

8

9 Safety First

or don't forget to pack your common sense!

From the coverage Florida has received in our media you would be forgiven for thinking any holiday to Orlando could be the equivalent of signing up for a vacation in Crime City, USA. This is simply not the case.

Make no mistake, America is a more violent, crime-worried country than ours, but the newspaper and TV images of Orlando as a mugger's paradise are a long way from the truth. If we were talking about New York or even Miami, there would be serious considerations of personal safety, especially for families. But, in pure statistical terms, you have more chance of being mugged in your local High Street than in Orlando. The only tourist destination in America with a LOWER crime rate than Orlando is Sante Fe in New Mexico, and that handles only a fraction of the numbers that central Florida does. Of course there have been incidents of violent crime in the city, no one could pretend otherwise, but on the whole these have been isolated and unusual and have drawn so much publicity simply because they are the exception rather than the norm. Again, in terms of the most recent statistics, crimes against visitors to Orlando account for 0.04 per cent of the total crime figures for the area, or something in the region of 4,000 incidents for every 13 million tourists. The area also has its own Tourist Oriented Policing Service (or TOPS), centred on International Drive, with more than 40 officers patrolling purely the main tourist areas, arranging crime prevention seminars with local hotels and generally ensuring that Orlando takes good care of its visitors. You will often see the local police in these areas out on mountain bikes, and they are a polite, helpful bunch should you need assistance or directions. Tourism is such a vital part of the local economy the authorities simply cannot afford not to be seen to be taking an active role against crime, hence the area does have an extremely safety-conscious attitude.

This is most evident in the use of state-of-the-art methods of crime prevention that have gone a long way towards driving tourist crime out of the area. These include the fitting of electronic locks on hotel rooms, designing new hotels with crime prevention criteria, like special landscaping, lighting and the use of particular colours, in mind, and putting extra police patrols on duty in motorway areas where tourists typically encounter difficulties through bad signposting or avoiding the tolls.

Having said all that it would be foolish to behave as if the villainous element did not exist and therefore there are a number of guidelines which all visitors to America, in general, and Orlando in particular, should follow. Put simply these are all a question of common sense. For example, just as it would be inadvisable to walk around the darker corners of Soho in London late at night alone, so it would in parts of Florida.

Emergencies

General: In an emergency of any kind, for police, fire department or ambulance, dial 911 (9–911 from your hotel room). It is a good idea to make sure your children are aware of this number, while for smaller-scale crises (mislaid tickets or passports, rescheduled flights, etc) your holiday company should have an emergency contact number in the hotel reception. If you are travelling independently and run into passport or other problems that require the assistance of the British consulate in Orlando, their office is located in Sun Bank Towers, 200 South Orange Avenue, with walk-in visitors' hours from 9.30am–noon and 2–4pm. Alternatively, you can phone between 9am and 5pm on 407 426 7855.

Hotels

While in your hotel, motel or guest house, you should always use door peepholes and security chains whenever someone knocks at the door. DON'T open the doors to strangers without asking for identification, and check with the

BRIT TIP: If your room has already been cleaned before you go out for the day, hang the 'Do Not Disturb' sign on the door and leave a light or the radio on.

hotel desk if you are still not sure. It is stating the obvious, but keep your room doors and windows locked at all times and always use deadlocks and security chains. It is still surprising how many people simply forget basic precautions when they

are on holiday (the local police also never cease to be amazed at how many people leave their common sense behind when they leave home!). Always take your cash, credit cards and car keys with you when you go out, and don't leave the door open at any time, even if you are just popping down the corridor to the ice machine. Lock your suitcases so they can't be used to

BRIT TIP: A handy idea for your journey over is to use a business address rather than your home address on all your luggage. It is less conspicuous and safer should any item be stolen or misplaced.

carry property out of the room and report any suspicious-looking characters to the hotel desk. And make a point of asking the hotels about their safety precautions when you make your reservation. Do they have electronic card-locks (which can't be duplicated) and do they have their own security staff?

Don't be afraid to ask reception staff for safety pointers in the surrounding areas or if you are travelling somewhere you are not totally sure about. Safety is a major issue for the Central Florida Hotel/Motel Association, so hotel staff are usually well briefed to be very helpful in this area. Keep a regular inventory of your belongings during the holiday so you won't get home and suddenly realise you have mislaid your spare handbag/camera/trainers. Using a bumbag (the Americans call them fanny packs!) is also a better bet than shoulder or handbags, and if you carry a wallet try to keep it in an inside pocket.

Nothing is guaranteed to get the

Silver Springs: glass-bottomed boat

Money

Following on from the advice about bumbags and wallets, it is completely inadvisable and totally unnecessary to carry large amounts of cash

> BRIT TIP: Be forewarned that all American banknotes are EXACTLY the same green colour and size. It is only the picture of the president and the denomination in each corner which change.

around with you. US travellers' cheques are accepted almost everywhere as cash and can be readily replaced if lost or stolen, as can credit cards, which are another widespread form of currency. Barclaycard (known in America as Visa), Access (or Mastercard) and American Express are almost universally accepted, but don't take unnecessary bank or credit cards with you. The Sun Bank in Disney's Magic Kingdom and Epcot 95 is open seven days a week should you need extra help with any financial transactions. It is also worth separating the larger notes from the smaller ones in your wallet to avoid flashing all your money in public view. Losing £200 worth of travellers' cheques shouldn't ruin your holiday — but losing £200 in cash might.

local police shaking their heads in disbelief and disgust than the tourist who goes round looking like an obvious tourist. The map over the steering wheel is one obvious giveaway, but other no-noes are wearing large amounts of ostentatious jewellery, masses of photographic equipment or flashing wads of cash around. The biggest single giveaway of all is leaving your camera or camcorder on the front seat of the car. In 1994, Orlando had fewer instances of tourist car crime in the year than Las Vegas on an average day, but it still doesn't pay to put temptation in a criminal's way. If you want to look a bit more like one of the locals, wearing the ubiquitous baseball cap is a good way of blending in, and wearing a hat is a good idea given the local climate.

Finally, and this is VERY strong police advice, in the unlikely event of being confronted by an assailant, DO NOT resist or try to 'have a go' as it more often than not will result in making the situation more serious.

In addition, most hotels will offer the use of safes and deposit boxes for your valuables, and many rooms now come equipped with mini-safes in which it is a good idea to leave your passports, return tickets, cameras etc, when you don't need them. Always keep your valuables out of sight, whether in the hotel room or car. Use the car boot if you're leaving a jacket or camera.

Driving

Car crime is one of the biggest forms of criminal activity in America and has led to some of the most lurid headlines, especially in the Miami area. Once again, it pays to make a number of basic safety checks before you set off anywhere. The first thing is to be SURE of the car's controls before you drive out of the hire company's car park. Which button is the air-conditioning, which side of the steering wheel are the indicators and where are the windscreen wipers? Check BEFORE you leave!

BRIT TIP: American freeways, highways and expressways (with the exception of the Florida Turnpike) do not have service stations, so if you need petrol you will have to get off the motorway (although not very far in most cases).

Also, make sure you know your route in advance, even if it is only a case of memorising the road numbers. Most of the hire companies now give very good directional instructions on how to get to your hotel from their car park so read them before you set off.

Just about the main item on the list of local police Dos and Don'ts is to use your map BEFORE you set off — trying to drive with the map over the steering wheel is just asking for an accident, let alone marking you out as an obvious tourist. Make sure, too, that you put maps and brochures away in the glove compartment when you leave the car to avoid leaving the obvious sign that says 'Tourist Parked Here!'. Check that the petrol tank is full and never let it get near empty. Running out of 'gas' in an unfamiliar area holds obvious hazards.

If you stray off your pre-determined route, stick to well-lit areas and stop to ask directions only from official businesses like hotels and garages or better still, a police car or station. Always try to park close to your destination where there are plenty of street lights and DO NOT get out if there are any suspicious characters lurking around. Always keep your doors and windows closed (if it's hot, you've got air-conditioning, remember?), and don't hesitate to lock the doors from the inside if you feel threatened by unlikely-looking pedestrians. As a general rule, be wary of car parks and get into the habit of glancing around and inside your car before you get in. And, please, don't forget to lock it when you leave it!

Miami crooks have also developed the habit of trying to get cars to stop by trying to look official or deliberately bumping into obvious hire cars from behind. The easily-identified hire car plates are now being phased out by most companies, but still NEVER stop for a non-official request. Go instead to the nearest garage or police station, and always insist on identification before unlocking your car and getting out of it for an official. It is comforting to know a unique aspect of driving in Orlando is none of the main tourist areas have any sort of no-go areas to be avoided. The nearest is the portion of the Orange Blossom Trail south of downtown Orlando. This houses a selection of strip clubs and 'adult bars' that are not particularly attractive and can be downright seedy at night.

Should you require any further information on being safe in Orlando, contact the Community Affairs office of the Orange County Police on 407 836 3720.

9

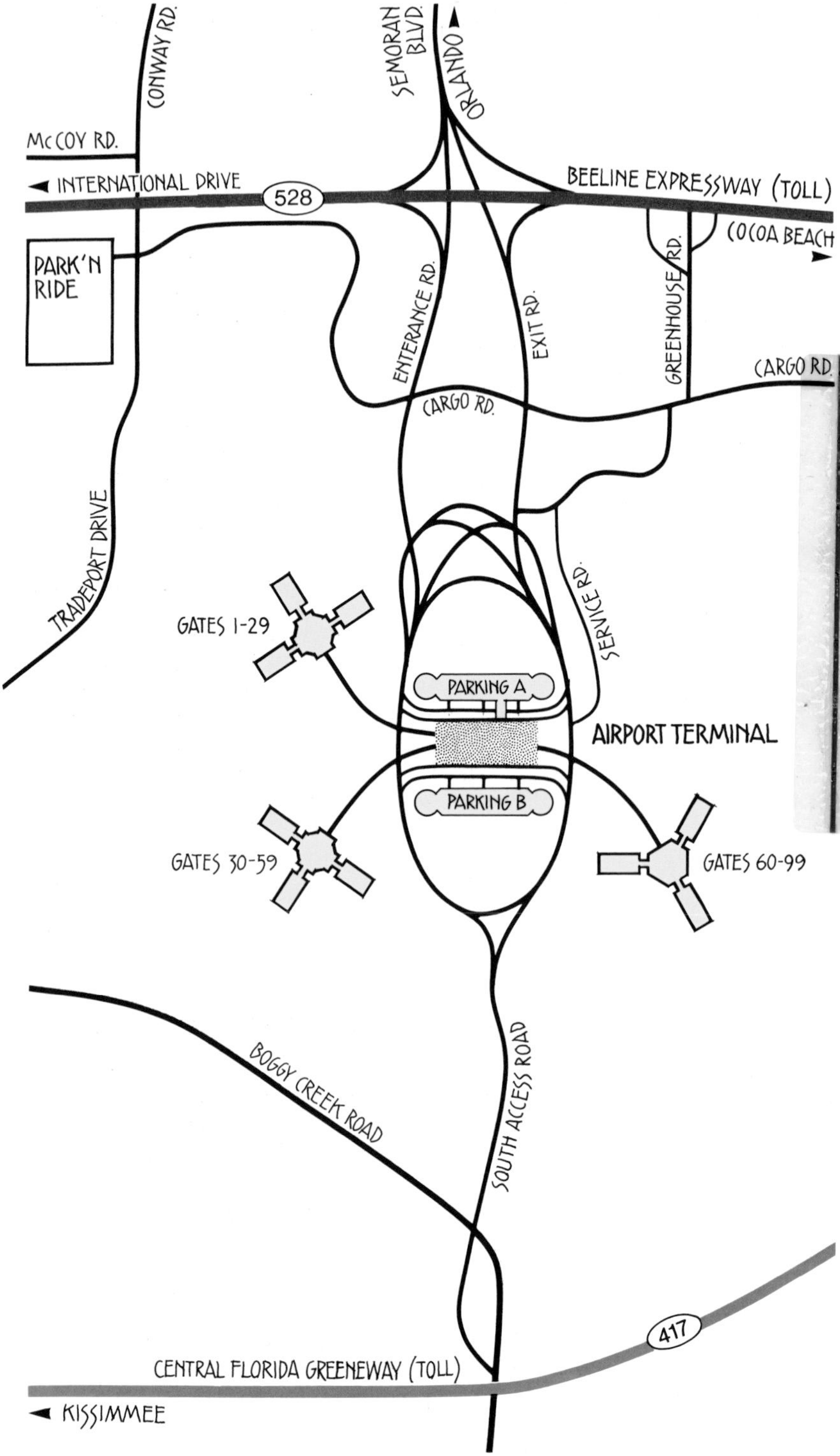

CONWAY RD.

McCOY RD.

SEMORAN BLVD.

ORLANDO

◄ INTERNATIONAL DRIVE

BEELINE EXPRESSWAY (TOLL)

528

COCOA BEACH ►

PARK'N RIDE

ENTERANCE RD.

EXIT RD.

GREENHOUSE RD.

CARGO RD.

CARGO RD.

TRADEPORT DRIVE

SERVICE RD.

GATES 1-29

PARKING A

AIRPORT TERMINAL

PARKING B

GATES 30-59

GATES 60-99

BOGGY CREEK ROAD

SOUTH ACCESS ROAD

417

CENTRAL FLORIDA GREENEWAY (TOLL)

◄ KISSIMMEE

Going Home
or where did the last two weeks go?

And so, dog-tired, financially crippled but (hopefully) blissfully happy and with enough memories to last a lifetime, it is time to deal with that bane of all holidays — the journey home.

If you have come through the last week or two relatively unscathed in terms of the calamities that can befall the uninformed or the plain unlucky (like coming out of Walt Disney World and being half way to Tampa before you realise you are going in the wrong direction!), there are still one or two more little pitfalls that can catch you out.

The Car

First and foremost, is the hire car. It has to be returned from whence it came — and that can take time. Remember how long it took to get mobile in the first place? Well, it can take just as long to return your vehicle, complete any necessary remaining paperwork, pay any outstanding bills and catch the hire company's courtesy bus back to the airport (if their operation is off-airport). The process tends to be appreciably quicker with the firms who operate directly from the airport.

The Airport

For reference purposes, the airport is 46 miles from Cocoa Beach and 54 from Daytona Beach on the east cost, 84 miles from Tampa and 110 from Clearwater and St Petersburg to the west, 25 from Walt Disney World and 10 from Universal

Studios; always allow yourself plenty of time for the journey.

As with all of the major tourist activities in Orlando, car hire return is a well-organised, highly efficient matter, but the simple numbers involved usually determine that here is one more queue to be negotiated, especially if you leave it until the last minute. Allow a good hour for this process ON TOP of the two hours you are advised to leave for checking in at the airport.

Having automatically tipped the bus driver for dropping you off at the terminal, you are now back where you started in terms of your Orlando adventure — in the impressively large, clean but rather daunting confines of the international airport (there are also two local, domestic airports, Orlando Executive, just east of the city, and Kissimmee Airport, just south of Highway 192, and should you end up at either of these you may have a rather long wait for the flight home!).

Orlando International

Orlando International is one of the fastest-growing airports in the world, handling an average of 1,000 flights and some 60,000 passengers per day at peak periods. The terminal complex covers 854 acres (and the whole airport a massive 15,000 acres), so it can swallow a lot of people comfortably, but its modern expanses can still get seriously busy. It handles almost half of the traffic of Heathrow and comfortably more than Gatwick and

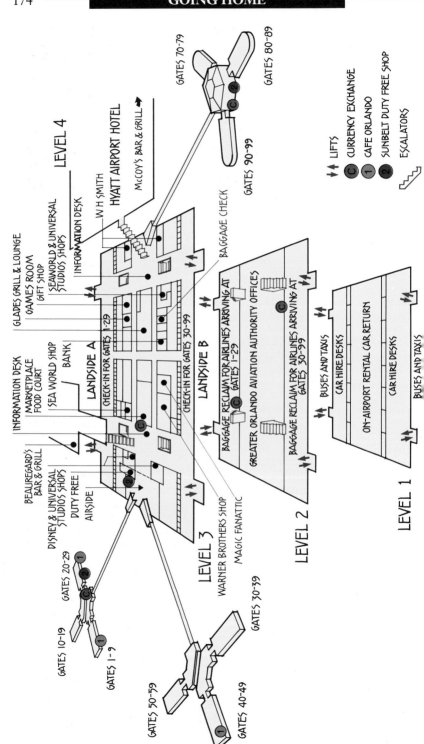

Orlando Airport – Great Hall

our other regional airports, so be prepared for one final battle with the crowds if there are several British charter flights scheduled at the same time. However, at all but peak periods, this is one of the most comfortable and relaxing airport terminals you will find anywhere in the world, and it was recently rated No 1 in America for customer service. Its provision of services and other facilities, like shops and restaurants, is second to none, and its airy, open concourses will make you feel you are in a top-quality hotel rather than an international airport (perhaps this is not too surprising when one end of the terminal is taken up by the airport-run Hyatt Hotel, a beautifully appointed and magnificently equipped establishment that is also open to airport passengers).

Ramps, rest rooms, wide lifts and large open areas throughout the airport ensure easy access for wheelchairs, and there are special features like TDD and amplified telephones, wheelchair-height drinking fountains, braille lift controls and companion-care rest rooms to assist disabled travellers.

You will also find plenty to do here to while away that final hour or two, and, should you have more than a couple of hours to spare, it is worth knowing you can leave your carry-on bags at the Baggage Checkroom and take the 15-minute taxi ride to the Florida Mall for any last-minute shopping or take in a film at the big cinema complex just to the north of the airport (a five-minute journey by taxi). The airport's two information desks (both on Level Three) keep all the cinema timetables, so if you think you have time consult them and hail a cab! Otherwise, you can stay in the airport and visit the Hair Salon, post office or travel agent(!), or have your shoes cleaned at one of three shoeshine stalls.

Landside

As with all international airports, you have a division between **LANDSIDE** (for all visitors to the airport) and **AIRSIDE** (beyond

10

which you need to have a ticket). Orlando's **LANDSIDE** is divided into three levels: **One** is for ground transportation, parking, buses and the car rental agencies; **Two** is the Baggage Claim level (you will probably hardly have noticed it on your way in); **Three** is where you should enter the airport on your return journey as it holds all the check-in desks, plus shops, restaurants, lockers, bank and information desks. Level Three is effectively sub-divided into four sections: **Landside 'A'** is the check-in section for Gates 1–29. Here you will find American Airlines, Continental, TWA and the British charters Leisure Air, Air 2000, Britannia and Monarch. **Landside 'B'** is home to the check-in desks for Gates 30–99 and the other main airlines, including Northwest, United, USAir, BA, Caledonian, Delta, KLM and Virgin Atlantic.

Then, once you have checked in, you can choose to explore the **East** and **West** sections of the main concourse which occupies the centre of Level Three. The **West** end houses the Great Hall, around which are the main shopping and eating areas. Inevitably, Disney & Co make one last attempt to part you from what's left of your money, so here you will find some more highly impressive, not to mention large, gift shops for Walt Disney World, Sea World and Universal Studios (and there is no airport mark-up either), Benjamin Books, The Grove Sweet Shop (great pic 'n mix!), two newsagents (one of which, the Keys Group News and Gifts, also sells toiletries and over-the-counter chemist's goods), a highly-varied food court (including Burger King, Pizza Hut, Nathan's Famous frankfurters and chili dogs and Mort's Deli, a stylish and inexpensive little restaurant) and, up the escalators in the centre of the hall, Beauregard's Bar and Grill.

When the airport begins to fill up Beauregard's is a very handy place to get away from the crowds, relax with a quiet drink, have a decent meal or put your feet up in front of their many TVs. The rest-rooms here are also exceedingly well maintained.

BRIT TIP: Overlooked by many travellers, Beauregard's bar and restaurant is the perfect little sanctuary to while away that final hour or two before the flight.

The **East** end of Level Three tends to be quieter and more picturesque as it is dominated by the eight-storey Hyatt Hotel atrium, featuring palm trees and a large fountain, and there are fewer departure gates and shops down here. Universal and Sea World both have secondary shops (and they're different, too!), WH Smith's has two outlets, while the Paradies Shop is also worth a look for other gift items. For food and drink there is a Starbuck's coffee shop and the Glades Grill and Premium Stock Lounge. There is also, up the escalator, the entrance to the Hyatt Airport Hotel if you fancy seeing out your visit in style. McCoy's Bar and Grill (up the escalator, turn right) is one of the smartest bar-restaurants you will find in Orlando, and it has the bonus of a grandstand view of the airport runways to watch all the comings and goings. It will cost you $4 for a glass of draught beer, $3.75 for an imported bottled beer and $4 or $5 for a cocktail, but it is worth it. The surroundings are immensely stylish and a long way removed from the average airport lounge. If you want to go really up-market in your Orlando farewell, go up the escalator, turn left and take the lift to the ninth floor and Hemisphere

Restaurant. Not only do you have an even more impressive view of the airport's workings, its northern Italian cuisine provides some of the best fare in the city. It's slightly on the pricey side ($8 for a starter like lobster and pasta in a cream sauce, and main courses from $14 to $20), but the service and food are five star.

The central access corridor between the East and West ends, which already houses some service facilities like a bank, travel agent, post office, baggage checkroom and hair salon, is also scheduled for a major facelift, with a mini shopping complex being added to include more impressive shops like Warner Brothers, Tie Rack, a Magic Fan Attic souvenir store and a family entertainment games and playroom.

If you still have time to kill after visiting all these establishments and buying those final gift items, wander round the concourse and examine some of the airport's magnificent art collection (a free brochure is available from the information desks) or view the large aquarium next to the Sea World shop at the East end — it's big enough to accommodate a diver when it needs cleaning or other maintenance, and that is quite an eye-catching sight!

Airside

Once you have decided it is time to move on to your departure gate, you have to be aware of the three satellite arms that make up the airport's **AIRSIDE**.

These are divided into **Gates 1–29, 30–59** (both at the West end of the main terminal) and **60–99** (at the East end). ALL the departure gates are here, plus the duty free shops, more restaurants, lockers and nursery services.

The airport is ultimately designed to have four separate satellite arms, each connected to the main building by a monorail shuttle service (as exists between the North and South terminals at Gatwick), so you need to keep your wits about you when it comes to finding your departure gate. As is increasingly the case these days, there are no tannoy announcements for flights, so you must remember to ask your departure gate and time when you check in on Level Three. However, there are three monitor boards in the main terminal which display all the necessary departure information. As a general rule, British Airways, Virgin Atlantic and Caledonian use Gates **60–99**, as do Delta. KLM, NorthWest, United and USAir usually use **Gates 30–59**, while charter airlines Leisure Air, Air 2000, Britannia, and Monarch all depart from **Gates 1–29**, along with American, Continental and TWA.

In most airports, once you have moved Airside it is not possible to return to the Landside area again. However, that is not the case here, and, if you find the crowds milling around your departure gate too much to bear, you can always return to one of the terminal hostelries, for a bit of peace and quiet.

Having said all that, you will find the Airside areas just as clean and efficient as the main terminal, with the added bonus of three duty free shops just in case your credit card hasn't already gone into meltdown.

As you pass through the ticket and baggage check at the West end of the terminal you will find the Sunbelt International Shoppers Ltd immediately on your right. This is the biggest of their three shops and is open only to departing international passengers, so you will need to have your boarding card handy. Unlike the duty free shops in Britain, you don't carry your purchases out with you. Instead, they are delivered to your departure gate for collection as you get on the plane. This is because the international flights are mixed in

10

with the domestic ones and, of course, duty free shopping does not

Orlando Airport – Atrium

apply to internal flights.

Having taken the shuttle to **Gates 1–19**, you will find another Sunbelt duty free shop (they're DETERMINED to get your money!), plus a newsagents (The Keys Group News and Gifts), a currency exchange, two bar/lounges of the Café Orlando and another mini-food court, featuring Burger King, Mrs Field's Cookies and TCBY (which really does stand for The Country's Best Yoghurt). **Gates 30–59** is the only satellite arm NOT to have its own Sunbelt shop, so remember to bag your duty frees back at their main store just past the Airside ticket check. However, you will still find a Café Orlando lounge bar, a Concessions International food outlet and a WH Smith's. Travelling from **Gates 60–99** gives you the options of another Sunbelt duty free shop, a Fenton Hill newsagents, Paradies gift-shop, currency exchange and food court containing Burger King (inevitably — it's always the busiest, too), Nathan's Famous frankfurters, etc, TCBY and the Premium Stock Lounge for that final beverage.

Just like back at your home departure airport, you still have to be near your departure gate a little before time so you can hear the individual rows being called for embarkation. You can also expect

your return flight to be somewhat shorter than the journey out thanks to the Atlantic jetstreams that provide handy tail-winds to high-level flights. Differences of more than an hour in the two journey times are not uncommon.

Finally, you will land back at Heathrow, Manchester, Glasgow, etc rather more jet-lagged than on the trip out. This is because the time difference is more noticeable on eastward flights, and it may take a good day or two to get your body's time-clock back on to local time. It is therefore even more important not to over-indulge in alcoholic beverages if you are driving home.

And, much as it may seem like a good idea, the best way to beat Florida jet-lag is NOT to go straight out and book another holiday to Orlando!

But, believe me, the lure of this great theme park wonderland will ultimately prove almost impossible to resist again.

Orlando Airport – Terminal

Your Holiday Planner

Example 1: with Four-Day Disney Pass

DAY		ATTRACTION	NOTES
SUN	DAY		
	EVE		
MON	DAY		
	EVE		
TUE	DAY		
	EVE		
WED	DAY		
	EVE		
THUR	DAY	ARRIVE 4pm local time	*N.B. 30 mins to drive to hotel*
	EVE	Transfer to hotel	
FRI	DAY	Welcome meeting/Drive around	
	EVE	Church Street Station	*Holiday company trip*
SAT	DAY	DISNEY MGM STUDIOS	*(Open until 7pm today)*
	EVE		
SUN	DAY	MAGIC KINGDOM	*(Open until 10pm today)*
	EVE		
MON	DAY	Typhoon Lagoon/Discovery Island	*(Open until 8pm)*
	EVE		

Example 1: with Four-Day Disney Pass (Cont'd.)

DAY		ATTRACTION	NOTES
TUE	DAY	KENNEDY SPACE CENTRE	
	EVE	Cinema	*Must see new Disney film!*
WED	DAY	SEA WORLD	
	EVE	Polynesian Luan	*Starts 6.30pm*
THUR	DAY	Balloon Flight, Water Mania	
	EVE	Fort Liberty Dinner Show	*Holiday company trip*
FRI	DAY	EPCOT 95	*(Open until 10pm today)*
	EVE		
SAT	DAY	Winter Park lakes/shopping	*(Must get new trainers!)*
	EVE	Relax!	
SUN	DAY	UNIVERSAL STUDIOS	*(Open until 8pm)*
	EVE		
MON	DAY	Fantasy of Flight or free day	
	EVE		
TUE	DAY	BUSCH GARDENS	
	EVE	Pleasure Island	*Holiday company trip*
WED	DAY	MAGIC KINGDOM	*Arrive late this time; open until 10pm*
	EVE		
THUR	DAY	Gatorland/Back to Airport	*Check-out by mid-day*
	EVE		*Flight 8pm; check-in by 6*
FRI	DAY	Return Gatwick 10am	
	EVE		

Example 2: with Five-Day Disney Pass

DAY		ATTRACTION	NOTES
SUN	DAY		
	EVE		
MON	DAY		
	EVE		
TUE	DAY		
	EVE		
WED	DAY		
	EVE		
THUR	DAY	ARRIVE 4pm local time	*N.B. 30 mins to drive to hotel!*
	EVE	Transfer to hotel	
FRI	DAY	Welcome meeting, + MGM STUDIOS	*(Open until 7pm)*
	EVE		
SAT	DAY	KENNEDY SPACE CENTRE	
	EVE	Fort Liberty Dinner Show	*Holiday company trip*
SUN	DAY	MAGIC KINGDOM	*(Open until 11pm today!)*
	EVE		
MON	DAY	Typhoon lagoon/Discovery Island	*(Open until 8pm)*
	EVE	Airboat Gator Hunt	
TUE	DAY	SEA WORLD	
	EVE	Polynesian Luan	*(6.30pm - 8.30pm)*
WED	DAY	Fantasy of Flight	
	EVE	Church Street Station	*Holiday company trip*

11

Example 2: with Five-Day Disney Pass (Cont'd.)

DAY		ATTRACTION	NOTES
THUR	DAY	MAGIC KINGDOM	*Arrive later (open until 10pm today)*
	EVE		
FRI	DAY	EPCOT 95	*(Open until 10pm)*
	EVE	Pleasure Island	
SAT	DAY	Winter Park lakes	
	EVE	Relax!	
SUN	DAY	Stowaway Adventures	
	EVE	EPCOT 95	*(Open until 10pm)*
MON	DAY	Cypress Gardens, or Silver Springs or free day	
	EVE		
TUE	DAY	BUSCH GARDENS	
	EVE	Wet 'n Wild	*(Open until 10pm)*
WED	DAY	UNIVERSAL STUDIOS	*(Open until 8pm)*
	EVE		
THUR	DAY	Gatorland/Back to Airport	*Check-out by mid-day*
	EVE		*Flight 6pm; check-in by 4*
FRI	DAY	Return Gatwick 8am	
	EVE		
SAT	DAY		
	EVE		
SUN	DAY		
	EVE		

Blank Form: Your Holiday!

DAY	ATTRACTION	NOTES

SUN
DAY
_____
EVE

MON
DAY
_____
EVE

TUE
DAY
_____
EVE

WED
DAY
_____
EVE

THUR
DAY
_____
EVE

FRI
DAY
_____
EVE

SAT
DAY
_____
EVE

SUN
DAY
_____
EVE

MON
DAY
_____
EVE

TUE
DAY
_____
EVE

WED
DAY
_____
EVE

11

Blank Form: Your Holiday! (Cont'd.)

DAY	ATTRACTION	NOTES
THUR	DAY ———————— EVE	
FRI	DAY ———————— EVE	
SAT	DAY ———————— EVE	
SUN	DAY ———————— EVE	
MON	DAY ———————— EVE	
TUE	DAY ———————— EVE	
WED	DAY ———————— EVE	
THUR	DAY ———————— EVE	
FRI	DAY ———————— EVE	
SAT	DAY ———————— EVE	
SUN	DAY ———————— EVE	

	BUSIEST	AVERAGE	LIGHTEST
MON	MAGIC KINGDOM	EPCOT 96 MGM STUDIOS UNIVERSAL STUDIOS	BUSCH GARDENS SEA WORLD KENNEDY SPACE CENTER CYPRESS GARDENS WATER PARKS
TUE	EPCOT 96 UNIVERSAL STUDIOS	MAGIC KINGDOM MGM STUDIOS	BUSCH GARDENS SEA WORLD KENNEDY SPACE CENTER CYPRESS GARDENS WATER PARKS
WED	MGM STUDIOS UNIVERSAL STUDIOS WATER PARKS	MAGIC KINGDOM EPCOT 96 BUSCH GARDENS	SEA WORLD KENNEDY SPACE CENTER CYPRESS GARDENS
THUR	MAGIC KINGDOM UNIVERSAL STUDIOS WATER PARKS	EPCOT 96 MGM STUDIOS BUSCH GARDENS SEA WORLD KENNEDY SPACE CENTER	CYPRESS GARDENS
FRI	EPCOT 96 SEA WORLD KENNEDY SPACE CENTER	CYPRESS GARDENS WATER PARKS	MAGIC KINGDOM MGM STUDIOS UNIVERSAL STUDIOS
SAT	MAGIC KINGDOM EPCOT 96 BUSCH GARDENS SEA WORLD CYPRESS GARDENS WATER PARKS	MGM STUDIOS KENNEDY SPACE CENTER	UNIVERSAL STUDIOS
SUN	MGM STUDIOS BUSCH GARDENS SEA WORLD CYPRESS GARDENS WATER PARKS	KENNEDY SPACE CENTER	MAGIC KINGDOM EPCOT 96 UNIVERSAL STUDIOS

PLANNING YOUR THEME PARK DAYS

DIAGRAM 2

11

When a tourist destination with the size and imagination of somewhere like Orlando decides it is time for a change, things change, and how! Hence the Brit's Guide introduces this Stop Press section to keep you fully up to date with exactly what to expect on your holiday.

Walt Disney World

October 1996 sees the beginning of **Disney's 25th Anniversary** in Central Florida, and the celebrations will last right through to December 97. All Disney World facets will have their own special attractions and festivities to mark the occasion, which will include exclusive shows and parades in the theme parks, special resort offerings and many surprises with a birthday or anniversary theme.

The **Disney Institute Resort** is scheduled to open its doors for a new kind of holiday experience for adults and older children in February 1996. The nine programmes on offer will be: Entertainment Arts (film, radio, television, video and nightclub performance); Sports and Fitness (from aerobics to advanced clinics in golf, tennis or basketball); Lifestyles (family history, personal development and community-building); Story Arts (worldwide traditions in story-telling, in the Disney tradition); Culinary Arts (the world's great cuisines); Design Arts (architecture and living design); Environment (gardening and landscaping); Youth (workshops in magic and comic book creation); and Performing Arts (interactive classes in pop, jazz and classical music, comedy, dance and film). The resort will include 28 studios, an outdoor amphitheatre, cinema, TV and radio station, sports centre, tennis courts, golf course, youth centre and FIVE swimming pools, as well as top class accommodation. Provisional charges are around $582/person for a minimum three-night stay. Call 407 827 4800 for more details.

Disney's Village Marketplace is under starter's orders for a development which will DOUBLE the size of the existing complex that also includes Pleasure Island. Two celebrity nightclubs, a 1,500-seat theatre, an expanded cinema complex, two star-name restaurants and two Disney superstores are all on the drawing board for 1997.

The Walt Disney World International Sports Complex is another mega-project that will take shape during 1996, opening in 1997 and featuring a baseball stadium, indoor arena, an athletics field, 12 tennis courts, a 2,000-seater show court, a golf driving range and facilities for 17 other sports.

Celebration, Florida is an ongoing creation of a whole TOWN to the south of Walt Disney World, the first phase of which is due to open mid-1996 and is scheduled to develop over the next 20 YEARS! Plans call for a traditional downtown district, with offices, shops, cinemas and restaurants.

But the big news is the announcement of the creation of a FOURTH new theme park for 1998, the **Wild Animal Kingdom**. This 500-acre park – easily the biggest in Disney World – will be divided into three sections, the Real, the Mythical and the Extinct, and the advance publicity promises a real environmental extravaganza of true-life adventure stories, safaris and other animal encounters. Creative director Joe Rohde says: "Guests will embark on a journey into the last wild sanctuaries of our planet, explore fable and fantasy, where dragons breathe real fire, and venture into realms of prehistoric danger."

Universal Studios

Universal Studios is already undergoing the transition to Universal City, Florida, thanks to the addition of another new theme park, Universal's Islands of Adventure, an entertainment complex along the scale of Church Street Station or Pleasure Island, five themed hotels, an 18-hole golf course, championship tennis centre and 16-screen cinema complex. **Islands of Adventure** promises a 21st Century-themed land of rides, shows and attractions, including the popular Dr Seuss creations (The Cat in the Hat, etc), Popeye, and the characters out of the Marvel comics, like Spiderman, the X-Men and the Incredible Hulk. Some parts of Universal City will come on line through 1997 and 98, while Islands of Adventure is planned for a 1999 opening. Of more immediate concern, though, is Universal Studios' next blockbuster attraction, **Terminator 2: Battle Across Time**, for summer 96. A four-dimensional, interactive show puts the guest at the centre of the action 'for a one-on-one showdown with the Terminator himself!"

JungleLand

This new cross-over between a zoo and an entertainment park has replaced the old Alligatorland Safari Zoo, on the Irlo Bronson Memorial Highway (Highway 192) eight miles east of its junction with I4, just past Medieval Times. It is an all new concept and challenges Gatorland's appeal, although Gatorland is still THE place for gators. Their Gator Show is equally as entertaining and amusing as the Gatorland version, while JungleLand also boasts the one-of-a-kind Carlton-Kevington stunt shows, a father and son team who put on dare-devil escape acts over an alligator pit and tiger cage. The emphasis is still more on the zoo elements, and to that end their range of animals is quite impressive, from parrots and macaws through monkeys, deer, a friendly llama and emus, to leopards, black panthers, lions and tigers. There is also a snack bar and gift shop, and JungleLand is open seven days a week from 9am–5pm (9am–7pm during peak periods). Admission charges are $9.95 for adults, $6.95 for kids (3–11), under 3s are free.

Daytona USA

Also opening in summer 1996 is the Daytona International Speedway's $18million "World Center of Racing" visitor centre which will present the history of racing in vivid fashion through the use of interactive media featuring drivers, cars, racing technology, live pit stops, multi-dimensional theatres and numerous historical memorabilia and exhibits.

Olympics 1996

With Atlanta and the 1996 Olympics only an hour's flight away, it is inevitable Orlando will have a strong Olympic flavour this summer, too. It will be in all the shops, on TV, in the adverts – and some of it will be

12

on the playing fields of Orlando itself. For the Florida Citrus Bowl stadium will be host to part of the Olympic soccer programme and Orlando will have its own Opening Ceremony and nine matches from July 20th–25th. There are six men's games and three women's at times varying from 4pm to 9pm. Tickets are already on sale for all matches, prices from $20–$40, and it could be a rare opportunity to sample such a huge event at first hand. Phone 407 423 2476 for more details.

Accommodation

Disney's Boardwalk Inn will be at the heart of a new entertainment district in the Epcot resorts area, with a 378-room deluxe hotel and meeting facilities, plus shops, clubs and restaurants all in a "village across the water" style. It occupies 45 acres on the shores of Crescent Lake and, in addition to the hotel, will feature a Duelling Piano Bar, an Atlantic Ballroom (1920s dance hall-style showcasing music from the 40s to 90s) and ESPN World, offering interactive and virtual-reality sports. Add an Italian restaurant, a bakery and more than 9,000 square feet of shops, and you are talking about another solid-gold attraction. Opening is likely to be July 1996. Beating Disney to the punch will be the third-largest hotel in Orlando (after The Dolphin and Marriott's Orlando World Center), the **Omni Rosen Hotel**, which is scheduled to open its doors in November 1995. This hugely-eyecatching monolith of a building is right next to the Beeline Expressway on International Drive and, while it will be catering primarily for the convention trade, it will also offer some excellent packages for tourists. Its 1,334 rooms and 80 suites all feature state-of-the-art security, while the hotel also boasts a huge swimming grotto, an exercise centre, tennis courts, three restaurants and two bars. It has underground parking for extra security and massive conference facilities, so expect it to be busy year-round. Call 407 354 9840 for more details. The **Caribe Royale Resort Suites** promises to be the largest suites hotel in the WORLD, with 1,218 spacious two-room suites set in three tower blocks around a tropically-landscaped pool area and with a truly immense reception lobby. The whole site exceeds 30 landscaped acres and some incredibly detailed thought has gone into features like security, en-suite amenities and extra provisions like a massive (free!) buffet breakfast and a poolside bar and grill. Caribe Royale is situated at the southern end of International Drive, very convenient for the Epcot Drive entrance to Walt Disney World and the Central Florida Greeneway route to and from the international airport. Expect the immediate surrounding areas to mushroom with shops, restaurants and cinemas once it is up and runnïng in the summer of 1996. For more details, call 407 238 8000.

Shopping

Seminole Town Center, a 20-minute drive north of downtown Orlando on I4 and State Road 46 into Sanford, is due to open early in the winter of 1995 with a brand new two-level shopping mall featuring no less than five department stores and 130 other shops and restaurants, plus a 10-screen cinema complex.

And there you have it, the future in all its glorious outline. There will, of course, be other developments that have beaten our deadline or have sprung up relatively unannounced, but that is simply the nature of the Orlando beast. I feel confident, however, you will not miss out on anything essential to your holiday enjoyment. It's all there waiting for you – go get it!

foulsham

The Publishing House, Bennetts Close, Cippenham, Berkshire, SL1 5AP, England

ISBN 0-572-02146-1

DEDICATION

To my wife, Karen, without whose non-stop support and assistance the Brit's Guide would never have become a reality.

ACKNOWLEDGEMENTS

The author also wishes to acknowledge the help of the following in the production of this book:

The Orlando Tourism Bureau in London.
The Orlando/Orange County Convention & Visitors Bureau.
The Florida Dept of Commerce, Europe Division.
The Kissimmee/St Cloud Convention & Visitors Bureau.
The Greater Orlando Aviation Authority, Community Relations Office.
The Walt Disney Company, Ltd.
Universal Studios, Florida.
The Anheuser Busch Entertainment Corporation.
The Orlando County Sheriff's Office.
HM Customs and Excise Office, Gatwick Airport.
Virgin Holidays Ltd.
Thomson Holidays.
Marriott's Orlando World Center.
Hawthorn Suites.
Westgate Lakes Resort.
Winter Park Chamber of Commerce.
Plus, Oonagh McCullagh (Orlando Tourism Bureau), Duncan Wardle (Walt Disney), Carolyn Fennell (Orlando Aviation Authority), Debra Johnson (Fantasy of Flight), Frank Langley (Spendid China), Fonda Ryan (Sea World), Ginger Taggart (Wet 'N Wild), Wanda Salerno (Winter Park Scenic Boat Tours), Crisa Marder (Mystery Fun House), Rich Renaud (Kennedy Space Center), Donna Turner (Gatorland) and others too numerous to mention. Thank you all.

Typeset in Great Britain by Poole Typesetting (Wessex) Limited, Bournemouth.
Printed in Great Britain by Cambus Litho, East Kilbride.

917.59
VEN

This book is due for return on or before the last date shown below.